FREUD'S SCIENTIFIC REVOLUTION

A Reading of His Early Works

SAUL HAIMOVICH

FREE ASSOCIATION BOOKS

First published in 2017 by
Free Association Books

Copyright © 2017 Saul Haimovich

The author's rights are fully asserted. The right of
Saul Haimovich to be identified as the author of this
work has been asserted by him in accordance with the
Copyright, Designs and Patents Act 1988

A CIP Catalogue of this book is available from
the British Library

ISBN: 978-1-9113830-6-2

All rights reserved; no part of this publication may be reproduced,
stored in a retrieval system, or transmitted, in any form or by
any means, electronic, mechanical, photocopying, recording or
otherwise, without the prior written permission of the publisher.
Nor be circulated in any form of binding or cover other than that
in which it is published and a similar condition including this
condition being imposed on the subsequent purchaser.

Typeset in Sabon 10pt by
www.chandlerbookdesign.co.uk

Printed and bound in Great Britain by
4 Edge Limited

CONTENTS

Introduction	1
PART I: From Mechanical to Evolutionary Psycho-physiology	22
1. The First Sub-period: From Neuro-anatomy to Psycho-physiology	
2. The Second Sub-period: The General Theory of Neurosis	
PART 2: Attempts to Solve the Brain-Mind Problem	97
3. The Project for a Scientific Psychology for Neurologists (1895)	103
4. The Fate of the *'Project for a Scientific Psychology'*	193
PART 3: The Scientific Revolution	226
5. The New Science	227
Bibliography	249
Glossary	259
Index	263

DEDICATION

To Elisa, my beloved wife, for her boundless help and support.

To my beloved Daniel and Maia Honey, for their deep love and the joy they brought to my life.

ACKNOWLEDGEMENTS

This book is the result of a long and lonely journey. I hope I have succeeded in conveying my ideas to my academic colleagues and other readers.

I want to express my deepest gratitude to Nina Reshef, the translator and editor of this book, for her dedication and immeasurable patience.

Introduction

This book offers what I consider to be a new interpretation of the Freudian opus. I here develop the argument that Freud, in his ground-breaking works – *The Interpretation of Dreams*, *The Psychopathology of Everyday Life*, and *Jokes and their Relation to the Unconscious* – published in the early 1900s, had begun to lay the foundations of a new science directed at the study of human phenomena.[1] My position differs from Freud's many devoted disciples who, while intent on embellishing their mentor's image, tend to apply the term 'new science', in its grandiose or inflated sense, to his work. To me, the introduction of any new psychological school or therapeutic approach does not represent the creation of a new science. Nor do I consider any specific psychological school or theory an independent science. Moreover, were we to adopt the traditional approach (which I discredit in due course) that views psychoanalysis as a site located in the field of psychology, we would be required to talk about psychology as a science and psychoanalysis as only one of the several schools within its domain.

My intention here, then, is to show that Freud began to formulate a *new science for the study* of human phenomena, rooted in precise *empirical* research. His work in the respective period thus reframes all

---

1 By human phenomena I mean all human activity and behavior, feelings, thoughts and sensations in all cultural spheres (e.g., the inter-personal, the economic, the artistic, religious, psychological, philosophical, etc.).

the disciplines commonly employed to delve into human phenomena as 'pre-scientific' fields of study. I openly admit that this argument is difficult to prove, and for various reasons. First and foremost, the plethora of beliefs distorting our perceptions of human reality trenchantly impedes any rigorous study of human phenomena. Even though these distortions are well-known, their elimination is exceedingly difficult because they have insinuated themselves into the way we think.

Second, Freud was forced to contend with many obstacles while paving the difficult route that would culminate in his formulation of what he considered a more-appropriate research methodology. The complexity of Freud's thinking can be considered to have directly resulted from his use of concepts and approaches gleaned from diverse scientific fields, done for the purpose of solving convoluted scientific and philosophical problems, but also from the numerous internal contradictions found in his work. Complicating this effort is the fact that Freud did not take care in his writings to clearly distinguish the revolutionary from the outdated concepts he employed.

Another source of the difficulty in substantiating my position lies in the strong tendency, adopted by his interpreters and encouraged by psychoanalysts, to prefer the later to the earlier Freud. Viewed from this perspective, the early Freud is quite obviously only a budding architect of psychiatric and psychological theories. Yet, as I will show, the young, revolutionary Freud, in addition to being a psycho-neurologist, was essentially a practical philosopher, bent on solving psychology's main issues according to the natural science paradigm. Most important, however, was his dedication to finding the best, and what would prove to be pioneering, scientific method to study human phenomena.

A common belief sustained even among devotees who view his work as a major contribution to contemporary culture is that Freud's ideas are old-fashioned. In contrast, I will demonstrate the nature and current value of Freud's work as well as its revolutionary character when contrasted to contemporary psychology, philosophy, and, quite bluntly, all the human sciences. I will also argue that Freud provided original, scientific solutions, what I will call his *empirics* or *empirical approach*, to several cardinal philosophical issues, the main two being the problem of dualism and the question of how psychological phenomena are to be researched scientifically.

I am convinced that the true essence of Freud's work has yet to be grasped because the scholars who interpreted and continue to interpret his work have focused mainly on his theories, while ignoring his empiricism together with his general research framework. In like manner, researchers – whether coming from psychology, psychiatry, the history of science, or philosophy – tend to study his work from the perspective of their own disciplinary premises; they are thus prone to finding extensive proof for the correctness of their own positions. This might be expected because Freud, after all, either practiced within these same disciplines or was thoroughly acquainted with them; his aim was, therefore, to solve common problems.

The challenge confronting us thus lies in discovering how Freud's mind worked during his feverish pre-revolutionary period (up to 1900), what principles he applied when organising approaches coming from those disciplines into an integral, coordinated whole at each stage of his development. We will also want to know what issues eventually become the main axes for understanding his thinking. When doing so, we will differentiate between the problems he solved from those he bequeathed to future generations of scientists and researchers. To the best of my knowledge, no student of the early Freud (the period of our concern) has examined the different layers of his thought in order to discern how they influenced his problem-solving efforts.

Freud's writings are therefore not given to a straightforward reading, as if they were just a compilation of publications in psychology, psychiatry, or philosophy. In this early period, while engaged in the study of mental illness, Freud's goal was to solve core problems without going outside the existing body of knowledge on human behaviour. One of the main problems he approached involved a fundamental philosophical issue: what is the relationship between the brain and the mind? However, despite its importance, I propose that this is not the major question preoccupying the young Freud; what did concern him were the methodological conundrums surrounding the study of human phenomena. Freud did not declare this to be the focus of his interest although this can be deduced from a reading of his *Project for a Scientific Psychology* (hereafter the *Project;* written in 1895 yet left unpublished until 1950) together with the mentioned three revolutionary works—*The Interpretation of Dreams*, *The Psychopathology of Everyday Life*, and *Jokes and their Relation to the Unconscious*—all published between 1900 and 1905.

It is quite astonishing to me that even those scholars who do deal with the mind-body connection and the methodology appropriate for the empirical study of psychic phenomena have never mentioned how much these issues preoccupied Freud throughout his pre-revolutionary as well as revolutionary periods.[2] It appears that Freud's interpreters, including those who fully appreciate his position in the history of science, have found it very difficult to imagine the radical implications of his negation of contemporary scientific and philosophical canons. This point cannot be sufficiently stressed: The young Freud was not proposing just another philosophical or psychological theory on the essence of human nature but a pioneering scientific method for the accurate study of mankind. Freud's aim, as a highly rigorous scientist, was to find *the* scientifically appropriate way to study human phenomena. This insight has guided me in my interpretation of his work.

Before continuing, I make a short detour to the literature I explored as I delved into the scientific character of the Freudian project, a subject that continues to arouse much debate. As I will show, numerous arguments have been advanced to undermine the scientific importance of Freud's work. In the course of this book I will resoundingly rebut the major contentions directed at convincing us of the pseudo-scientific character of his enterprise. In my opinion, Freud and his ideas have always suffered from attempts to delegitimise his science. Feeding those critiques is a narrow view of Freud's work as encompassing his therapeutic method and psychological theories exclusively, a position that ignores his research methodology in relation to normal human phenomena.

My purpose here is not to mine these critiques, which are often rooted in attitudes toward Freud's problematic personality as well as selected incidents in his personal history. I doubt that those same

---

2   See for example Erneling and Johnson, 2005.

critical philosophers and scientists would deny the importance of the theories put forth by Descartes, Kant, Russell, and Wittgenstein, for example, on the basis of these thinkers' personal issues, which were often quite acute, even pathological. For instance, we might conclude that Descartes' theories represent one of the most significant efforts found in modern philosophy to cope with psychosis by means of dissociation: His concept *cogito* can readily be taken to represent his yearning to disconnect thinking from disturbing physical and emotional needs.

When trying to persuade us that Freud's entire corpus is pure pseudo-science, some[3] have chosen to use the harshest of terms, labelling Freud a liar, a fraud, or an intellectual criminal. Their main philosophical arguments effectively represent some version of Karl Popper's contention that psychoanalytic notions are pseudo-scientific because no empirical data can refute them, a claim they tend to deliver rather offhandedly, without engaging in a thorough analysis of Freud's overall research methodology and without considering the fact that the place of theory in the study of human beings is very different from that of theory in the investigation of the non-human, material world. According to Popper, Freud's ideas, like those of Marx and of Darwin, are unscientific because they do not meet a specific set of logical as well as philosophical criteria, meaning that they provide no empirical data on the basis of which they can be refuted.[4] Popper was apparently unaware that all Freud's theories can be refuted without inflicting any damage to his scientific methodology. He, like other critics belonging to the same school, have paid no heed to the fact that as products of human activity, Freud's theories (like all philosophy), are themselves empirical objects, given to scientific investigation.

Another common critique, born of the same tradition, is that the empirical data on which Freud together with other psychoanalysts based their theories are unreliable reports of dreams and free associations rather than the products of controlled experiments.[5] Generally speaking, these authors have not bothered to examine the

---

3   Medawar, 1975; Thornton, 1986 [1983]; Crews, 1986; Webster, 1995; Cioffi, 1998.
4   See Popper, 1972: 34-39; 275, n. 52.
5   Kitcher, 1992: 189.

scientific structure that Freud proposed. They ignore that structure because they view his work from the methodological perspective of the pre-scientific disciplines (psychology, psychiatry, and the other human sciences) that Freud made obsolete. And, despite their admission that scientific research progresses in unanticipated ways, they appear unwilling to apply this same insight when approaching Freud's ideas. Their attitude is especially regrettable in light of the fact that these same critics[6] often do not meet their own criteria with the same level of consistency that they demand of others. What should we say about the contradictions found in the works of Popper, the philosopher who demands that we link material with non-material entities? Are we to declare him an intellectual criminal as well?

Others choose to deny the scientific status of Freud's work by stressing one or another aspect of Freud's notions that dresses him in the robes of a philosopher. Alfred Tauber has written that according to current, popular understandings of science, Freud's scientific pretensions undermine his own position, and that it would be more correct to treat him as a social philosopher and moralist. Tauber argues that Freud's program is basically an interpretation of experience, emotions, and human history. He goes on to say that this program is inherently hermeneutic rather than scientific in nature (Tauber, 2010: xvi). I have no intention of claiming that Freud did not exhibit a speculative, philosophical streak, especially in the years following his revolutionary turn, the period of Tauber's interest. Instead, I would conclude that Tauber, from within his own preoccupation with Freud's conservative psychological and philosophical notions, has overlooked Freud's empirics and methodology.

As to those researchers and philosophers professing a positivistic orientation, they seem convinced that research in the human sciences in general, but particularly in psychology, should apply the quantitative methodology and experimental approach that have so thoroughly attained paradigmatic status in the natural sciences. However, the fundamental problem with employing this approach in the human sciences is that it requires adaptation (or choice) of the researched phenomena to the research methods, which limits the range of properties

---

6   See ftn. 3.

to be investigated.[7] Alternatively, adherents of the hermeneutic approach forgo precise research, based on the premise that every explanation, especially of human phenomena, is itself an act of interpretation. They justify this position by claiming that the very act of explaining human phenomena is strongly influenced by the researcher's subjectivity, ideological stance, theoretical preferences and so forth. However, despite their overt rejection of positivism, promotion of this line of reasoning effectively reinforces its opponents' position. Why?

Since the late 19th century, the hermeneutic school has attempted, as I do here, to advance an alternative to the position that the study of human phenomena cannot be scientific because we are unable to conduct such research by means of precision-oriented tools, that is, experimentation and quantification. Advocates of hermeneutics have maintained that the human sciences do belong to the family of sciences; they simply require a different research methodology: interpretation. While admitting that interpretation offers explanations of lesser precision than those of the natural sciences, hermeneutics has rescued the human sciences from allegations of a metaphysical bent by including human phenomena among the objects of scientific study (Dilthey, 1989).

Hermeneutic interpretations of Freud's work[8] do not, however, adequately reflect the significance of his discoveries. In contrast to the hermeneutic school, I am convinced that Freud's mission was to discover a precise empirical research methodology that would avoid the positivistic trap, that is, it would study human phenomena while abstaining from the use of physical and mathematical tools. Evidence for the accuracy of this conclusion is found in the fact that subsequent to his development of psychoanalysis, Freud never once attempted to apply tools taken from the other natural sciences with which he was thoroughly acquainted. Instead, he proposed using new tools, such as free association, for the precise scientific study of individual human beings, and the analysis of combined individual and social (including cultural) phenomena whenever free association is inappropriate.

I would also suggest that these two philosophical approaches, the

---

7   A point that Wundt had already understood; see Danziger, 1998 [1990]: 34-39.
8   Ricoeur, 1970 [1965].

positivistic and the hermeneutic, do not truly contradict one another; rather, they complement one another. I am not the first to recognise the bias inherent in viewing the two approaches as essentially polar. What I do suggest, for the first time, is that the same empirical paradigm lies at the root of both, a proposition I elaborate later in this book (see Chapter 5). This paradigm differentiates between the concrete material phenomena studied by physics and biology, in addition to presumably empirical psychological phenomena (behavioural, functional, cognitive) on the one hand, and abstract nonmaterial phenomena, studied by humanistic psychology as well as the humanities (that is, hermeneutic and non-scientific) on the other.

I thus argue that Freud contrived a dialectical solution to the taken-for-granted opposition between the two types of phenomena. He dwelt on the precise description and presentation of the phenomena in question while simultaneously searching for the scientific tools appropriate for examination of the observed objects' unique empirical character. I am referring to research exhibiting two main characteristics: (a) description and delimitation of each human phenomenon studied while avoiding any distortion of its specific features; and (b) direction of that research by one sole interest: precise investigation of human phenomena, free of extraneous interests, be they philosophical, academic, commercial, religious, political, and so forth. I do not mean to claim that quantification and experimentation would be absent from this new science, but I do maintain that their use would necessarily comply with these two characteristics. This, I suggest, is the type of rigorous approach needed for the research of human phenomena.

Attempts to characterise Freud's thought according to the current and conventional criteria applied in philosophy and psychology have also done little to shed light on his new research direction. His writings nonetheless reveal extensive involvement with the philosophical dichotomies so familiar to him and his peers.[9]

In the last few decades, however, a small group of authors, after exploring the diverse aspects of the Freudian project, have come to understand that all past attempts to categorise Freud according to

---

9   See Draenos, 1982; Kitcher, 1992.

philosophical criteria have failed. These authors have contended with the very broad range of Freudian notions while scrupulously examining his arguments regarding the foundations of a new natural science for the study of human phenomena. Moreover, they have done so while refraining from adjusting his research methodology and criteria, necessary to fluidly merge with those of the established natural sciences.

Patricia Kitcher (1992), for instance, has argued that Freud's objective was to outline a comprehensive, interdisciplinary theory of the human mind, one that would integrate approaches and knowledge originating in diverse scientific spheres, both natural (neuro-psychology, behavioural psychology, and evolutionary theory) and humanistic (linguistics, sociology, cultural studies, and anthropology). She has also noted that despite his own failure, Freud offers a model for others to follow when formulating a cognitive science. José Brunner (1994) has further argued that Freud's scientific system is much more sophisticated than the reductionist dichotomy (natural science versus hermeneutics) employed by his supporters as well as detractors when attempting to categorise his work. Brunner continues by saying that the dialectic between explanatory theories and hermeneutics is crucial for psychoanalysis. He suggests that Freud's program was aimed at developing a view of the human mind that would avoid this dichotomy by replacing it with a synthesis of explanation and understanding (1994: 97).

Among the scholars aware of the impossibility of capturing the essential Freud with philosophic terms exclusively, Bhargavi Davar and Parameshwar Bhat (1995) have proven themselves to be especially profound. They, too, see the Freudian project as an attempt to construct an interdisciplinary science. The two have criticised the failures of hermeneutic as well as positivistic thinkers to comprehend Freud through the science-versus-humanities prism. Davar and Bhat consider positivism (empiricism) and hermeneutics (humanism) to be two versions of the same philosophical stance they call *Foundationalism*. Knowledge, when viewed through the Foundationalist lens, is indisputable, or true, when it complies with some predetermined, ultimate criterion (sensory data, observation, or intuition). These criteria are pre-theoretical, axiomatic; they require no explanation. They function as the foundations of epistemic certainty, established at the preliminary stages of knowledge construction, meant to guide us in determining what knowledge is true and which theories are correct.

With respect to Freud, Davar and Bhat argue that the aim of the Foundationalist critique is to formulate strict philosophical criteria that would deny psychoanalysis any entry into the world of knowledge. This philosophical critique is rooted in the meta-scientific tradition inspired by Popper and his disciples but also in the humanistic constructs belonging to phenomenology and existentialism (1995: 8-9). They argue that positivists (Popperian or empiricist) employ epistemological criteria and norms to determine what they consider to be 'true' scientific theory as a means for rationalising allegations of pseudo-science directed at the Freudian system. Alternatively, they insist, humanists (hermeneutic, phenomenological, or existential) use ethical norms to banish what they consider to be dehumanising theories from the sphere of knowledge while promulgating science's ethical obligations to society.

Davar and Bhat, not content with pointing out the failures of positivistic as well as hermeneutic approaches, go on to investigate the source of those failures. They argue that these philosophical deconstructions of psychoanalysis express, in effect, the crisis of philosophy, implying that they must themselves be subjected to analysis and criticism. According to Foundationalism, even though the primary subject for the empiricist is physical phenomena and for the humanistic the self, the two share one basic assumption regarding the knowledge–mind relationship: 'a theory is sound only if it satisfies a single criterion of knowledge, provides a single interpretation and adopts a single method' (1995: 14). Consistency cannot be demanded of psychoanalysis so long as the philosophy of science is itself replete with contradictions, paradoxes, and internal inconsistencies (1995: 22). Foundationalism, which has guided philosophical thought since Plato, responds to the philosopher's need to protect philosophy's superiority over science in determining the norms governing theorising in addition to the conduct of science (1995: 14-16).

Despite the significant advances these new interpretations contribute to our understanding of the Freudian project, I maintain that they nonetheless err in their continuing tendency to place the type of science that Freud attempted to formulate either within the framework of psychology and psychiatry, or within the interdisciplinary mode, an approach meant to unify diverse disciplines, explanations and interpretations, science and humanism. They consequently remain blind to Freud's unique contribution to scientific research per se. As previously stated, scholars trained in the traditional disciplines of philosophy, psychiatry and psychology tend to apply only the tools available in their attempts to understand Freud's work.

This 'conservatism' has prevented them from understanding the three features of the Freudian project that underlie his new science: (1) it reaches beyond the boundaries of the mentioned disciplines; (2) it encourages a revolutionary perception of the empirical human world; and (3) it offers a new methodology, targeted specifically at research of human phenomena. Hence, I maintain, these features remain incomprehensible to those resisting academia's trenchant change. In order to continue developing while also applying Freud's new science, we need to revise the entire traditional structure, internal divisions, and academic classification of the human sciences. If we are to recognise and adopt the revolutionary features in Freud's writings, we cannot limit ourselves to investigating either his therapeutic system or his psychological and psychopathological theories. We must go further, to painstakingly examine how he perceived the empirical phenomena he researched together with what led him to his views.

Before continuing, however, I should underscore the fact that my stress on the empirical aspects of Freud's research does not flow from any empiricist philosophical stance (which stresses phenomena over theory) but from my understanding that the most fundamental changes Freud introduced into the human sciences involved his unique empirical perspective, the *new way in which he viewed* human phenomena.

These claims bring us to what philosophers call the *ontological problem*. However, because I reject philosophical rules of reasoning and am uninterested in ruminating into questions about the mind's existence, I turn to *epistemological* arguments. I therefore claim that psychology's core concepts distort our perception of human behaviour. To me, Freud's proposed science of human phenomena, especially his empirics, promises to finally free the human sciences from the influence of religion together with philosophy's fundamental concepts and dichotomies – the soul and its derivatives (mind, self), body vs. mind, analytic reduction of phenomena into mental elements and functions, the natural vs. the humanistic sciences, explanation vs. interpretation, objectivity vs. subjectivity, psychology vs. sociology – all of which induce an incorrect view of human reality while deterring acquisition of more precise knowledge about human phenomena.

The most appropriate time frame within which to investigate Freud's submergence into philosophical and scientific matters is what I call his 'pre-revolutionary' period in the years prior to 1900. A review of his activities during this period reveals what factors troubled him most together with what directions are most conducive to understanding his work. By this I mean what led him toward the most innovative elements of the revolution he initiated in 1900, what he yearned to alter in the dominant philosophical and scientific approaches to studying human phenomena, his identification of the factors that may provide the basis for a new human science, the points at which these developments stalled as well as the beginnings of Freud's retreat from his revolutionary ideas.

In my first book[10] I was able to show that Freud's investigations into his patients' stories, his linguistic perspective and fundamental theoretical concepts surpass, in their descriptive power, the definitions of illness and their symptoms resting at psychiatry's foundations to this very day. I was able to demonstrate that Freud's innovations showed psychiatry to be a pre-scientific discipline due to its distorted view of empirical phenomena, framed by its basic concepts. My purpose in the current book is infinitely more complex because I extend my horizons to touch upon the fundamental notions applied by psychology, culture, philosophy, religion, and folk beliefs when considering human phenomena.

The main arguments I develop in this book are tightly interrelated and not given to isolated analysis. Freud, I argue, laid the foundations for a revolutionary approach to the study of humanity in general, not simply the ailing individual, or the mind.

---

10 Haimovich, 2010.

He did so in three works, which I call the 'revolutionary trilogy': *The Interpretation of Dreams*, *The Psychopathology of Everyday Life*, and *Jokes and Their Relation to the Unconscious*. I do not employ the term 'revolutionary' lightly; my aim is not to glorify change per se, no matter how major. Instead, I address myself to the scope of the structural transformation, its depth as well as its breadth, a shift similar in its significance to that experienced by physics with the birth of Newtonian science, the theory of relativity, and quantum mechanics. My argument regarding the Freudian revolution is therefore especially far-reaching because it rests on the claim that the most revolutionary elements in Freud's work lie in his *empirics* and methodology, which I show to be superior to and more precise than that offered by today's recognised human sciences.

My second, complementary argument is that Freud renounced the concept of 'mind' as the prism through which to observe and categorise human phenomena. I would stress here, however, that my comments are limited to the empirical field and the work Freud published during a relatively short, unusual period. Despite these restrictions, I contend that his nascent but sophisticated empirical notions are sufficient to redirect the research of human phenomena.

My third argument states that in the wake of the Freudian revolution, conventional psychiatry and psychology should be treated as pre-scientific disciplines, resting on primitive empirical concepts.

The fourth argument I develop at the book's conclusion is that in line with Freud's methodology, philosophy in all its aspects, as the product of human thought and activity, must be considered another of the empirical objects to be examined.

Fifth, in suggesting a new empirical perspective on human phenomena, Freud established a revolutionary, uncompromising methodological precept: We must first accurately perceive and then describe the objects of our study, without neglecting their essential features – a tendency observed in the human sciences as well as positivistic-hermeneutic philosophy to this very day – before choosing our research tools (observation, experimentation, quantification, interpretation, explanation, intuition, or others). I expand on this point throughout the book, but especially in Part Three, which is devoted to Freud's empirical approach and scientific methodology.

As I have noted, the thread connecting all of Freud's interpreters is their tendency to examine his theory and research suggestions according to the traditional division of the human sciences into psychology, biology, psychiatry, and sociology' or, alternatively, the humanities (the humanistic model) and the natural sciences (the positivistic model). Contrary to these interpretive avenues, which maintain the common disciplinary distinctions, I suggest viewing Freud's thought as an arena in which concepts and theories belonging to different disciplines have the opportunity to intermingle; in the struggle between them, a new, previously non-existent empirical view of human reality is created. This approach, which led me to an interpretive strategy for reading and exploring Freud's writings, was applied in my previous book. Three interpretive strands comprise this strategy, each devised to cope with a specific set of the texts' core difficulties.

According to the *first interpretive strand*, I separate the revolutionary from the conservative elements of Freud's theories. This task is far from simple as the revolutionary features of Freud's scientific work are entwined with those more appropriate to the older paradigm. Hence, the main purpose of this aspect of my research was to clearly distinguish between the two while giving priority to those revolutionary elements more supportive to the construction of the new science.

The *second strand* of my interpretive strategy emerged from the realisation that the most revolutionary feature of Freud's thought was his empirical approach rather than his theories or therapeutic methods. As I demonstrated in my previous book, Freud had forsaken the notions 'symptom' and 'illness'; in this book I show that Freud had also abandoned those basic concepts used in psychology to comprehend and classify empirical (presumably psychic) phenomena. Freud's empirics differ greatly from the system for perceiving phenomena by means of 'mind,' 'function', and 'element'. My contention is especially difficult to sustain because the notion 'mind' is so deeply entrenched in the public consciousness as well as the academic discourse, whether speaking of philosophers, psychologists, or theorists in general, that it has become central to the academic mapping of the human sciences, which positions psychology among the scientific disciplines.

I should note here that my argument regarding the inappropriateness of 'mind' for the study of human behaviour greatly diverges from the ontological arguments offered by materialistic philosophers and positivistic psychologists (psycho-neurologists, psycho-biologists, psycho-physicalists). Whereas these deny the existence of mind in order to claim, by way of contradiction, that mental processes are simply neural processes, I reject all references to the concept of mind, together with its adequacy for the scientific research of human phenomena. As I elaborate in Part Three, I am convinced that Freud paved the way for a view of human phenomena that had no recourse to 'mind', 'functions' and 'elements'.

Because such an approach significantly deviates from the accepted schools of Freudian interpretation, I should mention Georges Politzer (1902-1942), a leading French psychologist and philosopher, who greatly influenced French psychology and psychoanalysis primarily through his students. Politzer, writing in the late 1920s (1965-1966 [1928-1929]; 1994 [1928]), had already suggested that the subject of Freud's research was not 'mind.' His argument, which is similar to my own, states that psychology – any stream of psychology – replaces everyday events with psychological phenomena. Politzer is unknown to English-speaking circles; his profound critique of traditional philosophical psychology covers Freud's psychological theories as well. In Europe, Politzer's ideas comprise the foundations of important elements in Jacques Lacan's work on the 'subject'.[11] Lacan, however, ignores Politzer's conclusions regarding the object of Freud's research just as he ignores Politzer's critique of philosophy.[12] Politzer's characterisation of the subject of Freudian research as the 'drama of everyday life' ('drama' is used here in its original Greek sense of doing and acting; see Giorgi, 1994: xxvi), greatly inspired my own work even though I disagree with his description as well as with his critique. My reason: Politzer, like other philosophers, based his analysis on Freud's theories without discerning the altered place of theory in Freudian research.

---

11 For comprehensive references to the notion "subject", see Lacan, 2006 (1966): 854-855.

12 Among the numerous psychologists and philosophers influenced by Politzer I mention only Merleau-Ponty, Leclaire and Laplanche (Apprey, 1994: x).

Added to the difficulties inherent in my arguments was the necessity of contending with the way in which Freud himself interpreted his own findings within the framework of his later psychological theories, in which 'mind' plays a central role. In order to cope with Freud's own self-interpretation, I added a third strand to my approach, as explained in my first book:

> The third aspect of my interpretation of Freud emerged as a result of the considerable difficulties that my research aroused. These difficulties can be characterised as the differences of opinion that arose between Freud and me regarding the essence of his scientific enterprise [...]. A vast literature exists regarding the disparities between the various interpretations, between those of the author and those of his readers. The two main issues causing these difficulties are: (1) over-interpretation of the texts; and (2) the legitimacy attributed to the reader's right to disagree with the author.
>
> My view of the second issue is that even when the reader's interpretation appears to resemble that of the author, it remains her interpretation. Her task is, of course, easier because she is not required to justify her interpretation. In my own case, justification of my interpretation, so different from Freud's on the one hand, together with my wish to avoid over-interpretation, an act inimical to me on the other, led me to treat Freud's texts with awe. My approach entailed staying as close to the text as possible, even compulsively, while trying to avoid any act of over-interpretation. I am therefore convinced that my disagreements with Freud are the result of my attitude toward his texts. This loyalty, together with some logical deductions, led me to discover the gap between Freud's practice and his theories.
>
> Additional support for my heretical interpretation was provided by Freud himself. I contend, without repeating here any of the proof so abundantly found in his late texts, that Freud's aspiration was to develop a new human science, confined to neither a 'psycho(patho)logical' theory nor a therapeutic method. This science would ignore the boundaries of established disciplines (psychiatry, psychology, sociology) as well as their respective empirical positions. Freud's treatment of his empirical objects, observed in his late research, ruthlessly crosses these disciplinary boundaries. My allegiance is thus to Freud's scientific spirit, not to the letter of his writings. It is Freud's scientific spirit that lent support to my 'over-interpretation' (Haimovich, 2010: 14-15).

In order to keep track of Freud's changes in attitude toward psychology, we must conscientiously examine his early work, written from the start of his medical studies in 1873. Freud, who began his research in the fields of biology and neurology while attending the laboratories run by Karl Claus and Ernest Brücke, turned to clinical psychiatry in May 1883, after transferring to Theodor Meynert's Institute of Brain Anatomy (Bernfeld, 1951). Greatly influencing his development were Freud's initial acquaintance with psychology and its fundamental lexicon during the courses he took with Franz Brentano (a dualist and idealist) and his laboratory work under Meynert (a materialist and positivist).[13]

In the first part of this book I therefore describe the process Freud underwent while moving from neurological to psycho-physiological models of investigation. My main reason for doing so is to follow Freud's preoccupation with the problematic relationship between the brain and the psyche (or 'mind'), between neurophysiology and psychology. The analysis of this phase is essential for our understanding of what brought him, in 1895, to try to explain mental processes on the basis of neuro-physiological and evolutionary causes (the subject of Part Two), prior to the scientific revolution he initiated in 1900 (discussed in Part Three). This revolution directly emerged from the reductionist failure as well as the trends accelerating in his own thinking.

Careful examination of selected neuro-physiological papers from the early period of Freud's research is crucial if we are to understand why he felt the need to contend with the dualist problem but also the progress of his revolutionary empirics. I am convinced that the tremendous effort Freud expended during those momentous three weeks in the late summer–early fall of 1895 was nurtured by his years of work as a neurologist together with his reflections on the problems associated with the reduction of mental into material processes. I suggest that the brain-mind relationship did more than provide the framework for Freud's neuro-anatomical and physiological research; it was a central preoccupation during the early stages of his psychiatric research and budding interest in his patients' stories. He eventually reached the point where he could not focus on other issues without

---

13 See Gay, 1988: 29-31, 42; Tauber, 2010: 29ff, 155-156.

first seriously attempting to solve the conundrum. Freud's approach, combining science with practical philosophy, came to distinguish him from his colleagues in the fields of neurology and philosophy.

The dynamics of Freud's development prompted me to divide his pre-revolutionary period, the focus of this book's Part One, into two sub-periods, based on the degree of his success in propounding a psycho-physiological explanation for hysteria. The first sub-period begin in October 1885, when Freud travelled to Paris in order to study with Jean-Martin Charcot (1825-1893). The onset of the second sub-period came in early 1893, the year in which Freud published his *Preliminary Communication,* and ended some time in 1897.

In the first chapter of Part One, following a short description of his academic studies, the intellectual atmosphere that he absorbed and the neurological research he conducted, I turn to a discussion of Freud's initial attempts to explain psychiatric phenomena as he understood them. The preliminary buds of those ideas can be found in his first published psychiatric articles on hysteria and hypnosis, which he further elaborated in the theoretical articles accompanying his clinical research. I discuss his writings on psychopathology in connection with selected neurological writings as they appear to belong to the same scientific discipline – neuropathology.

The main neuro-psychopathological work I examine is his essay 'On Aphasia' (1891). In this essay we find Freud's initial attempt to describe human phenomena as they are observed in reality, as linguistic rather than psychological phenomena. 'On Aphasia' thus represents a milestone in Freud's intellectual development that, throughout the period of his neurological research, progressed from the study of simple to highly complex neurological systems. This was the path he took toward understanding the most sophisticated of neurological systems – human beings. Here I trace the outlines of the theoretical model that Freud adopted, his fundamental notions, and his attitude to the psychology-neurophysiology relationship through an analysis of the studies he undertook during this period.

After a detailed investigation into his psycho-physiological explanation of hysteria in the second chapter of Part One, I dwell on those articles, written at the same time that he began to formulate a new approach to sexuality and defence mechanisms, in which Freud applied this explanation to other neuro-psychiatric phenomena. I then refer to all his published as well as unpublished works, written during the period between his letter to Josef Breuer (26 June 1892) and his letter to Wilhelm Fliess (16 August 1895), shortly before he commenced to write the *Project*. Hence, the precise chronological demarcation of this sub-period of research is very important. I note the few deviations from this chronology by means of citations from Freud's later writings while making the maximum effort to relay the period's special character without confusing the order of events.

The main goals of Part One are: (1) to highlight the homogeneity of Freud's thinking throughout this period as well as its dependence on the structure of psycho-physiological theorizing. This explanatory model played a central role in guiding Freud as he processed his discoveries; it channelled as well as filtered his theoretical choices while serving as a sort of 'mixer' into which Freud fed everything he wished to explain; and (2) to identify the core problems that he encountered, those that motivated him to write the *Project* in September-October 1895.

In Chapter Three (the first in Part Two), I introduce the *Project*, which I consider to be one of Freud's two most important, impressive works, the other being, of course, *The Interpretation of Dreams*. The two are closely linked. The *Project*, which Freud himself never published (it appeared posthumously), is the main work that led him toward realisation of the most revolutionary element of the research methodology described in *The Interpretation of Dreams*, specifically, his approach to linguistic phenomena, an approach he had begun to refine in 'On Aphasia.' The *Project* is not open to easy interpretation; as far as I know, no comprehensive study of all its features has yet been attempted. I focus here on the psychological elements and functions Freud borrowed from philosophy (as they were and are still used in psychology) for the purpose of categorising and explicating mental phenomena, in addition to his approach to the brain–mind problem. The latter, I argue, was one of the two main theoretical issues preoccupying Freud throughout the pre-revolutionary period. It remained in the background of his psychopathological writing until 1895, when his attention turned to its resolution in the *Project*.

One major factor impeding our understanding of the *Project* is causing it to be viewed as aberrant or speculative. Freud had, in effect, digressed from what was considered accepted practice, then as now, among his fellow neurologists. Scientists generally do not examine the fundamental premises governing their disciplines because this type of thinking is considered to be philosophical in character. The average scientist tends to adopt a materialist or dualist stance toward the brain–mind problem without delving into its nature. In contrast, Freud probed into the principles underlying psycho-neurology. It therefore appears to me that we can view his work during those years as situated at the seam between science and philosophy. Freud, with the aid of the most advanced concepts, approaches and theories of his time, examined the possibility of explaining psychological processes in materialist terms. In other words, he attempted to solve the dualist problem and unite the two entities, body and mind, what science and philosophy, in conformity with religiously based popular notions, had previously separated.

The second chapter of Part Two dwells on the changes in Freud's thought from the time he sent the *Project* to his friend Fliess (1895), up to the year 1900, when he published *The Interpretation of Dreams*. Publication of this work initiated an entirely new phase. During the interim between the two works, Freud almost completely abandoned psycho-physiological explanations to concentrate on the construction of an evolutionary model of psychological and psycho-pathological causation. Concurrently, he immersed himself in research on linguistic phenomena (dreams and mistakes) while developing a totally new research direction, a task, I believe, he successfully completed.

In Part Three, I unfold Freud's new science, the elements whose development he closed together with those he left open. I reveal the structure of the new science by describing how Freud resolved the problem of psychology's materialist foundations while expanding on the epistemic rupture separating the old from the new science. *The Interpretation of Dreams* thus captures the crux of the revolution he attempted to initiate in all the human sciences, not just psychology.

In the course of my argument, I suggest general outlines for the interpretation of Freud's later work. I deal with those human phenomena that Freud studied in order to describe how he expanded the reach of his research methodology into other areas. On the basis of that same methodology, I conclude by elaborating my own proposal for a reclassification of the human sciences.

PART I: From Mechanical to Evolutionary Psycho-physiology

Even though comprehensive studies of the texts I am about to examine are already available in the literature, I propose that their authors were unable to identify the unifying structure underlying those of Freud's works written during this early period, nor how the various parts are connected. My analysis takes into account that this period is commonly perceived as a preliminary stage in Freud's development of his innovative psychological ideas. Although some of these same researchers stress the physiological aspect of Freud's theories from this period, they present them as an amalgam of psychological discoveries mixed with physiological concepts and theories. There are some authors who, after stressing the physiological aspects, argue that Freud sought a comprehensive psychological explanation for the illnesses he was studying (Stewart, 1969: 28-30). In contrast, neurologically inclined authors, who better understand this period's neuro-psychological spirit, view this phase as the beginning of Freud's construction of a dynamic neuro-psychological approach (Solms, 2002).

My intention here is to present Freud's efforts as a single unit, characterized by a neuro-psychological structure having a deep internal logic. I therefore view this period as the commencement of his attempts to confront the essential philosophical problems inherent in the fields of psychology and physiology, and to understand the relationship between the two. This confrontation set Freud apart from colleagues who, then as now, construct their theories on the basis of accepted principles without deeply pondering their validity. Freud's application of those same principles eventually led him to understand that they were inappropriate for the investigation of human phenomena. Only after rejecting the psycho-biological model was he able to arrive at a totally new methodological approach to the human sciences. Freud's advances during this period thus represent a preamble to a new science. I therefore prefer the term 'pre-revolutionary period' to the commonly accepted 'pre-psychoanalytic period'.

1

The First Sub-period:
From Neuro-anatomy to Psycho-physiology

Freud's various biographers have noted his outstanding achievements while in school; they have described the young Freud as passionate for knowledge, a tireless reader, having broad intellectual horizons and showing interest in numerous scientific and philosophical subjects.[1] What most interested him in the area of philosophy was the study of human nature. Freud's medical studies, begun in 1873, had been less than enthralling him.[2] Peter Gay has stressed that Freud had a fondness for philosophers such as Feuerbach, who was intent on eradicating idealist philosophy and who is thought of by many as the father of German materialism.[3] During the 1874-1875 semester after commencing his medical studies, Freud studied philosophy with Franz Brentano, the founder of empirical psychology who, for a short time, was able to soften Freud's atheistic and anti-metaphysical beliefs.

---

1 Freud's personal life lies outside the confines of this book. References to biographical details are limited to those directly related with his ideas and the problems he dealt with. The text is based primarily on the biographies authored by Ernest Jones and Peter Gay as well as prominent works on specific topics, cited so long as they contribute important information. Regarding Freud's secondary school studies, see Trosman, 1976: 46-70.

2 See Freud, 1925, SE 20: 10; Bernfeld, 1944; Jones, 1972, Ch. 3.

3 See Lange, (1880[1877]): V. Two, 246ff; Gregory, 1977: Ch. 1; Gay, 1988: 28-29; Levitt and Turgeon, 2009.

In March 1876, Freud began working on his first research project with Carl Claus, head of the Institute of Comparative Anatomy and a leading Darwinist. Freud delved into Darwin's theory while taking courses in biology and zoology parallel to working with Claus, in the course of which he became acquainted with precise, rigorous scientific research methods.[4] Freud later worked in Brücke's physiology laboratory from 1876-1882,[5] after which he joined the staff of Meynert's neuro-anatomy laboratory (1882-1885).[6]

Freud's initial research investigated the development of the neurological systems of primitive creatures (under Claus' supervision, he investigated the gonads of eels, a primitive marine invertebrate), after which he gradually approached research of the human brain (Gay, 1988: 33). His first neurological articles dealt with genetic changes of the nerve cells in the spine of the petromyzon, a lower-order fish. Freud was able to prove the existence of a connection between the nervous systems of vertebrates and of invertebrates. His research thereby contributed to the scientific efforts aimed at demonstrating the 'evolutionary continuity of all organisms' (Solms, 2002: 19). Freud's other anatomical articles dealt with methodological issues (the techniques he developed to improve observation by means of the microscope); the structure of the nerve cells and fibres of crayfish; and the mapping of unknown regions in two small sections of the brain stem, the medulla oblongata and the pons. Over the course of this research, Freud progressed from study of the spinal cord to study of the brain, from individual cells to groups of cells, and from the nervous system of animals to that of human beings. Between 1884 and 1887, Freud also published six articles on the effects of cocaine use.

It is worth noting that Freud did not abandon his neurological research when he began to practice psychiatry after his return to Vienna in 1886, following his studies with Charcot in Paris. His last

---

4   See Ritvo, 1965, 1972, 1974, 1990.

5   For more on Brücke's personality and his influence on Freud, see Freud, 1925, SE 20: 9-10; Bernfeld, 1944: 348-351; Dorer, 1932: 118-120; Amacher, 1965: Ch. 1; Jones, 1972, Ch. 4. For more on this environment and the reigning scientific spirit under which Freud was trained and worked, see Rothschuh, 1973: Chs. 6-7.

6   On Meynert's influence on Freud see Bernfeld, 1951; Spehlmann, 1953: 11-14; Amacher, 1965: Ch. 2. On Freud's neurological research see Spehlmann, 1953: 18-52; Ritvo, 1990: Part 2; Solms, 2002; Gamwell and Solms, 2006.

purely anatomical article, 'The Brain' was published in 1888. Freud also published hundreds of articles on organic, neurological illnesses together with his early psychiatric works on hysteria and other neuroses. In these articles he described neurological syndromes, reviewed works written by his most important colleagues in the field of neurological research, established the foundations for paediatric neurology and wrote signal works on infantile cerebral palsy (the last published in 1897) that earned him an international reputation as the leading expert in the field. He also served as director of the Neurology Department of Vienna's Institute of Children's Diseases. These facts provide clear evidence that during the entire period, generally considered as the era when psychoanalysis was born, Freud in effect worked and thought as a neurologist. This explains why his first psychological theories reflect the innovative neurological conceptions current at the time. Numerous biologists, neurologists and historians of these disciplines are convinced that Freud's psycho-neurological ideas remain valid and innovative to this very day.

In order to understand Freud's first neuro-psychiatric works, which appeared late in his career as a neurologist, we must relate to the two scientific approaches then dominating academia as well as the program of the research laboratories headed by Claus and Brücke: physiological reductionism (Galaty, 1974) and Darwinian evolution. Brücke was one of the four founders of Helmholtz school of physiology and neurology. The other two were Emil Du Bois-Reymond and Karl Ludwig, two of the period's foremost, internationally recognized scientists.[7] The school's ideal was to establish a new physiology, based solely on chemistry and biophysics. In his elaboration of the school's approach, Du Bois-Reymond had stressed:

> No other forces than the common physical chemical ones are active within the organism. In those cases which cannot at the time be explained by these forces one has either to find the specific way or form of their action by means of the physical mathematical method, or to assume new forces equal in dignity to the chemical physical forces inherent in matter, reducible to the force of attraction and repulsion (quoted in Bernfeld, 1944: 348).

---

7   See Bernfeld, 1944; Temkin, 1946; Cranefield, 1957; Galaty, 1974.

The problem Freud and others encountered with this approach was that these forces explained only how organisms operated but not the mechanisms by which they developed or adapted to their environments. At this time, Darwin's biological theory had replaced religious, metaphysical and vitalistic explanations. Organic development was now being explained on the basis of natural forces, without any need to introduce non-material factors such as the vital force suggested by natural philosophy. Darwinism thus dominated Vienna University's School of Medicine as well as the laboratories headed by Claus and Brücke in addition to the Helmholtz school.[8] Although the School did not directly teach Darwinism, the physiological research it conducted reinforced the existence of evolutionary processes. Freud's own research on the nervous system of fishes also found evidence supporting Darwinism.[9] I should stress this fact because several of Freud's interpreters[10] have ignored the influence of evolutionary theory on his work while others have under-estimated its impact on his early thinking (Sulloway, 1979). The young Freud could thus be considered a proponent of *naturalistic materialism*, an approach blending physiological and evolutionary explanations (Flanagan, 1984: Chs. 1 and 2).

The Description and Explanation of Neurosis – Freud's First Steps in Psychiatry and His Psycho-neurological Approach

In 1882, Freud's economic straits forced him to leave his position in Brücke's laboratory and to begin engaging in medicine. He thereupon joined Vienna's General Hospital, where he stayed for three years until his departure for Paris, working for short periods in different

---

8   Du Bois-Reymond, in his 1870 lecture 'On the limits of the knowledge of nature *(Sur les limites de la connaissance de la nature)*', argued that: '...the evolution theory in connection with the doctrine of natural selection forces upon him the idea that the soul has arisen as the gradual result of certain material combinations and, perhaps, like other hereditary endowments that are useful to the individual in the struggle for existence, has advanced and perfected itself through an innumerable series of generations'. Cited in Lange, 1880 [1877], II: 312. See Also Gamwell and Solms, 2006: 9-10. Freud's Project (1895) obviously gave full and exact expression to the Darwinist notions suggested by Du Bois-Reymond.

9   See Gay, 1988: 36; Solms, 2002.

10 See Amacher, 1965; Pribram and Gill, 1976.

departments in order to acquire clinical experience. As part of his internship, he worked in Theodor Meynert's psychiatric clinic for six months, where he began to study nervous diseases as well as to treat patients privately. Freud also continued his research on the nervous system's anatomy, with Meynert giving him access to his neuro-anatomical laboratory, where he could work independently. While doing so, Freud moved from investigation of the spinal cord to study of a more advanced part of the system, the medulla oblongata.[11]

Freud's neurological works and initial psychiatric articles show a conceptual consistency because the same psycho-physiological perspective guided them both, with Freud perceiving psychiatric phenomena as neurological illnesses (Solms and Saling, 1990). The considerable conceptual continuity between this early period and his psycho-pathological theories was based on the psycho-physiological ideas he would formulate in the second sub-stage of his development. As we shall see, this continuity is also apparent in the subjects and problems that troubled him. Freud's psycho-neurological articles help us grasp the conceptual framework in which he worked and the important place the mind-body problem occupied within them. As I begin to show below, some of the changes observed during this period can be viewed as harbingers of his new psychology but also of his innovative empirical approach.

With his return to Vienna from Paris, Freud adopted a new approach to neurological functioning, distinct from Meynert's, which he articulated in his unpublished article 'Introduction to Neuropathology' (*Einleitung in die Nervenpathologie*), and in the article 'The Brain', his contribution to the medical dictionary edited by Albert Villaret.[12] The main innovative that Freud offers in these articles relates to the connection between the body and the cortex, which he describes as functional rather than topological, that is, the body's periphery is not, as Meynert believed, directly reflected but represented in the cortex. As a critique of Meynert's neuro-anatomical approach, this notion is one of the most important comprising the functional and dynamic views that would guide Freud in the coming

---

11 Freud, 1925, SE 20: 10-11.

12 See Solms, 2002; Gamwell and Solms, 2006.

years.[13] In embracing this approach, which well-fitted Charcot's view of hysteria as a functional-dynamic defect, Freud joined ranks with the prominent neurologist John Hughlings Jackson, who applied Darwinism to understand the brain and mental functioning. We may conclude that Freud joined contemporary efforts to develop a functional and evolutionary model so as to provide a more precise account of complex psychological phenomena (Flanagan, 1984: 24). His article 'The Brain' thus launches his long journey toward a scientific method for the research of human phenomena as they appear in reality rather than according to any philosophical and psychological 'scientific' analysis.

Freud significantly distanced himself from his German teachers and their neuro-anatomical views in the psychiatric context as well. Neuro-anatomic psychiatrists viewed all psychic disturbances and illnesses as expressions of an anatomical injury of the nervous system (localization theory). Hence, the psychiatrist's task was to discover the location of these disturbances somewhere in the brain. Should that location not be discerned, patients were viewed imposters, exemplified by hysterics.

Defining Hysteria — Hypnosis, neuro-anatomy, psychology and neuro-physiology

In his report of his studies with Charcot, Freud stressed the latter's seriousness, in contrast to his German colleagues who viewed French researchers as uncritical and tending toward investigations of the strange as well as the staging of performances meant to impress the public.[14] Freud harshly criticized those of his colleagues and German psychiatrists in general for viewing hysterical patients as imposters, and for defining hysteria as an illness incurred exclusively by women;

---

13 See Amacher, 1965: Ch. 2; Solms and Saling, 1990: 97-102.

14 Charcot's fame as a neuropathologist was immense. The French government established a chair in neuropathology in Paris medical school and a clinic at the La Salpètriére hospital especially for him. Patients and physicians from all over the world came to Paris in order to receive treatment and learn from him. Freud studied with Charcot from October 1885 until the end of February 1886. On Charcot's work and its influence on Freud see Freud, 1886a: 5; Chertok, 1970; Jones, 1972, Chs. 10-11; Major, 1974; Sulloway, 1979: 28-35; Gelfand, 1988; Harris, 1991.

he also chided them for not taking hypnosis as seriously as Charcot did.[15] Freud was especially impressed by the transition Charcot had made from research on cerebral illnesses originating in anatomical changes to the study of neurosis, especially hysteria, and from his conceptualization of hysteria (and neuroses in general) as caused by some functional, dynamic, psychological defect located in the cortex.[16] We should note here that within this conceptualization, physiology and psychology were almost considered synonyms. In the coming years, Freud's main purpose would be to unearth the character of the functional (that is, psycho-physiological) defect that was unique to hysteria. In his *Report* on his studies (1886a), and still more precisely in the preface to his translation of Charcot's *Tuesday Lectures*, Freud cited his mentor as commenting that he, Charcot, was dealing with pathological anatomy, with the hope that someone else would deal with patho-physiological aspects (1892-4: 135). By viewing hysteria as the product of a neuro-psychological defect, Charcot, an expert in neuro-anatomical pathology, revised the principle dominating psychiatry until then, according to which he himself had worked. According to this principle, psychiatrists defined as illness solely those phenomena that could be explained in terms of anatomical damage.[17]

In his early patho-psycho-physiological writings, Freud dealt with the same issues as did Charcot: neurological functioning, hysteria, hypnosis, suggestion and aphasia. Charcot was convinced that in order to discover the essence of the functional modification associated with hysteria, it was important to isolate this illness as well as to precisely defined it systemically, as a nosographic entity, distinct from other illnesses. This stance differed from that taken by other physicians who were wont to clump hysteria together with a plethora of other illnesses, the majority of which were indistinguishable one from the other (1888a: 12-13). He thought it especially important to differentiate hysteria from those cerebral phenomena resulting from anatomical changes.

---

15 See Freud, 1886a; 1886c; 1888a; Möbius, 1895.

16 See Charcot, 1991 (1889), Lectures I, XXI, XXII, XXVI; Havens, 1966.

17 Freud: 1886a: 10-12; 1886b; 1888a: 41-42; Charcot, 1991 [1889]: 12-13, 360; Levin, 1978: Ch. 2; Harris, 1991: xxvii-xxxviii.

Three facts were especially difficult for contemporary academic psychiatry to digest given its adoption of the neuro-anatomical explanation for mental illness: that no cerebral damage could be found during autopsies of patients suffering from hysteria; that hysterical symptoms were extremely changeable, with one symptom appearing and then disappearing within one patient, sometimes for long periods and sometimes never to return, accompanied by the appearance of new symptoms; and that hysterical symptoms neither fit the nervous system's anatomical divisions and functioning nor resembled known organic symptoms.[18] For instance, although paralysis of the right hand and leg could be expected to occur together, paralysis of the hand alone appeared. In consequence, when symptoms appeared illogical in terms of the anatomical approach, doctors would treat the patient as an imposter.

These facts, which contradicted the anatomical model of hysterical symptoms, aroused Freud's curiosity from his very first meeting with Charcot, when the elder physician demonstrated that traumatic differed from organic paralysis and amnesia and that he could induce instances of paralysis by means of hypnosis.[19] In concurrence with Charcot, Freud began to compare hysterical with organic symptomology. In his article 'Hysteria', published in 1888, Freud stated his conclusion that the anatomical structure of the brain was irrelevant to the explanation of hysterical paralysis (1888a: 47, 48-49). This conclusion raised a complex problem: If hysteria is not connected with the brain's structure, how can we relate to it as an illness of the brain?

Prior to Charcot's presentation of his view of hysteria as non-anatomical in origin, several physicians had suggested an alternative physiological explanation to the illness, but to no avail. The definition of hysteria as an organic disorder was problematic not only because no organic proof for this contention had been located, but also because researchers who thought it was only a physiological disorder had been unable to describe its nature. Freud brought attention to the need for a physiological formulation that took account of conditions

---

18 See Freud, 1886b, 1888a, 1892-3; Ackercknecht, 1959; Havens, 1966; Levin, 1978.
19 See Charcot, 1991 [1889]: 274; Levin, 1978: 45; Sulloway, 1979: 30; Harris, 1991: xlii.

of excitability in different parts of the nervous system (1888a: 41; 57). Freud was convinced that hysteria was a neurological disorder, requiring a search for its causes in physiological changes occurring in the nervous system.

In an article published in 1893, Freud suggested his physiological formulation of hysteria and established the fundamental characteristic of this disorder as lying in *'the abolition of the associative accessibility of the conception* [idea, representation]*'* of the organ (1893c: 170-172), implying the impossibility of one's idea of an arm, for example, becoming associated with other representations. Throughout this period, Freud's psychological approach remained entrenched in the neurological framework of his contemporaries despite adhering to Charcot's conviction that we must turn to psychology to explain hysteria.

Despite Freud's clear pronouncements, several of his interpreters have argued that Freud had formulated a psychological rather than neurological conception of hysteria (e.g., James Strachey, 1956: 3). Kenneth Levin in particular has claimed that Freud, from the beginning, made no attempt to provide a physiological explanation for hysteria but did expend considerable effort to develop psychological explanations. For Levin, Freud, after his meeting with Charcot in 1886, was already a psychologist (1978: 6).

In contrast to the preceding authors, I argue that Freud's statement regarding his move to the field of psychology and focus on representations does not entail any deviation from traditional psycho-neurology, either then or now. Freud's definition of hysteria as an expression of damage in a representation's associativity is inherently psycho-neurological in nature. It did not increase psychology's importance in his thinking and should not be interpreted as the abandonment of psycho-physiological principles. Psychiatrists and neuro-anatomists alike upheld such psychological ideas. For example, consider the detailed, comprehensive psychological theories espoused by Meynert, important aspects of which were adopted by Freud.[20]

In order to present a precise description of the evolution of his thinking at this early stage, it should be clearly understood that Freud

---

20 See Meynert, 1885: 138-278; 1892; Amacher, 1965: Ch. 2.

did not bid farewell to neurology in order to deal with psychology and psychopathology; instead, he forsook anatomical neuro-pathology in order to devote himself to psycho-physiological neuro-pathology, a field within neurology's boundaries.

Clear evidence of this continuity is found in Freud's preoccupation with the controversy regarding the character of hypnotic phenomena (1888b). One group, known as the Nancy School, whose outstanding representative was Hippolyte Bernheim, maintained that hypnotic phenomena resulted from suggestion. That is, hypnotic phenomena were observed after a conscious idea had penetrated the hypnotized brain as a result of some external influence and was then perceived as some spontaneous event. The second group, headed by Charcot, upheld that at least some hypnotic behaviours were based on physiological changes, meaning changes in the nervous system's excitability without participation of the neural elements active in consciousness.

Freud, however, was not content with this division of hypnotic events into the physiological and the psychic; he was intent on finding the link that connected the two (1888b: 81-84). He found a solution to his queries in auto-suggestion. He believed that in this type of suggestion, physiological elements interceded between external pressures and their outcomes. Although psychic in character, this suggestive process is unconscious. Freud thus concluded that indirect auto-suggestive events were physiological (i.e., unconscious) and psychic to the same degree (1888b: 82-84).

After eliminating the antithesis between psychic and physiological events in hypnosis, Freud sought to determine whether all hypnotic events are subject to psychic intervention. Within this context, Freud provided what was, to him, the only meaning of the concept 'psychic': changes in excitability taking place exclusively in the cortex (1888b: 84). He argued that it is inappropriate to detach the cortex from other parts of the nervous system, and that deep functional changes in the cortex must be accompanied by changes in excitability occurring in other parts of the brain (Spehlmann, 1953: 33). Later, Freud would contend that no single criterion exists capable of differentiating between psychic and physiological processes, between cortical and sub-cortical events.

At this point we can clearly witness the difference between the psychological and the physiological, and what Freud discerned as the distinction between the two. The *physiological* refers to every neural process that operates independently of those parts of the brain responsible of consciousness, whereas the *psychological* relates to a neural process in which the cerebral sections responsible for consciousness participate. That is, Freud perceived both processes as cerebral in location. At this stage, he agreed that suggestion-based explanations were preferable to physiological explanations because suggestion is a clear and undeniable process whereas neural excitation remains obscure in character. Without rejecting his reductionism, Freud made room for psychological explanations. Freud likewise offered a clear psycho-physiological approach in his presentation of August Forel's notion that suggestion is successful when the change has sufficient force to remain within the domain of the nervous system's dynamics (1889: 100-101). A comprehensive and detailed psycho-physiologic perspective is also in evidence in his neurological essay *On Aphasia*,[21] written in the midst of his search for a psycho-physiological explanation for hysteria.

On Aphasia

The subject of aphasia attracted Freud's interest already in the early stages of his work as a neuro-pathologist. A lively debate was being conducted at the time about the relationship between physiological mechanisms and mental processes.[22] Antonio Damasio has written that aphasia research constituted the intellectual as well as practical focus of neurology and those scientists and philosophers interested in psychology at the close of the nineteenth century.[23]

Siegfried Bernfeld considered *On Aphasia* to be the first 'Freudian' book 'with all the precious simplicity of style, lucidity of presentation and tantalizing hiding of ideas' (1944: 357). Since

---

21 Full title: *Zur Auffassung der Aphasien: Eine Kritische Studie*.
22 See Riese and Hoff, 1950-1; Riese, 1958a, b, 1959; Marx, 1966, 1967, 1970; Scherrer, 2003: 184.
23 Cited by Greenberg, 1997: 3.

its publication, the essay's hidden ideas have lost their allure thanks to the researchers who have burrowed into its intricacies. The essay nonetheless maintains, and will continue to retain, its impressiveness due to the richness of its ideas, which do not fall below those presented in *The Project* and *The Interpretation of Dreams*. Walther Riese found the essay to be a brilliant and rare work of medical thinking (1958a: 289), whereas Valerie Greenberg viewed it as a 'narrative of nineteenth century European intellectual culture' (1997: 5). From her perspective, the book is to be situated at the junction of multiple disciplines at different stages of development (1997: 1): anatomy, physiology, pathology and clinical neurology in addition to what we now call anthropology, archaeology and psycho-linguistics (1997: 5).

On Aphasia has been studied primarily for the purpose of discovering the prolegomena to psychoanalysis. Some have viewed it as proof of the importance of the connection between psychoanalysis and neurology, whereas others consider the book as evidence of Freud's first steps away from neurology and toward creation of a distinctive, autonomous psychology. Freud, who had begun his research on invertebrates, the simplest of neurological systems, now began probing into how language, the most highly developed of neurological systems, functioned. He had come to understand that in order to conduct scientific research of human beings, he would have to study language, that is, human phenomena as manifested in reality.

On Aphasia, which represents his first steps toward research of linguistic phenomena, was written while Freud was still chained by the two features of pre-scientific, philosophical views of these phenomena. On the one hand, its analysis into psychological and physiological elements and functions, and on the other, the reductive assumption that it was possible to explain linguistic phenomena down-top, by means of psycho-neurological premises, an approach still dominating contemporary psychology and neurology.

Similar to my view of *The Project* as a work characterizing Freud's later development, I consider *On Aphasia* to be Freud's most important work during the first sub-period precisely because it contains all the elements that, after considerable reworking, would bring Freud to his revolutionary approach to the study of human beings.

The What and Why of Freud's Critique of Localization Theory

Diverse researchers, but especially historians of neuro-psychiatry, are quite aware of the fact that Freud did not fully reject localization theory.[24] The psychoanalytic literature on the subject is nevertheless quite confused and difficult to classify. Researchers are divided between those who deny that Freud rejected localization claiming that his approach was not less locational than the theory he criticized, and those who argue for his departure from localization. In addition, some researchers view his functionalist theory as conceived by Freud the neurologist while others deny that Freud viewed 'functional' and 'psychological' as psycho-physiological terms rather than pure psychology.

As I will show, *On Aphasia* can be better understood once the reader accepts that one of the issues preoccupying Freud was the problem of what we can localize and what not, detailed by Friedrich Lange in his book *History of Materialism (Geschichte der Materialismus)*.[25] Freud's declared purpose for writing this essay was to critique the premises on which the accepted theory of aphasia had been constructed. The first premise differentiates between aphasias that are nothing more than the outcomes of lesions in the brain's speech centres and those caused by lesions in the areas connecting these centres one to another ('conduction aphasias'). The second premise relates to the topographic relationship between the various speech centres. Freud stated that these premises are strongly connected to the idea of localization, that is, to the confinement of neural functions to specific anatomical sites (E, 1; G, 1).[26]

This is not the place to fully elaborate either the neurologists' arguments for localization or Freud's counter-arguments on the nature of the various types of aphasia. I will only note that when Freud rejected the accepted explanations for conduction aphasias, his aim was to establish that there are no functional differences in the cortical area in which speech activity takes place. He maintained that within

---

24 See Spehlmann, 1953: 34-39; Riese, 1958a: 293-8; Marx, 1967: 820-821.

25 Lange, 1880 [1877], V. III: 111-161.

26 The page numbers in the parentheses refer to the original German 1891 edition and to Stengel's English translation of 1953.

the speech area, these activities are spread throughout very broad areas, making it impossible to differentiate between speech centres and associative areas, with every area in the speech area performing the different functions (perceptual and motoric) simultaneously. In addition, Freud wanted to prove that there are speech problems more amenable to explanation when we do not treat them as lesions in the connection between two speech centres but as a change in the functional state of the entire speech apparatus (E 29; G 30).

I should stress in this regard that Freud was unwilling to entirely reject localization theory. For example, instead of the explanation of transcortical motoric aphasia formulated by Ludwig Lichtheim, who attributed the condition to a lesion in the link between the motor centre of speech and one of the other cortical centres likely to stimulate the speech apparatus to act, Freud proposed viewing the disturbance as the outcome of some damage in the sensory area of speech, or a disturbance in the motor centre, now functioning at a lower level (E 28-29; G 29-30). However, in other instances, such as amnesic aphasia, Freud concluded that the condition could not be explained without assuming the presence of localized damage (E 43; G 45).

In the fifth chapter of his book, Freud criticizes the basic assumptions of the theory of aphasia, that is, the general premises of the localization theory as elaborated mainly by Meynert. The basic assumptions of this theory, to which Freud assigned the label *corticocentrischen* (E 46; G 47), were (a) the cortex, due to its location at the brain's surface, is especially suited for the reception and storage of sensory stimuli; (b) the cortical regions are connected by means of sub-cortical areas containing associative fibres. Between these regions we find an empty cortical zone that Meynert had originally called *functionelle Lücken* (functional gaps - E 45; G 46), meant to be filled with new memory impressions; and (c) the cortex contains point-by-point representations of the body, similar to a snapshot. Meynert called this kind of representation a 'projection' (E 47; G 49).

Freud also mentions that new anatomical and clinical discoveries negate Meynert's premise regarding the crucial importance of the cortex in the brain's organization. Based on these empirical findings, Freud concluded that the organization of the brain was based on two main systems: (a) the cortex, the more recently developed system; and

(b) the forebrain's ganglia (*Vordenhirnganglions*), which fulfil some of the brain's original, primitive functions from a phylogenetic point of view (E 49-50; G 51).

Freud also opposed Meynert's approach to the body's representation in the cortex, based on his (Freud's) adoption of an important element in Jackson's theory, which proposed that projections are to be found solely in the medulla whereas those representations are exclusively representative in the cortex,[27] meaning a less-detailed registration of the body's periphery. In other words, not every point in the body's periphery rests in the cortex even though some connection between them may exist, meaning that no precise topographic image of the body is to be found in the cortex. In a charming metaphor, which appears to herald the solution that he would later assign to the psycho-physical dilemma and the direction of his future research, Freud states that the body is contained in the brain's regions just like 'a poem contains the alphabet' (E 53; G 55). That is, the body is represented in the brain by means of different arrangements, composed of numerous and diverse associations of the elements, some of which may sometimes be represented whereas others attain no representation at all. The leading principle, Freud argued, is functional; topographical relations exist solely to serve brain functioning.

Two additional, very important elements of the many belonging to the localization theory promulgated by Meynert and Wernicke that were subjected to Freud's criticism entail assumptions regarding the localization of psychic functions and elements in the brain, and the view of perception and association as two distinct physiological processes. Freud's critique is essential for determining, with a good level of certainty, the degree to which he accepted – or rejected – localization theory. His main criticism of the premise that psychic elements were inscribed in the brain (that is, ideas could be located in the brain) was that in the brain, parallels of simple ideas, whether recurring or new, are processual rather than static events. This process, he continued, does not, however, completely reject localization. It begins at some location in the cortex and then disperses along diverse

---

27 This redundancy is necessary to understand the difference between the two kinds of inscription.

paths. Such events leave a change in the affected part of the cortex, and with it the possibility of memory (E 56; G 58). In other words, what Freud wished to negate in this context was the notion of physiological processes, parallel to psychological processes, as being static processes, as well as the premise that representations are registered in the nervous system as static 'copies' of the external world. Freud proposed an alternative premise, one stating that the registration occurs after representation has taken place. His suggestion was meant to counteract the conception of cortical centres as storage bins for ideas received directly from the external world, without undergoing any change, and not, as is commonly thought, to totally deny the existence of inscriptions in the brain.[28]

The second assumption regarding the localization of elementary units with which Freud found fault was the view of perception and association as distinct physiological processes. Although Freud noted that from a psychological perspective, perception and association were different one from the other and that ideas were separate units, he rejected this analysis from a physiological perspective; he thus assumed that the localization of the physiological parallels of perceptions and associations was identical. These physiological processes are part of a single, uniform process, not given to segmentation, which begins at one point and spreads throughout the cortex. What Freud could not accept from localization theory was the differentiation between speech centres and the associative pathways involved in producing

---

28 An extreme example of this approach is offered by Ana-Maria Rizzutto. Based on Freud's criticism of those locating representations in brain cells, as well as on Jackson's parallelism, Rizzuto argued that representation, according to Freud, is a psychic rather than a physiological phenomenon. She does so even though she herself refers to two facts: first, Freud's distinction between two types of external object inscription in the nervous system, the projective, in the medulla, and the representative in the cortex; and second, that the physiological parallel of representation leaves a change in the cortex, making memory possible (1990: 242-244). Freud's (and Rizzutto's) inconsistency is most prominent because he declares he doubt that something psychic remains after the occurrence of the physiological process parallel to the representation. But, if the change following the physiological process, parallel to representation, is not psychic, how can Freud explain memory providing the foundations for all linguistic and higher psychic activity? Freud's lack of success in resolving this contradiction in *On Aphasia* involved stating that psychic 'memory images' (*Erinnerungsbild*) will appear when the same cortical situation is later stimulated (E 55-56; G 56-57). Irrespective of Freud's declarations that the psychic is not physiological, and vice versa, what does the last statement mean? Is it purely psychological?

speech. Freud assumed that every part of the cortex where speech is ingrained has the same functional value, with no differences existing between them. He maintained that there was no need to assume that sub-cortical elements were involved in the association of ideas (E 57; G 59). For the same reason, Freud rejected Meynert's premise regarding the existence of memory-free zones in the brain, as well as another, related premise: responsibility for speech and language, the highest and most developed psychic functions, belongs to the sub-cortex, whereas the cortex (a more-recent and also the most-developed part of the brain) is responsible for the simpler functions of perception and memory. He believed that this scheme did not comply with evolutionary logic. Freud similarly stated that the speech zone is continuous and all speech acts take place within it. What he meant was that no functional differentiation is to be found in this area and that it is impossible to distinguish perceptual and motoric centres from the areas connecting the different centres (E 62; G 64).

But Freud did not renounce localization. He tried to explain the localization of speech centres, especially the Broca and Wernicke centres, established by pathological anatomy, while integrating the two theories (E 62-67; G 64-69). Freud's explanation was based on the localization of these two centres in the brain: the Broca area, located next to the centre of the bulbar motor nerves; and the Wernicke centre, located in the area containing auditory nerve endings (the exact location of which was then unknown) and the visual centre of speech, itself bordering on those sections of the occipital hemisphere where optic nerves endings are found (E 63; G 65). A sizeable distance divides these two centres, with the entire zone devoted to speech. Speech centres, Freud continued, mark the external borders of the speech zone.

As part of his critique, Freud also differentiated between the pathological and the physiological significance of the speech apparatus (E 63-64; G 65-66).[29] Freud clearly delineated how he connected the established localization theory with the new physiological conception to explain the clinical findings. As stated, Freud viewed the organization of the speech system as a continuous cortical zone,

---

29 See Riese 1958a: 293-294.

spreading between the ends of the visual and the auditory nerves and zones containing specific motor nerves, found in the left hemisphere (E 67; G 68-69). From the perspective of pathology, the importance of these zones is fully sustained. Topography, according to Freud, exerted its influence under two conditions, when the lesion was located in a speech centre, meaning one of the most peripheral zones of the speech area; and when the lesion decisively paralyzed that centre. The result of these lesions is the loss of one of the elements active in speech association. In all other instances, the functional in addition to the topographic factor need to be considered. Should a lesion be located in one of the centres without fully destroying it, that centre will continue to work while altering its functioning.

In his discussion, Freud noted that in order to describe how the speech apparatus operates under pathological conditions, he had chosen to adopt Jackson's theory, which stated that all modes of pathological responses by the speech apparatus in situations of damage originate in the retrogressive functioning (disinvolution) of a higher-level system. Each instance of pathology fits an earlier stage of physiological development, implying that an arrangement appearing relatively late will be the first lost (E 87; G 89).

As stated, Freud attached great importance to localization while incorporating the theory with physiological premises advanced for his time. Freud's primary purpose was to negate the theory's applicability for explaining speech as well as associative and intellectual activity while accepting the distinction between localization of symptoms and localization of functions, presented by Lange and Jackson.[30] Under normal conditions, the speech area functions as a single unit, providing a basis for the higher psychic activity related to speech and language.

Here it is important to note that Freud did not reject the physiological importance of the diverse centres as receptors for specific stimuli (E 66; G 68). What this implies is that although Freud was interested in broadening his assumption regarding the lack of functional differences between the sensory and the motoric centres, he was unable to dismiss those differences in terms of anatomy. This meant that he accepted the anatomical-localization theory not

---

30 Riese and Hoff, 1950: 65.

only because of its pathological but also due to its physiological importance. Stated more precisely, Freud was dissatisfied solely with the premise that the speech association zone was directly connected to the body's periphery, meaning that this zone was directly influenced by the projective information received by sensory nerves, and perhaps by motor nerves, from the external world. A careful reading of the text clearly indicates that premises regarding localization and projection did not disturb Freud when his subject was lower-level cerebral functions, such as sensation and movement, which do not involve the higher associative activity grounding speech. It is nonetheless worth noting that within the context of his premise that linguistic activity involves the different centres, Freud was hinting at another, non-projective premise stating that sensory stimuli change in the process of their reception. To achieve a more precise evaluation of Freud's success in constructing a purely physiological theory, devoid of anatomical premises, we should recall that Freud himself noted that he had inferred the complex structure of words from pathology (E 73, 78; G 75, 80).[31] Freud thus acknowledged that a word's elements (as he conceived them) exactly respond to the anatomical description of the cerebral activity centres (visual, auditory and motoric).

We now briefly review the localization premises that Freud dismissed when explaining speech functions as well as his main physiological objective, as deduced from the text *On Aphasia*:

1) Within the context of speech, the anatomical differences found in the neurological system are important.

2) Projective imprints of sensations and perceptions are found in the speech zone.

3) The physiological processes parallel to ideational processes are static and discrete. We should stress that

---

31 Riese coherently summarized the difficulties Freud encountered when developing his approach to physiological processes. Riese thought that Freud was unable to avoid inferring the composition of speech from its disruptions and to pass from pathology to physiology even though he did reiterate his disbelief in the possibility of localizing the physiological processes accompanying speech (Riese 1958a: 293).

Freud accepted the notion of ideas as psychologically discrete units; he even used it as a pillar of his description of the speech apparatus.

4) Perceptions (ideas in general) and associations are different physiological processes.

This criticism enabled Freud to pave his way toward a physiological model of the cortex in which associative and representational activities freely take place when thinking and speaking. In that model, the cortex's functioning is not confined by ingrained objective information. The endless possible combinations of associative-representative activity are not limited by the preordained, fixed meanings, received from the external world. In his physiological descriptions, Freud sought to approach the way in which people speak in everyday life. For this, he found support in Jackson's writings.[32] I argue that this was Freud's main reason for rejecting localization's four premises regarding thought and speech at the same time that he retained them with respect to the motoric and perceptual functions uninvolved in speech. He consequently developed a dichotomous model of neural systems. The first, sensory-motoric system, related to the body's periphery by means of projective links; the second, verbal system, was not directly related to the body's periphery.

Later, in the *Project* (1895), Freud went on to provide a fully developed version of the psycho-physiological system as comprised of two sub-systems, described as the first and last stops in the neural system's phylogenetic development. The first, simpler sub-system, based on the reflexive arc model, was responsible for perceptual and motor functions. One pole of this system ended in the brain's receptive centres, which receive sensory stimuli; its second pole is responsible for response activity by means of the body's motor mechanisms. The second sub-system operates on the basis of the first. As we have seen, Freud envisioned these two zones as residing in a broad area free of physiological differentiation given its responsibility for speech and higher intellectual activities. This area operates on the basis of the two ends of the reflex arc and includes those ends within it. Freud's

---

32 See Jackson 1958, V. 2: 130, note 2; 138, note 2.

implicit assumption was that the connection between the sensory and the motoric centres of speech was indirect. Lying between them was a sort of expanse in which a broad and diverse range of activities took place between the time that stimuli were received in the sensory centre and responses were elicited in the motoric centre; this stimulus was potentially capable of eliciting a response by the motoric centre. That is, according to this premise, there is no connection between stimulus and response without the intermediation of representational activity.

Freud and the Mind-Body Problem

According to Otto Marx, the psycho-physical problem was the main theoretical issue to be confronted by all those dealing with aphasia (1967: 818). The nature of this problem as it appears in *On Aphasia* is important for two reasons. First, even though Freud deals with psychological issues (perception, association, words and speech) within the framework of his neuro-physiological research, he frequently states the need for separating psychology from physiology. Second, this problem is generally ignored by almost all the authors contending with Freud's book or his ideas during this period. Their analyses seek to determine the degree to which the psycho-physical problem is either psychological or physiological in character. Ernest Kris, for example, argues that in *On Aphasia*, Freud began to contend with the relationship and very appropriateness of the division between physiology and psychology (1950: 115).

Erwin Stengel argued that Freud's most important step at this phase was the limited autonomy he assigned to the psychic, as a result of which he freed himself from the shackles of physiology and neurology in contrast to Jackson, who was unable to distinguish mental processes as such and who never deviated from the psycho-physiological framework despite the theory of concomitance he had formulated (1954:88). Mark Solms and Michael Saling have argued that it is in *On Aphasia,* rather than the *Project,* that we are to search for the lost connection between Freud's neurological and psychoanalytical work. They claim that the important decisions enabling Freud to develop psychoanalysis related to his rejection of the localization of psychological processes in distinct anatomical zones (this rejection represents his leave-taking from orthodox German neurology), and his adoption of Jackson's dynamic evolutionary theory (1986: 407).[33] Freud was thus able to construct an independent psychological theory without discarding neurology. In order to make their case, Solms and Saling repeat Mark Kanzer's (1973) argument stating that the *Project* does not present a truly neurological model but a series of psychological statements in neurological dress (1986:400). They do not seriously relate to Freud's declarations or to the fact that in the *Project*, psychological processes are rooted in physiological explanations. Their argument regarding Freud's unwillingness to construct an independent psychological model free of neurological connections ignores Freud's wish to undo those connections. In addition, Solms and Saling do not explain how psychology can remain an independent discipline if simultaneously linked to neurology. Statements of this kind were generally used to introduce a reductive approach in which the psychological is reduced to a product of neurological anatomy and physiology.

I contend that these and many other researchers do not fully comprehend the complexity of Freud's approach with respect to the psycho-physical problem. My critique states that the standard treatment of Freud's approach to disciplinary demarcation is very superficial, with the respective authors not relating to the issue in principle, as Freud did. Freud was not interesting in discovering the appropriate distance between psychology and neurology, expressed in trivial self-contradicting statements such as 'independent psychology, tied to neurology', 'autonomy limited to the psychic', and 'the appropriate level of separation between physiology and psychology'. What is crucial here is that Freud was immersed in achieving two contradictory aims, the first, rejection of the link between neurology and psychology; the second, preservation of that link. Most of all, he aspired to solving the psycho-physical dilemma. Indeed, the *Project*, considered by some as a psychological work in disguise, provides the clearest statement of this purpose, one that distinguished Freud from all his colleagues and his interpreters, then as now. In the *Project*, Freud, by adopting a scientific – or practical philosophical – approach,

---

33 See also Davison, 1955.

attempted to overcome the basic problems burdening the human sciences, meaning those revolving around the connection between the body and the mind.

Freud's work demonstrates just how much he was neither an ordinary physician nor psychiatrist. His genius was expressed in his fantastic ability to relate to the major contradictions of modern thought while attempting to resolve them. In *On Aphasia*, he succinctly describes the heart of the psycho-physical problem:

> 'But does not one in principle make the same mistake, irrespective of whether one tries to localize a complicated concept, a whole faculty or a psychic element? Is it justified to immerse a nerve fibre, which over the whole length of its course has been only a physiological structure subject to physiological modifications, with its end in the psyche, and to furnish this end with an idea or a memory?' (E 55, G 56).

Beginning with these questions, Freud transforms the scientific issue of localization into a much more fundamental query: Is it possible to assume that physiological processes are transformed into psychological processes? Freud's query can be carried even further: Is it possible to assume that physiological processes take place within the psyche?

At this stage, Freud was, it appears, unable to fully abandon the premise regarding the link between the brain and human phenomena. Even though he spoke to the psycho-physical problem in his first question, its formulation evades any deep resolution by arguing, as scientists and philosophers often did, that when discussing the localization of psychic events, they were in fact referring to the physiological processes accompanying psychic processes rather than the psychic processes themselves. In this case, a psycho-physical interaction cannot be found because no connection exists between the psychic and the physiological given that both phenomena are in fact one and the same physiological process. Here is an example of the absolute reduction of the psychic into the physiological. Freud was well aware that the researchers he was criticizing were conscious of their problematic formulations. He was tolerant of their positions because he knew that when they referred to the localization of ideas or functions, they were actually referring to the localization of physiological processes. In this context, Freud's critique was limited to their phrasing, which was confusing (E 55, G57). However, if localization advocates were in fact concerned with physiological rather than psychic processes, why raise such a fuss?

Freud's second question in the above quotation had a radical, extreme character. Only two of his many interpreters, Marx and Riese, related to this knotty problem. Nevertheless, Freud's own response was inadequate to his question:

> 'The relationship between the chain of physiological events in the nervous system and the mental processes is probably not one of cause and effect. The former do not cease when the latter set in; they tend to continue but, from a certain moment, a mental phenomenon corresponds to each part of the chain, or to several parts. The psychic is, therefore, a process parallel to the physiological, "a dependent concomitant"'[34] (E 55, G 56-57).

This statement indicates that Freud adopted the dualist approach expressed in Jackson's writings, specifically, that physiological and psychological processes are parallel and autonomous, one from the other, yet connected in some way. Jackson phrased his approach in these terms:

> 'Now, I speak of the relation of consciousness to nervous states. The doctrine I hold is: first, that states of consciousness (or, synonymously, states of mind) are utterly different from nervous states; second, that the two things occur together--that for every mental state there is a correlative nervous state; third, that, although the two things occur in parallelism, there is no interference of one with the other. This may be called the doctrine of Concomitance'.[35]

The question is why was Jackson so persistent in relating to psychological phenomena (e.g., awareness, the ego) as a distinct segment of his physiological research and theorizing? If the two processes were so different and devoid of mutual influence, an idea

---

34 This phrase, in English, appears in the original.

35 See Jackson 1958, V. 2: 72.

hinted at in Freud's questions, why did Jackson and Freud have need of any premise regarding some kind of link between the two? Furthermore, if these processes were so inherently different, what did one indicate about the other? Is the parallelist approach truly dualistic, as various researchers have claimed,[36] or is it actually monistic and reductionist? We can, in effect, ask the same question of the entire dualist approach. Dualism, I argue, in all its variations, can be treated as a monistic and materialistic doctrine. Hence, the body-mind problem requires formulation in a more radical way than we have done to date.

According to Marx, despite the fact that Jackson had warned about the confusion between psychology and physiology as well as anatomy, he himself was prey to this error (1966: 340). Jackson's position regarding the psycho-physiological problem meant that he was uninterested in the character of the connections between body and mind, and that for him, concomitance theory was serviceable for the study of brain diseases. On other occasions, he stated that for clinical purposes, our beliefs about the nature of the links between psychical and neuronal states were unimportant; the assumption of their parallelism would do.[37] Riese has also noted that Jackson was persistent in his search for the physiological basis of psychical phenomena and for the '"nervous arrangements" their "psychical side"' (1965: 815). My conclusion is that Jackson, by turning to psycho-physiological parallelism, had tried to avoid dealing with the psycho-physical problem but without losing the assumed benefits gained from integrating psychological and neuro-physiological explanations (this and similar approaches are quite common in medicine, psychology, biology, philosophy, etc., among dualists as well as materialists).

The same muddle appears in Freud's work. On the one hand, he wrote that because one idea is clearly given to differentiation from another idea, it is impossible to deduce that the physiological parallel is likewise simple and localizable. Freud in fact argued that it is incumbent upon researchers to independently differentiate

---

36 See for example Sulloway 1979: 48-50.

37 Jackson 1958, V. 1: 52; Marx 1967: 818.

the physiological modification from the concomitant psychological processes (E 55-56; G 57-58). That is, he clearly distinguished between physiological and psychological processes on the basis of Jackson's parallelism. On the other hand, Jackson's and Freud's parallelism raises two important questions: If no connection exists between the psychical and the physiological, and if these two phenomena are completely different, what is the meaning of the premise that they are concomitant and parallel? Furthermore, why is it at all necessary to assume the existence of a connection between two so highly distinctive processes?

The answer to these questions is that parallelism is not less organismic than is localization or any other theory linking the organic to the psychic. The sole benefit that Freud could reap from parallelism was support for his premise that physiological processes are dynamic rather than static, and not given to discrete anatomical localization. This conception differs from the psychological approach asserting the existence of discrete ideas or representations. We should nevertheless recall that Freud's parallelism, despite its dynamics, is not less localizational, reductionist and psycho-physiological than that of his colleagues. A concise example of this is found in a single sentence, from which Freud erased all traces of parallelism: 'Yet whenever the same cortical state is elicited again, the previous psychic event re-emerges as a memory' (E 56; G 58). And even though Freud rejected any causal links between physiological and psychological processes, this sentence can be used to definitively demonstrate that he remained loyal to parallelism while simultaneously remaining convinced that the physiological caused the psychological.[38]

Marx has observed that after trying to convince us of the necessity of clearly separating physiology from psychology, Freud himself ignored his own warning when discussing the physiological parallels of perceptions (1967: 820). He notes that when Freud uses the term 'association' in this text, he often means the association of physiological processes (1967:822). Another of Marx's comments clarifies the interpretive confusion found in the literature regarding

---

38 In *On Aphasia*, then, Freud took an approach similar to that taken in his introduction to Bernheim's book.

the degree of physiologism and psychologism found in Freud's work. Marx argues that the most important aspect of *On Aphasia* lies in Freud's critique of Wernicke. According to Marx, Freud had realized that Wernicke's main flaw rested on his translation of psychology into physiology. The interesting point Marx raises (Riese, 1958a: 289, made a similar claim) is that Wernicke (like all the psychiatrists and neurologists active in the 19th century) had constructed his anatomical model on the foundations of a psychological model of language while convinced that these foundations rested on anatomical data. In short, psycho-linguistics had been effectively translated into neuro-physiology and neuro-anatomy.

Marx further states that the most significant contribution of Freud's critique is his revelation that these anatomical and physiological explanations were, in effect, crypto-psychological (1967: 822-823). We can therefore agree with Levin's argument (see above) that Freud's theories, even at this early stage, were primarily psychological in nature. I agree with Levin but only under the condition that we amend his statement by adding that all psychiatry and neurology was rooted in psychological assumptions at that time. Hence, the criterion crucial to understanding the changes in Freud's thinking is implicit in the following question: Did Freud remain committed to solving the psycho-physical problem on the basis of monistic materialism (often referred to in dualistic dress) and, in this sense, to the view that psychology was a materialistic science, meaning that it was grounded in neurology? With respect to this early period, the answer is clear: I fully agree with Riese (1958a: 300) when arguing that Freud unhesitatingly supported 'brain materialism', that is, he believed in basing psychology on cerebral (anatomical or physiological) foundations in order to endow it with the aura of natural science.

We can now better understand the place of *On Aphasia* in Freud's development. Marx's observation remains pertinent in that all the existing research, when searching for the sources of Freud's later concepts and theories among its pages, seeks to situate the book's importance in the history of the illness and the evolution of later psychoanalytic reasoning. The consensus reached, irrespective of the approach adopted, is that *On Aphasia* is one of the last neurological works Freud wrote after immersing himself in psycho-pathological research and the formulation of a psycho-therapeutic method.[39] Contrary to these views, I believe that this book is important because, first of all, it helps us penetrate Freud's early psycho-pathological thinking once he began to search for a neuro-physiological explanation adequate for the neurotic (functional, psycho-physiological) phenomena he was researching. The book, an integral part of his budding psycho-pathological research, provides evidence of the uniformity of his neuro-psycho-pathological work during that period. It also represents Freud's first attempt to provide a neuro-physiological explanation for a neurosis.

This book is not, however, the only work indicating the strong connection between Freud's research on aphasia and his work on hysteria (Marshall, 1974: 355). To begin with, hysterias, like aphasias, were considered to be neuroses, that is, nervous illnesses. Neuroses were therefore categorized as neurological rather than psychiatric illnesses. This explains why neither hysterias nor aphasias were included on the list of psycho-neuroses in contemporary psychiatric textbooks.[40] At this point, psychiatry limited itself to the treatment of psychosis, with neuroses considered 'non-physical diseases of the nervous system' (Erben, 1890).[41] Perhaps the best evidence of the close proximity between hysteria and aphasia is found in Charcot's famous *Tuesday Lectures*, attended by Freud, which dealt with both phenomena together (Charcot, 1991 [1889]). Aphasia was one of the types of paralysis that Freud, under Charcot's encouragement, began to research in order to differentiate it from hysterical paralysis (Freud, 1893c: 161, 163).

These and other facts lead us to conclude that Freud took great interest in his colleagues' research on aphasia due to their contribution to the understanding of hysteria. And so, it was the

---

39 Freud himself as pointed out by Kris, 1954: 19, note 1; see also Riese: 1958b; Marx, 1967; Jones, 1972: 233-237.

40 See for example Krafft-Ebing, 1890.

41 Quoted by Chertok and de Saussure, 1989: 423-424, note 6. These authors note that such a definition of neurosis appeared in Erben's 1890 article, published in the same medical textbook where Freud published his article on psychotherapy. That definition is particularly interesting because it provides a blatant example of the contradictions characterizing the medical-psychiatric discourse.

study of aphasia that nurtured the neuro-physiological conceptions that Freud developed in expectation of discovering physiological explanations for psychological phenomena without (seemingly) undermining their independent character. Freud, on his part, was searching for functional, that is, neuro-physiological explanations for the two conditions. Their resemblance appeared stronger in those cases of aphasia not rooted in some anatomical disorder, as in the case Freud described of paraphasia resulting from decreased functioning as distinct from those phenomena elicited by fatigue in healthy people (E 13; G 13-14). Freud saw a deep connection between diverse abnormal phenomena (e.g., between the repetitious sentences of hysterical patients and of those suffering from aphasia), which he viewed as expressions of different brain disorders.

It is clear that in turning to research of his patients' psychology, and in formulating the new psycho-physiological theory presented in *On Aphasia*, Freud did not deviate from the psychological principles underlying the neuro-psychiatric research of his colleagues (Riese 1958a: 293-294, 298). In addition, *On Aphasia* allows us to understand Freud's thinking when he attempted, somewhat later, to differentiate between organic motoric paralysis and hysteria. His efforts were, in fact, not directed toward differentiating between an organic malady and a psychological disorder but between two organic illnesses. By this I mean that he considered paralysis to be a result of an organic disorder to be explained in anatomic and physiological terms, versus a functional paralysis, caused by a physiological disorder in the absence of any anatomical injury. In consequence, *On Aphasia* presents us with Freud's nascent psycho-physiological theory for the explanation of a range of brain diseases, including aphasia and hysteria. It therefore follows that this work represents neither the beginnings of Freud's transition to psychology nor his departure from neurology. Freud would elaborate this theory in a series of articles and other documents, among them the *Preliminary Communication* and the article on organic and hysterical paralysis, all written between 1892 and 1894.

Another class of symptoms pointing to the tight link between the two illnesses relate to the central role played by diverse functional linguistic disorders (Charcot, 1991 [1889]: 130). Freud was greatly attracted to research on the physiology and pathology of language and speech, required for the investigation of aphasia. Freud dwelt on linguistic phenomena throughout his analysis of his hysterical female patients.[42] His interest in aphasia strengthened when he came across Jackson's writings while researching brain functioning. These offered more than an innovative neuro-physiological approach; Freud found in them a new way to understand how perceptions, words, ideas and memories were integrated in an associative stream of speech. Jackson's influence on Freud was deep and far-reaching, going beyond physiological explanations of aphasia.[43] His influence can be felt throughout Freud's theorizing in this period, loosely observed in *On Aphasia* but fully developed in the *Project*.

Freud's main ambition at the time was to describe the cortical area as the site of representational activity, completely unfettered by localization and projective models. But why was he so intent on doing so? I am convinced that from the beginning, Freud had no intention of completely negating localization theory, only of denying its importance when explaining the role of language, speech and

---

42 Rizzutto (1989) has raised an argument similar to my own. She contends that Freud wrote *On Aphasia* in order to explain the linguistic phenomena of three of his patients: Anna, Emmy and Cecilie. She is convinced that Freud's book is to be assessed against the background of contemporary psycho-pathological research. According to Rizzutto, Freud turned to the research of aphasia and to the construction of a general theory of linguistic phenomena because he sought to explain his patients' pathological and spontaneous speech. However, Freud's interest in aphasia was more general, going beyond those three patients. In contrast to Rizzutto, I argue that Freud wanted to explain normal not less than pathological linguistic phenomena. Although Rizzutto does not exaggerate the importance of language to Freud's thinking, even at this early stage, she totally ignores his determination to understand normal linguistic phenomena as well as the most developed normal brain functioning. Hence, contrary to Rizzutto, I argue that Freud investigated pathological linguistic phenomena in order to understand normal phenomena. In doing so Freud was consistent with his initial neurological studies. The last, highly important difference between Rizzutto and myself lies in the place assigned to the concepts *object representation* and *word representation* in Freud's understanding of linguistic phenomena. On the one hand, Rizzutto is correct in drawing attention to these terms because they represent cornerstones in Freud's psychological explanatory model. On the other, Rizzutto erred in not referring to the use Freud made of these concepts for the purpose of grounding, reductively, linguistic and other phenomena in psychological explanations according to traditional neuro-pathology and psychology.

43 See Stengel, 1954: 87; Fullinwider, 1983.

higher representational intellectual functions. That is, in addition to explaining aphasia by combining the functionalist approach with localization premises, the overt aim of his research, he had another, latent purpose.

As previously stated, what most bothered Freud about localization theory, in addition to its conceptualization of speech pathology, was the way in which it explained speech per se. It is important to repeat that Freud was not averse to the idea of miscellaneous brain centres whose purpose it was to receive projective information originating in the external world as well as the body, and of motor centres responsible for speech activity. He was unhappy with the explanation of the representational activity that prepares the speech mechanism for action as grounded in functionally differentiated brain centres. In contrast, Freud was convinced that the cortical area (which included the sensory and motoric areas) responsible for the brain activity expressed in speech and representation activity was a very large area, lacking internal physiological differentiation. In this area, stretching between the diverse perceptual and motoric centres, speech associations (that is, all representational activities) took place. Freud was also certain about the impossibility of distinguishing between perceptions, memories and ideas and their associations within different linguistic acts. As stated, in the speech area, representation of the sensations received from the sensory organs is a representative rather than a projective process. This means that ideas are not precise reproductions of physical reality and that sensory stimuli constantly change in accordance with the infinite number of interpretations they acquire and with the endless connections they create with each new perception or recollection.

I argue here that Freud was driven by a broader purpose than explaining aphasia; he wanted to explain speech phenomena among normal as well as hysterical persons once he obtained a clear image of those phenomena during his early clinical research. His rejection of any physiological difference between perceptions and associations provides outstanding proof for my argument. Even though Freud argued that conceptions (representations, perceptions and ideas) are to be considered elementary phenomena in psychological terms, that is, they are separate and distinct from their associations, he immediately afterwards describes psychological perception and association as a single process, similar to his physiological view (E 55-57; G 56-59). I therefore conclude that Freud, in his clinical research and conceptualization of normal speech, was struck by the continuity and associativity of language and speech, by the plethora of word's meanings and their diversity. All these led him to conclude that language's very nature allows us to make only arbitrary distinctions between ideas and words. *On Aphasia,* gives physiological expression to this insight.

Here I must return to Jackson and the great influence his views on the propositional (judgmental) character of speech had on Freud. The crux of Jackson's model was that single words or unconnected sequences of words lack meaning. Words acquire meaning only within a sentence. Hence, sentences, rather than words, comprise the essential units of speech.[44] It is worth noting that Jackson's premises presaged one of the basic tenets of modern linguistics (see the works of Ferdinand de Saussure). Freud, who intuitively perceived some fundamentals of language and normal speech, did not elaborate any linguistic principles either in *On Aphasia* or in any of his later works. Those of his later works that do deal with linguistic phenomena were based on the psychological reductionism of words and ideas as discrete units. Marx and others have already remarked that Freud, despite his discovery that contemporary physiology's fundamental flaw rested on its being a crypto-psychological field of study, never critiqued its basic premises; he adopted them instead (1966: 346). Although Freud was unable to formulate his solution in theoretical terms, he overcame his psychological reductionism and went beyond it by proposing an empirical approach to purportedly psychic phenomena that differed completely from that of philosophy, psychology and physiology.

---

44 See Jackson, 1958, V. 2: 130, note 2; Riese, 1965: 812-813.

The Psycho-physiological Explanation of Hysteria

After some years spent researching hysteria, Freud, in collaboration with Breuer, had the opportunity to present his psycho-physiological explanation for the condition's symptoms. This account represents the conclusion of this stage of study and of his initial acquaintance with psychiatric phenomena. At the same time, it represents the onset of a new stage, during which Freud developed his general theory of neurosis and some selected psychoses.

Freud's formulation of his trauma-based psycho-physiological theory of hysteria was completed only in 1892, irrespective of his initial adoption of Charcot's two views of the sources of hysteria. The first of these views argued for the impairment of the neuronal functioning, expressed in the system's over-excitation (1892-4: 137-138; 1893c: 168-172), whereas the second, the etiological model, located the source of impairment in the emotional trauma experienced by persons having an inherited tendency for hysteria (1888a: 50-51; 1893d: 22-23). In parallel, Freud had also accepted Breuer's view that the recollection of a traumatic experience would eliminate the related symptom (Freud-Breuer, 1893b: 7; Jones, 1972: 246).

Despite the purposes of Freud's research on the symptomatology of hysteria, which had been clear from the very start, formulation of a psycho-physiological explanation of the condition was confounded by numerous problems. However, before turning to the solutions Freud found for these problems, I discuss Levin's argument, which denies the physiological underpinnings of Freud's thought at the time. Although Levin admits that Freud had suggested seeking a physiological explanation for several aspects of hysteria, he argues that Freud was in fact influenced by psychological rather than physiological models. Levin further argues that Freud abstained from contemplating the precise meaning of the physiological impairment causing outbursts indicative of hysteria (1978: 65). He also states that the majority of Freud's comments on the illness are, in effect, psychological discussions on the pathogenesis of hysteria's primary symptoms, such as paralysis, and their cure by means of hypnotic suggestion (1978: 68).

As we will see, Levin erred when contending that Freud shirked from a physiological formulation. The most we can say is that

Freud evaded the issue throughout the years of his psychiatric studies. He simply felt incapable to the task. Once he overcame this feeling, he invested considerable effort in providing the desired physiological formulation and to convincing Breuer to collaborate in its publication. The texts themselves provide the best response to Levin's contentions.[45]

Freud and Breuer ultimately elaborated an explanation that integrated the psychological with the physiological. Their approach, based on their empirical experience, provided the structure for the '*Preliminary Communication*'. The psychological perspective, outlined in the article's first section (1893b: 3-7), treated the representations stimulated by external events, as might be expected. We should recall here that representation was considered a process taking place in the cortex, with psychological conceptions adjusted to the structure of physiological thinking. To achieve a thorough understanding of the Freudian text we should also remember that at this stage, Freud considered a phenomenon as psychological not only if it was based on representation but also if it occurred in response to an external stimulus.[46] Following Charcot, Freud and Breuer stated that hysterical symptoms were the outcomes of some psychic (that is, external) trauma experienced by the patient. The causal relationship between them, they stressed, is far from simple. The trauma, they suggested, did not function solely as the cause of a symptom that disappears, with the latter continuing its independent existence. The traumatic memory, they proposed, functions as a foreign body once it penetrates the patient's psyche. Proof of their proposition is that every hysterical symptom disappears if we succeed in raising the memory of the traumatic event and releasing its associated energy (*affect*). It thus appears that hysterical patients suffer primarily from their memories (1893b: 7). We therefore

---

45 Marx has shown that 19th century physiology was based on psychological models throughout (Marx, 1966, 1967). His conclusions support my argument that the type of speech and the models employed cannot serve as criteria for determining the level of any scientist's physiological or psychological orthodoxy. The essential criterion for determining their conceptual allegiance is the total practical (not only the explicit) attitude toward the body-mind dichotomy and the reduction of psychic to physiological phenomena.

46 Freud 1888b, V. I: 77.

see that together with the psychological aspects of hysteria as described in their article's opening section, Freud and Breuer describe the empirical phenomenon on which they base their physiological explanation. Specifically, they had noticed that raising memories themselves was insufficient to cause the symptom's evaporation, that is, recollection in the absence of *affect* brought almost no results (1893b: 6).

In the next section of their article, while presenting the physiological aspect of their approach, Freud and Breuer explain why hysterics suffer from memories. They argue that the detrimental impact of traumatic memories resulted from the fact that these memories, unlike other memories, did not fade away; the reason: during the harmful event, the injured person does not appropriately respond. An appropriate response, they state, was any action, from tears to revengeful acts, voluntary or not, which allows the associated energy to dissipate. They add that the second avenue for dealing with trauma involves connecting the memory with other experiences and associations that might correct it. To illustrate, when a person is humiliated, he can turn to his sense of self-worth to correct the hurt. In the absence of such an appropriate response, memories are stored in their full strength, lacking any access to consciousness in normal circumstances. In short, traumatic memories are those whose energy has neither been discharged nor deteriorated, unlike those memories that remain connected with their associations.

Although Freud and Breuer did not offer an explicitly psycho-physiological formulation in this paper, the physiological character of this explanation remained obvious in Freud's numerous papers and documents from that period: in his notes to his translation of Charcot's book *Tuesday's Lectures* (1892-4: 137-138), in his lecture 'On the Psychical Mechanism of Hysterical Phenomena' (1893a: 36), in his paper on the comparison between organic and hysterical paralysis (1893c: 171-172), and his article 'The Neuro-psychosis of Defence' (1894c: 60-61). In this last article, Freud filled in the gaps and explicitly stated that the theory of abreaction, mentioned in the *Preliminary Communication*, was based on his hypothesis regarding quantities of affect. Because numerous researchers have argued that Freud had already changed theoretical direction and turned toward psychological interpretations in this period,[47] we should review his description of hysterical symptoms in his comparison between organic and hysterical paralysis, published just a few months after the *Preliminary Communication*. In this article (1893c), Freud presents his physiological explanation, following his psychological definition of hysterical impairment as the elimination of a conception's accessibility to associative interplay. This he does in order to describe the process inducing paralysis. Freud argued that paralysis of an arm, for example, would appear under conditions in which a person's conception of his or her arm was part of a highly charged association; once the quantity of excitation (affect) was discharged, the organ would cease to be paralyzed. If a person is incapable of or unwilling to rid him or herself from that excess quantity, the event's memory becomes traumatic and causes permanent hysterical symptoms. Freud named this theory 'The Abreaction of Accretions of Stimulus' (*Das Abreagieren der Reizzuwächse*, 1893c: 171-172).

This explanation reiterated the one presented with Breuer although now its neuro-physiological character is no longer blurred. When Freud states that Charcot was the first to teach that a turn to psychology is warranted when searching for an explanation for

---

47 Among all those cognizant of the importance of the psychological-physiological dichotomy in Freud's work, it is interesting although difficult to understand the case of Ola Andersson. Andersson did not deny the physiological aspects in Freud's early psychotherapeutic writings. He also did not deny the strong connection between Freud's physiological formulation of hysteria and its psychic mechanism (1962: 87). Else, he argues, Freud's formulation, as presented in a note to Charcot's *Lectures*, was the type of 'physio-pathological model of hysteria' that Freud had sought. Andersson adds that in his 1888 contribution to Villaret's dictionary, Freud was still unable to do so, although he did so later, in 1892 (1962: 91). Andersson also argues that Freud and Breuer's theory of abreaction (*Preliminary Communication*) had far-reaching physiological implications (1962: 92). However, Andersson introduces a most peculiar and quite contradictory change by stating that Freud's attempts were inconclusive, and that his efforts to construct a physiological formulation in 1892 and 1893 were completely hypothetical (1962: 95). Andersson attempts to justify his new claim by referring to Freud's later revisions (for example, in the 1894 *The Neuro-psychoses of Defence*) of his physiological formulation, done to present it in a more psychological language. Contrary to Andersson, I maintain that even those more-psychological formulations are an extension rather than a nullification of the physiological model. I mention two reasons for doing so: Although Freud was already deeply immersed in the life histories of his patients, he still wanted to solve the core psycho-physiological problem: Is it possible to base psychological phenomena on physiological processes? Moreover, Freud's 1894 presentation of his formulation was not less physiological than its previous versions.

hysterical symptoms, his reference was to physiological psychology. Freud further remarks that Charcot had stated that hysteria was a physiological impairment of the neuronal system. The clearest evidence for the neuro-physiological reductionism in Freud's explanation is found in the statement that a person's conception of his or her arm, once denied entry into the arena of free association, continues to exist in the material substratum (1893c, I: 171). What exactly did Freud mean by this term if not the neuronal system? What other material might he view as the material infrastructure of psychology?

My conclusions regarding this subject are simple: At this stage in his theoretical trajectory, Freud could not yet imagine any other kind of psychology, one that was not based on the functioning of the nervous system; without the brain, psychology would cease to be a natural science. For Freud, the very thought of psychology free of any material foundations was equivalent to forsaking the natural science for metaphysical psychology. In addition, we should cluster together all the terms that Freud considered to be quantitative in nature (e.g., excitation, affect, discharge, etc.) within the category of physiological concepts and not, as Levin argues, quantitative psychology. Despite his success in outlining a reasonable psycho-physiological framework that could not be considered inferior to others in its reduction of psychological to physiological processes,[48] Freud remained dissatisfied and thus continued to search for a more comprehensive formulation. Once he began to understand these processes in terms of his theory of defence, he considered his previous theorizing wanting with respect to its explanation of the appearance of hysterical and neurotic symptoms in general. And so, despite Freud's progress in providing a physiological explanation for hysterical

---

48 The plausibility of Freud's formulation was particularly noticeable when comparing it with statements made by Breuer and others. Breuer had stated that he would discuss psychic processes in the 'language of psychology' but thereafter referred to them in unquestionably physiological terms. Breuer had said that the term *Rindenerregung* ('excitation of the cerebral cortex') is a postulate (1895: 185), implying that his physiology is purely hypothetical. Herman Oppenheim, one of Freud's contemporaries, who Levin describes as representing the physiological approach to hysteria (1978: 67), declared that his approach was also 'hypothetical' and that he was satisfied with only hinting at a speculative explanation of the physiology of hysteria (1890: 554). In the case of Oppenheim, the literature tends to ignore his statement while presenting him as an unalloyed physiologist.

symptoms, the main riddle he was determined to solve – how to present a physiological model of the conflict waged by psychic forces between themselves – remained intact.

2

The Second Sub-period:
The General Theory of Neurosis

This chapter dwells on the deep uniformity and deep dependence on the structure of the physiological model marking the work done in this period. The physiological explanation thus constituted the main conceptual force guiding Freud's elaboration of his empirical findings while functioning as a filter in his choice of concepts and theories. The psycho-physiological model was the sieve through which Freud sifted all that was in need of explanation during this early stage of his development. I therefore describe this period as consisting of one unit, characterized by a deep internal logic that would gradually dissipated. Some of its core elements (such as the energy terms) would continue to influence Freud throughout his life, and even colour current psychoanalysis. I will also try to identify the central problems that Freud encountered during his work, problems that motivated him to write the *Project* in September-October 1895.

The full psycho-physiological explanation of hysteria

As we saw in Chapter 1, Freud and Breuer had together concluded that hysterical symptoms resulted from traumatic events. They also noted that the majority of these symptoms were not produced directly by the trauma; unlike the case in physical trauma, they did not exist independently of their cause. Freud and Breuer consequently deduced that it was not the emotional trauma but its memory that produced these symptoms. This memory acted as a foreign body in the nervous system, provoking pathological effects long after it had penetrated the individual's nervous system (1893b, II: 6; 1893a, III: 35). They saw proof of their assumptions in the fact that when patients remembered the traumatic event and expressed the accompanying feelings, they found relief from their symptoms.

Although this explanation was adequate to their empirical findings, Freud and Breuer felt that it aroused a theoretical problem awaiting explanation: How was it possible for a memory to be active so many years after the traumatic event took place? Why was it not forgotten and deprived of its force and clarity? To explain this pathological process they suggested some hypotheses regarding normal and abnormal psycho-physiological functioning. They proposed that ideas became pathological when they retained their energy, resulting from interruption of the normal 'wearing-away' or dissipation of that energy. An idea's affect *(Affekt)* was thought to fade away in two ways, first, when an adequate energetic response to the trauma takes place, what they referred to as 'abreaction' or 'catharsis', and second, when, even without abreaction, the trauma's memory becomes connected with other associations that contradict and thereby 'correct' or 'change' it (1893b, II: 8-11).

In his lecture on the mechanism of hysteria (1893a), Freud developed his description of the physiological aspects of normal and hysterical phenomena along lines that were described in two separate documents, Sketch A and Sketch C.[1] He wrote that when a person experiences a psychic stimulus, the *sum of excitation* [sic] of his neuronal system increases. And yet, this system also exhibits a tendency to diminish this excitation. A healthy nervous system is thus achieved under two conditions: through associative thinking or by an adequate motor response. This premise provided the physiological grounds for explaining the traumatic ideas inducing hysterical phenomena: ideas become pathological when the nervous system fails to discharge surplus energy.

---

1   The June 26, 1892 letter to Breuer, known as Sketch A, I: 147-148; and a draft, Sketch C ('On the theory of hysterical attacks'), of Section IV of the *Preliminary Communication* (1892, I: 151-154).

The clearest evidence of the physiological character of Freud's psychological explanations is found in Sketch C, where he defines psychic trauma as: 'any impression which the nervous system has difficulty in disposing of by means of associative thinking or of a motor reaction...' (1892, SE I: 154).

Like emotional trauma, the ample variety of hysterical symptoms (paralyses, functional inhibitions, hallucinations, tics, etc.) was also subjected to psycho-physiological reduction, expressed in the conceptualization of hysterical symptoms as representations, expressions or symbols of traumatic events, and as failed attempts to discharge their blocked 'affect'. According to Freud, symptoms are unsuccessful expressions of ideas that appear wherever a breach occurs in a logical associative sequence. In other words, hysterical symptoms are ideas registered in an incorrect or inappropriate place, in this case, the body, rather than in memories. But symptoms, as substitutes for ideas, are (manifest) elements of an ideational sequence. That is, for Freud, ideas are impressions left by stimuli on the nervous system; they constitute the psychic aspect of nervous functioning.

To illustrate, Freud described paralysis of the arm as a consequence of the 'abolition of the associative accessibility of the conception of the arm' (1893c, SE I: 170-171); it captures one aspect of his attempt to equate the concept 'symptom' to psycho-physiological explanations. Completing the reduction is the second aspect, which Freud conceived as the inaccessibility to association consequent to the strong energetic charging (originally *valeur affective* in French, quota of affect in English, and *Affekbetrag* in German) of the respective idea, for instance, the mentioned arm.

It is important to note that the concepts 'affect' (*Affekt*) and 'quota of affect' (*Affektbetrag*) were used by Freud in another reductive formulation, that of emotion. This he did by using the terms *Affekt* and *Affektbetrag* in their two different meanings, that is, in the term's usual sense as feelings, and its special sense as the energetic aspect of the rejected idea. As Freud used a list of terms when referring to the energy infusing the nervous system – e.g., 'excitation' (*Erregung*) and 'sum of excitation' (*Erregungssumme*) -- I maintain that he used 'affect' and 'quota of affect' in an energetic-physiological sense, as part of his effort to reduce emotions to physiological phenomena.

And yet, the psychoanalytically prone authors who viewed Freud's theories as a *pure psychology* have continued to argue that Freud could not possibly have applied those terms in connection with energy.[2] While doing their best to ignore this reduction, they confused the empirical level of Freud's research, where emotions are fully explored, with the theoretical level, where the psycho-physiological conception of emotion constitutes one of the most-unhappy aspects of his impressive enterprise. It is especially interesting that Hermann Oppenheim, whom Levin referred to as a physiologist, formulated a psychological definition of emotion. Like Freud, Oppenheim stated that sensory and motor functions, blood vessel activity and secretions, are influenced by feelings; the involuntary influence of emotions on these functions was, moreover, one manifestation of hysteria (1890: 554).

As stated, Freud did not used the terms 'affect' and 'quota of affect' to refer to emotions exclusively. When comparing hysterical with organic motor paralysis, Freud used 'quota of affect' in a clearly physiological and energy-related context (1893c, I: 170-172). It is highly doubtful that Freud, when speaking of associations having great energy values and existing in the 'material substratum', was referring to purely psychological phenomenon. 'Material substratum' can only mean the 'nervous system'. Additional evidence of the physiological character of his theory is provided by its title: 'The Abreaction of Accretions of Stimulus' (1893c, I: 172), with similar expressions appearing in a note to his translation of Charcot's lectures, in Sketch C, and in his lecture on the psychic mechanism of hysterical phenomena.

But Freud's use of 'affect' and 'quota of affect' is not the sole indication of the physiological reductive character of his theory of emotions. The central thesis suggested by Freud and Breuer in their *Preliminary Communication* is that hysterical patients suffer from memories because the affect attached to those memories has not faded away. To reiterate, the dissipation of a memory's energy is achieved through a motor reaction or through association with other memories that are capable of amending the original memory. Their premise that it is possible to mitigate a memory's traumatic force by means

---
2 See Strachey 1962a: 66-68; Levin, 1978: 89.

of motor discharges (body actions) contradicts the psychological interpretation of their explanation of hysteria and invites the following question: If we assume that 'affect' is a psychic element, how can it be discharged by bodily actions? It seems impossible to accept this assumption without an additional assumption about the functioning of the psycho-neuronal system, which I now explain.

During this period, the main premise of Freud's psycho-physiological theory of hysteria was that the nervous system tends to maintain a constant level of excitation by means of either an associative elaboration of each energy increase or by a motor reaction (1892, I: 153-4). In the psychoanalytic literature, this premise is known as the 'principle of constancy'. Freud, in his lecture of January 11, 1893, returned to this premise to explain the extinction of the affect connected with memories. As I will show, it is implausible (as Strachey argued, 1962a) that Freud used those terms to speak of experienced emotions exclusively. For Freud, a repressed memory's affect is a latent emotion. He viewed emotion as only one of several possible expressions of the nervous energy discharged in the direction of some motor mechanism. In contrast to emotions, excitations not discharged through a motor mechanism remain energetic charges, accompanying ideas inscribed in the 'material substratum'.

Freud made this view explicit in two later fragments. In the third section of his essay 'The Unconscious', he wrote that 'there are no unconscious affects as there are unconscious ideas'. Ideas are cathected 'memory traces' whereas emotions correspond to processes of discharge, manifestations perceived as sensations (1915, 14: 178). A similar formulation appears in Lecture 25 of his *Introductory Lectures to Psychoanalysis* (1916-7, 16: 395).

These fragments clearly show that even in this very late stage of his work, Freud was still influenced by the psycho-physiological approach; he was incapable of saying, as we do today, that there are unconscious feelings just as there are unconscious ideas. Feelings, according to this definition, result from the discharge of the energy charging those memories comprised of conscious sensations of motor actions as well as of pleasure and displeasure. I therefore conclude that what Freud referred to as emotional structures were not emotions per se but memories inscribed subsequent to emotional experiences.

In addition to the ideas 'idea' and 'affect', the core of Freud's psycho-physiological explanation, Freud harboured others, still of secondary importance at this stage. I present them here for the purpose of completing the theoretical picture. Some are remnants of accepted psychiatric ideas while others would play a central role in Freud's theorizing only at a later date.

The first idea is based on an important observation: traumatic experiences whose energy has not dissipated do not appear, or appear only schematically, in the patient's memory when that patient is in a normal state, irrespective of their freshness and vividness (1892, 1: 153; 1893 b, 2: 9). Memories not abreacted in a normal way may be recalled during abnormal periods of consciousness (hypnoid states). Freud and Breuer further argue that in any manifestation of hysteria, we find the dissociation of consciousness upon the appearance of these states, which function as the illness's basic manifestation. Furthermore, despite their acute intensity, the memories appearing in hypnoid states remain unconnected to other conscious associations.

Freud and Breuer subsequently distinguished between two kinds of hysteria: *dispositional*, when the hypnoid state exists before the illness's appearance; and *acquired*, when the hypnoid state results from severe trauma or long repression. Furthermore, even though they continue to uphold the premise regarding the existence of dual states of consciousness, inklings that hypnoid states may be consequences of trauma begin to appear.

The second of Freud's ideas contains his nascent conceptualization of defence as inherent in the psycho-physiological explanation.[3] Freud and Breuer spoke of defence as one of the factors impeding the dissipation of traumatic events, encountered when patients do not react due to the nature of the trauma, as in the loss of a loved person when social circumstances prevent the appropriate reaction, or when the trauma is accompanied by memories that the patient wants to forget (i.e., to repress, reject, inhibit, suppress or strangulate), or to the appearance of hypnoid states, in which traumatic experiences take place (1893b, 2: 11; 1893a, 3: 38-39).

---

3 The concept 'defence' encapsulates all the different terms used by Freud and Breuer when discussing this phenomenon.

Although Freud knew of the tendency of patients to 'forget', he deferred his analysis of defence because he was intent on clearly describing the passage of energy between ideas, symptoms, feelings and motor innervations, a step necessary for the completion of his psycho-physiological explanation. Freud's main goal at this stage was to describe the outcomes of defence mechanisms, such as difficulties in remembering, and the accumulation of energy in memory, rather than research into defence per se.

The general psycho-physiological explanation of neurosis

Parallel to his publications on the psycho-physiology of hysteria, Freud began to research other neuroses. He first attempted to apply Breuer's cathartic method[4] when hypnotizing patients in the course of Emmy's treatment (1888 or 1889 - 2: 48). Based on his descriptions of Elizabeth's and Lucy's treatment (which he began later, in the autumn of 1892) we can conclude that Freud had abandoned hypnosis by the time he had published the *Preliminary Communication*. In Elizabeth's case, after trying other new techniques (concentration and pressure on the forehead), he turned to free association (2: 135).

In the interim, Freud began his formulation of two other notions that would play a central role in his later thought: the theory of sexuality and the theory of defence. Freud began work on the first, which initially focused on clarification of the sexual aetiology of neurosis, two years before the second. Originally, Freud had only pointed to the rejection of unpleasant and traumatic memories from consciousness. Although defence was an important element in the psycho-physiological explanation, Freud left its full theoretical explanation for a later date. I note this because psychologistic interpreters tend to stress his defence theory in their efforts to diminish the importance of Freud's psycho-physiological model at this stage. Despite this intention, Levin, for instance, is

---

4 See Laplanche and Pontalis, 1973, entry: Cathartic Method (or Therapy). This method was based on the idea that the remembrance of traumatic experiences and their affect will led to their abreaction (catharsis), thereby liberating the patient from her symptoms.

only able to point out Freud's attentiveness to the phenomenon and its definition. Almost the entire chapter that he dedicates to defence theory dwells on the theory's sources and Freud's discussions with Breuer on whether hypnoid states, rather than defence, cause hysteria (Levin 1978: Ch. 5).

Parallel to his abandonment of hypnosis as a treatment, he began to understand the great importance of patients' resistance to relating their memories. He also conceived the idea of conflict between antithetical forces, what would be central to his theory of defence. In his paper on a treatment accomplished by means of hypnosis, Freud had explained his patient's symptoms as the consequence of contradictory and burdensome ideas. He had labelled the rejected idea *counter-will*, in contrast to the patient's *conscious will* (1892-1893, 1: 122-123). During the initial years (1892-1894) of his work on an explanation of neurosis, description of its sexual aetiology acquired a higher level of priority. He subsequently concluded that sex is the only cause of neurosis by the time he wrote his first papers on the subject; in Draft B, he declared that neurasthenia was indisputably of sexual origin (CL 39 - February 8, 1893).[5]

In addition to his notions of affect, sum of excitation and material substratum, three other developments contradict allegations regarding the purely psychological nature of this period. The first is that he began to outline his sexual hypothesis within the context of neurasthenia, anxiety neurosis and melancholia. Freud would later call these three conditions 'actual' (physiological) neuroses, while distinguishing them from defence psycho-neuroses: hysteria, obsessions, paranoia and hallucinatory confusion. The second, is that up until he began drafting the *Project*, Freud effectively abstained from working on his theory of repression; the third is the positioning of his theory of sexuality totally within the framework of his psycho-neurological explanation. Only after the failure of the *Project* did Freud turn to the two other theories, which he developed within an

---

5   Freud added various documents to his letters to Fliess. Their dates are not always precise. There are a total of 14 documents, the last being Draft N, attached to a letter dated May 31, 1897. When the date is precise, I cite it in my first reference to the *Draft*; in other cases I refer the reader to the notes prepared by J. Moussaieff Masson, publisher of *The Complete Letters of Sigmund Freud to Wilhelm Fliess*.

evolutionary and dynamic framework while divesting himself of the greater part of his psycho-physiological premises.

Although Freud applied diverse criteria to distinguish between actual and defence neuroses, he considered it important to stress that the differences he identified in their sexual aetiology were what had led him to this differentiation. I would argue that this interpretation, which became the accepted one,[6] is incorrect.

Freud often returned to the centrality of a sexual aetiology in his nosography.[7] In *Studies on Hysteria*, he affirmed that after he had established the sexual aetiology of neurosis and that different sexual factors caused different neuroses, he began to apply the same model to obtain precise diagnoses of the diverse categories in his system (2: 257). The impression obtained is that Freud first identified the specific sexual causes of the illnesses he researched and only later did he distinguish between those illnesses. His tendency to stress the fundamental importance of sexuality also found expression in his use of the term *actual* to neurasthenia and anxiety neurosis. With this term, chosen relatively late (1898), he called attention to what he perceived as the main factor differentiating between the two kinds of neuroses: timing. While neurasthenia and anxiety neurosis were the outcomes of current, still operating aetiologies (sexual activities such as masturbation and *coitus interruptus*, which do not lead to complete satisfaction), the source of psycho-neuroses rested in the past, in childhood (i.e., in traumatic memories).[8]

In diverging from Freud's overt declarations, I argue that he constructed his nosography on the organic-psychic distinctions characterising the three dimensions according to which he categorized the respective illnesses: the symptomatic, the aetiological and the psycho-physiological. Hence, despite the profound importance of sexual factors, the main criterion in his classification appears to have been psycho-physiological differences. Only after identifying these factors did he search for their sexual causes while making a great effort to integrate

---

6   See Laplanche and Pontalis, 1973, entry: 'Actual Neuroses'; Jones, 1972, Ch. XI.

7   1895, SE 2: 257; 1896a, 3: 149; 1898, 3: 268.

8   Freud raised this argument for the first time in 1896a (3: 152), after fully developing his nosography according to his initial criteria.

them into his psycho-physiological definition of each illness. That is, throughout Freud's nosographic work, the psycho-physiological model remained dominant. My understanding of Freud's thinking at this stage thus differs from what is commonly believed. Sexuality, I conclude, gained in importance only after he completed writing of the *Project*, when he reinterpreted his work and played down the mechanistic explanations he had incorporated into his sexual aetiology.

I am convinced that it is precisely this distinction between the two kinds of neuroses, one physiological, the other psycho-physiological (nervous, not psychiatric, as these illnesses were considered at the time), that led Freud to distinguish between the two temporally grounded types of sexual causes, the first present (actual), the second past. We can also conclude that Freud originally turned to the research of neurasthenia, anxiety neurosis and melancholia on account of their accepted classification as psychic *and* purely physiological illnesses (this distinction is pivotal for the precise portrayal of psychiatric conceptions then as now) but also because sexual factors were commonly considered to be crucial in their causation. Freud apparently expected that the study of patients with actual neuroses would help him understand the sexual roots of psychic illnesses.[9]

The centrality of the body-mind dichotomy in his nosography and his uncertainties can be better understood when we examine its role on each of the three levels previously mentioned.

> 1) *The symptomatic aspect*: Freud resolutely attempted to differentiate between the phobias associated with obsessive neurosis and those with anxiety neurosis. One essential difference between the two was that the affect (in terms of energy) of anxiety neurosis was *'not further reducible by psychological analysis, nor amenable to psychotherapy'* (italics in the original), indicating that the neurosis was not the result of a repressed idea (1894b, 3: 97). In other words, the actual somatic symptom neither symbolized nor possessed any psychic significance, making psychotherapy inadequate for treating actual neuroses (Draft B, CL 43).

---

9 Draft B, CL 44.

2) *The aetiological aspect*: As stated, Freud argued that he had separated the two types of neurosis because he had discovered two distinct sexual aetiologies: present disturbances and past traumatic sexual events. In this formulation, accepted by all of his interpreters, Freud emphasizes the influence of aetiology in his classificatory decisions. However, Freud himself contradicted this interpretation on several occasions, when indicating the other factors guiding his categorizations. In what follows, I show that the distinctions he made on this basis implicitly suggest the true sources of their differentiation.

We should not forget that when Freud spoke of 'actual sexual life', he was not referring solely to the patient's present sexual activity; this phrase referred to the entire period of sexual behaviour, beginning with puberty (1898, 3: 267). When Freud wrote that the details of a patient's sexual life were not repressed, he meant that the source of actual neuroses was to be found in physical sexuality (the physiological sphere), and not in ideas (i.e., the psychic sphere). As we will see, Freud based his distinction between the two types of neurosis precisely on this last differentiation, meaning that somatic sexual causes, in which the psycho-physiological level takes no part, were the sources of actual neuroses. By using the term `actual`, Freud minimized the psycho-physiological to the benefit of secondary, sexual facets of neuroses. He thereby circumvented direct confrontation with psycho-physiological issues.

Although the later Freud did mention actual neuroses on various occasions, I am confident that he became convinced that this nosographic entity had no solid foundations in empirical reality. Evidence for this conclusion can be found in his gradual yet consistent interpretation of actual phenomena as the products of defence. This is why, I suggest, the concept (i.e., actual neuroses) almost completely disappeared from his writings and from psychoanalysis in general.

The most glaring contradiction among Freud's remarks on the nature of the sexual criteria differentiating actual from psychic neuroses appears in a paper on the defence psycho-neurosis. In complete opposition to his previous, published statements, Freud claimed that actual neuroses can be produced by traumatic memories

(1896b, 3: 168). This diametrically opposed aetiology raises a crucial question: If neurasthenic and anxious patients exist whose illnesses were provoked by traumatic memories, what remains of the sexual criterion by which Freud had distinguished between them? In a similar vein, Freud also began to believe that masturbation and *coitus interruptus*, or at least their alleged damaging outcomes, were products of repression and trauma, that is, psychic events. In response to these blatant contradictions, we can only conclude that aetiology did not provide a consistent rationale for his nosographic distinctions.

> 3) *The psycho-physiological aspect*: I differ from Freud's account in maintaining that psycho-physiological principles were the main criteria guiding him during construction of his nosography. It is important to point out that the psycho-physical problem found very strong expression in his mechanistic explanations, the same explanations he used to distinguished between illnesses.

But first, I wish to draw attention to a subtle distinction, missed by several researchers, in their haste, that will allow us to grasp that when, on various occasions, Freud spoke of the sexual aetiology of neurosis, he was actually referring to psycho-physiological mechanisms, not sexuality. During this period, his aetiological explanations included two factors: one, that the immediate causes of neuroses are disturbances of the psycho-physiological mechanism; and two, that the sources of these disturbances lie in the patient's sexual life (1896a, 3: 149). (This distinction must be borne in mind in order to discern when Freud referred to one or the other of the term's meanings and to understand how Freud incorporated sexual explanations in his psycho-physiology.)

The somatic versus psychic character of the mechanism causing an illness appears in many of Freud's statements, with the following fragment being one of the clearest:

> 'The anxiety neurosis, too, has a sexual origin as far as I can see, but it does not attach itself to ideas taken from sexual life; properly speaking, it has no psychical mechanism. Its specific cause is the accumulation of sexual tension...' (1894c, 3: 81).

Here, Freud refers to the tradition characterizing every psychic process as one involving ideas. In contrast, he treats every somatic process as a purely energetic process, lacking ideas. Another aspect of this distinction appears in a paper on anxiety neurosis, in which Freud argues that anxiety is a sub-cortical discharge of sexual excitation rather than a psychic elaboration of the same excitation (1894b, 3: 109). From this, we can deduce that when Freud distinguished between what he called 'actual' (i.e., somatic) neuroses and psycho-neuroses, he was relying on the distinction between (a) physiological, sub-cortical phenomena and (b) psychic, ideo-energetic cortical phenomena. These distinctions became increasingly problematic as Freud continued in his efforts to formulate psycho-physiological explanations of different neuroses, especially that of melancholia (see below).

In addition to hysteria and obsession, Freud included two other syndromes among the defence psycho-neuroses: hallucinatory confusion and paranoia. However, neither Freud nor his interpreters assign their inclusion any relevance for understanding his thinking at the time. Interpreters rarely refer to them, what I consider clear proof that they consider them irrelevant to the understanding of Freud's theories. By not clearly differentiating between these psychoses in his papers, Freud gave credence to this later assessment.

I contend that this devaluation of any inquiry into these psychoses is erroneous because it blinds us to the unique factors that Freud indeed indicate. He veritably designated three groups of pathological phenomena at this time. Other than the two known groups, he provided a preliminary differentiation between defence psycho-neuroses and psychoses (hallucinatory confusion and paranoia). Although he considered them as emanating from defence mechanisms, explicitly labelling them 'defence psychoses', he did not view them as psycho-neuroses. As I later show, they played a central role in his construction of a general theory of neurosis. What is most relevant here is that while trying to explain them, Freud encountered some of the core issues that would eventually shatter his psycho-physiological model. Furthermore, in a departure from common beliefs, it was psychosis, not neurosis, that most-profoundly challenged Freud's general psychology, questions that continued to perturb him throughout.

Freud's desire to find a physiological explanation supporting his assumption that only sexual disturbances caused psychical illnesses would become a major motivation for his work on his psycho-physiological model. As we will see later, despite his inability to substantiate this notion, he continued to believe in sexual causality and its empirical reality, done by citing the repeated references to sexuality in his patients' stories. Although Freud later abandoned the psycho-physiological explanatory framework, he retained a belief in its main elements, those of ideas and energy, throughout his life. As proof of his consistency, in what follows I show how he devised, during the period in question, a classificatory structure that is most impressive in its logic and internal consistency, a beautiful system based on combinations of ideas and quantities of energy.

Somatic Actual Neuroses
Neurasthenia and anxiety neurosis

Freud began his investigation of the sexual aetiology of psychic illnesses with his study of neurasthenia. He adopted George Beard's view of this illness, which reflected the psycho-physiological principles they held in common.[10] Freud, like Beard, considered neurasthenia to be an expression of the nervous system's fatigue.[11] In energetic terms, neurasthenia resulted from an *impoverishment of excitation* (1894b, SE 3: 114) throughout the system.[12] Its characteristic symptoms were general and sexual fatigue, intra-cranial pressure, dyspepsia, constipation, etc.[13] Sexual exhaustion was considered one of the main causes of nervous exhaustion.

I begin my analysis of Freud's theories of neurasthenia and other neuroses by turning to Draft B. From the beginning of his study of neurasthenia, Freud's aim was to demonstrate that it could be categorized as a sexual neurosis.[14] To achieve his aim, his first step was

---

10 Beard, 1890: 15-17.

11 Draft B, CL 40-41.

12 Freud adopted Beard's terminology and used the term 'Verarmung an erregung' (GW 1: 341).

13 1896a, SE 3: 150.

14 February 8, 1893; CL 39.

to establish that every (acquired, not hereditary) case of neurasthenia is sexual in origin.[15] As part of this process, he felt it important to establish that physical illness, depressive affects, and other toxic influences (e.g. overwork) were able to produce only normal fatigue, sadness and physical weakness; neurasthenia originated only in exhaustion of sexual origin, in the presence of other, facilitating factors.

Freud distinguished between the occurrence of neurasthenia in women versus men. In men, he considered the illness to result from either masturbation (beginning in puberty, with symptoms appearing in one's twenties) or *onanismus conjugalis* (incomplete intercourse). In women, the illness is mainly a product of male neurasthenia. If masturbation is actively practiced for a long time it will, by itself, result in neurasthenia and weakened potency. If the intensity of masturbation is low, it will produce only a predisposition for the illness, which will erupt only after the appearance of some supplementary cause. Freud also distinguished between two kinds of neurasthenia, rooted in secondary motives, the *cerebral*, which appears when the facilitating factor is intellectual work, and the *spinal*, a product of normal sexual activity. That is, Freud proposed that a man who masturbates at puberty will be unable to maintain normal sexual activity due to the fatigue induced by it, like any other activity. Incomplete intercourse is the second cause of neurasthenia; it results from the desire to prevent conception or by an early predisposition (again, masturbation during puberty).

Girls and young married women, Freud argued, 'are sound and not neurasthenic'.[16] He considered that in its pure form, neurasthenia is rare in married and elderly unmarried women. As to married women, he described this illness as resulting from the husband's neurasthenia although it could appear simultaneously with the husband's symptoms. Freud also pointed out that neurasthenic men aroused hysteria and hystero-neurasthenia (hybrid neurosis) in women.

---

15 CL 40.

16 Freud assumed that women generally do not masturbate. Another preconceived and biased notion appears in the assumption that male neurasthenia will motivate appearance of the illness in women. Here the implicit supposition is that the couple's sexual pleasure depends on the man's potency, with the woman remaining passive. This interesting case allows us to examine the role of prejudice in the creation of psychiatric nosologies.

Freud also suggested cleansing the following symptoms, which he collectively labelled anxiety neurosis, from the definition of neurasthenia: diminished self-confidence, pessimistic expectations, a tendency for distressing antithetical ideas, hypochondria, agoraphobia, claustrophobia, vertigo, and anxiety in relation to decisions and memory (worries about psychic functioning). In his 1894 paper on neurasthenia and anxiety neurosis,[17] Freud presented a more detailed list of the latter's symptoms by adding general irritability, anxious expectations, different kinds of anxiety attacks, night fears, digestive disturbances (especially diarrhoea), paraesthesias, hallucinations, weakness, sadness, and so forth. Freud divided these symptoms into three variants of anxiety neurosis: chronic attacks, sporadic attacks, and periodic mild depression (Draft B, CL 42-43).

Although Freud clearly distinguished between neurasthenia and anxiety neurosis in *Draft B*, he did not do the same with respect to their sexual aetiology. He considered *coitus interruptus*, the second cause of neurasthenia, to be the cause of anxiety as well.[18] This fact contradicts the accepted assumption that Freud made nosographic decisions on the basis of his new conception of sexuality.[19] I argue that despite the importance of sexual aetiology for understanding Freud's ideas, his classificatory approach was rooted in the psycho-physiological model, with all his early sexual theories coloured by it. In *Draft B*, Freud did not indicate what led him to set anxiety apart from neurasthenia although the reason is clear: anxiety and its symptoms, unlike neurasthenia, cannot be an expression of nervous exhaustion but only of heightened nervous activity.[20] This difference is clarified in *Draft E* and his 1894 paper, where Freud explains

---

17 Although this paper was published in 1895, the Standard Edition assigns it to 1894. I follow the SE's dating.

18 Freud assumed that anxiety neurosis is acquired by married women and men during 'the second period of sexual *noxae*, through coitus interruptus' (CL 43). Freud referred here to his identification of the two causes of neurasthenia that appear in different periods of life: the first, puberty masturbation; the second, marriage masturbation (coitus interruptus), CL 41.

19 Laplanche and Pontalis, 1973, Actual Neurosis; Stewart, 1969: 47; Andersson, 1962: 119.

20 See list of symptoms, anxiety neurosis, in Drafts B and E, and 1894b, 3: 92-99.

that anxiety results from a sub-cortical discharge of the somatic stimulation accumulated in the nervous system following sexual abstinence.[21] That is, only after defining the two neuroses according to their neuro-physiologic features did he begin a more detailed examination of the sexual causes of anxiety.[22]

In that same 1894 paper, Freud clearly stipulated that the distinction between neurasthenia and anxiety neurosis lies in the polarity observed between excitation's accumulation and its depletion.[23] Moreover, the cause of anxiety is any sexual behaviour that leads to accumulation of excitation in the nervous system. This conception, which remained somewhat inchoate in *Draft B*, left Freud with a problem. The assumption that anxiety is a product of the discharge of accumulated excitation led him to conclude that anxiety is yet another hysterical symptom. He was unable to accept this logical outcome because he needed to retain anxiety neurosis as an independent pathological category.

Before delving into how Freud separated anxiety neurosis from hysteria, it is important to note that although he did not directly contend with the psycho-physical problem here, its deep influence is felt in his classificatory doubts and decisions. From the beginning of his involvement with anxiety neurosis, he felt it incumbent upon himself to verify if this illness was a psychophysical or purely physical phenomenon. In *Draft A*, he asks the following question:

> 'Is the anxiety of anxiety neuroses derived from the inhibition of the sexual function or from the anxiety linked to their aetiology?'[24]

In other words, he asked whether anxiety was only a physiological disturbance, derived from the accumulation of excitation occurring during inhibition of sexual discharge, or negative feelings conducive to the inhibition of sexual functioning. In the first case, the symptoms felt by the patient were only somatic, not psychic; in the second, as we shall see, he spoke of anxiety as a psychic phenomenon conducive to

---

21 CL 79-80; 1894b, 3: 109-110.

22 1894b, 3: 99.

23 1894b, 3: 114.

24 CL 37.

the inhibition causing accumulation of excitation, a dynamic identical to the case of hysteria.

At first, despite his assumption regarding its 'actual' (i.e., physiological) sexual origins, he attributed anxiety's source to an idea, worries about pregnancy, or a psychic trauma.[25] In *Draft E*,[26] Freud explains that he wrongly assumed anxiety to be another hysterical symptom because he thought that its source in women was their worry about becoming pregnant whereas in men, it was their distress over the possible failure of the precautions taken. Later, he came to believe that anxiety can appear in anaesthetic women as well as in cases where those fears were not present.[27] The significance of this notion is that Freud's shift, regarding the source of anxiety as physical, meant that it is not psychic. He now considered anxiety neurosis to be a purely physiological, sub-cortical phenomenon,[28] neither cortical nor psycho-physiological. Walter Stewart attributes this change in Freud's thinking to his encounters with diverse clinical cases (1969: 52-53).

Despite Freud's and Stewart's statements, I doubt that clinical experience could be the main source of Freud's revised position because the sexual anaesthesia of anxious women can also be understood as a hysterical symptom caused by psychic trauma. Even more, in his paper on anxiety (published after having sent *Draft E* to Fliess), Freud argued that intense anxiety neurosis appears only in non-anaesthetic women. A truly anaesthetic woman, he added, is 'little susceptible [sic]' to suffering from anxiety!ced[29] The question about what brought Freud to interpret anaesthesia and anxiety as purely physiological rather than psycho-physiological symptoms thus remains open.

And yet, the answer may be found in the same paper on anxiety neurosis. There, Freud indicated that his first insight into its mechanism was that the illness resulted from an accumulation of excitation and that, most importantly, it is impossible to find a

---

25 Draft B, CL 43.
26 Date unclear, perhaps June 6, 1894, see CL 78.
27 CL 61, 78.
28 1894b, 3: 110.
29 Id, 3: 102.

psychic source for anxiety.[30] From this I conclude that during this preliminary stage, Freud was attuned mainly to the physiological differences between anxiety neurosis and neurasthenia. He therefore found it sufficient to indicate the differences between the two along the axis of low/high excitation. Had he assumed that anxiety is an accumulation of excitation caused by psychic trauma or some other ideational factor, he would not have been able to present anxiety neurosis as distinct from hysteria.

Aside from its descriptive advantages, the distinction between anxiety neurosis and hysteria provides another benefit: it exhausts the combinatorial possibilities offered by Freud's nosographic structure. Without introducing a pathology characterized by a high level of purely somatic excitation, Freud's structure would have remained incomplete at the high somatic end of the axis, while including two somatic phenomena of low-level excitation (neurasthenia and melancholia). This leads me to conclude that architectural concerns of internal beauty, harmony and combinatory equilibrium, rather than simple fidelity to clinical phenomena, guided Freud as he constructed his psycho-pathological model. Although his various expositions are full of doubts and not especially convincing in relation to the purely physiological character of anxiety (in *Draft E*, Freud wrote that this is the weak point of his theory), we can say that Freud's explanation of anxiety was quiet acceptable and relatively free of major difficulties when compared to those of his colleagues who were also intent on explaining psychological phenomena in physiological terms.

At this stage, the main problem afflicting Freud's concept of anxiety revolved around how such a high level of excitation is obtained without any psychic – that is, cortical – involvement. As Freud wrote: '...why this transformation into anxiety when there is an accumulation [of physical sexual tension]?' (CL 80). I would add: as opposed to a transformation into the psychical sexual excitation that, according to Freud, is the usual destination of energy accumulations from any source? To solve this problem, Freud developed a model combining his assumptions on neuro-physiological functioning with his nascent views on the physiology of sexuality.

---

30 Id, 3: 107.

Freud first indicated how organisms cope with accumulated tension, based on its source, external or internal. In the case of external stimuli, the process is simple: any reaction diminishing psychic tension in an intensity equivalent to the external stimulus is easy to cope with it. It is, however, more difficult to do so when the excitation is endogenous (hunger, thirst, sexual drive). In this case, only specific and adequate reactions (eating, drinking, sexual activity), those that prevent excitation of the external organs of the stimulated system, can diminish the tension.

Freud assumed that the accumulated internal energy is noticeable only when it rises beyond a certain threshold (CL 80) and overcomes resistance by the paths conducting excitation to the cortex (1894b, 3: 108). Only after passing this threshold does excitation acquire psychic value and connect with the ideas that make it possible to provide an adequate and targeted reaction. That is, physical sexual tension awakens psychic libido only after overcoming psychic resistance.[31] At this point, sexual ideas become cathected and appear as a psychic libidinal tension, leading to a specific tension-reducing action (in the present instance, coitus). If the response is inadequate or does not take place, psycho-physical tension increases immeasurably. At this stage, the tension may disturb the person but is not transformed into anxiety. Anxiety results once this tension reaches the threshold at which it can arouse psychic affect (libido) although various factors (abstinence, *coitus interruptus*, unsatisfied excitation) prevent its connection with sexual ideas. That is, the impediment inherent in anxiety neurosis rests in the absence of the psychic libido that generally allows the channelling of somatic sexual tension and thus prepares the person to act.

Freud's indecision regarding the psychic versus somatic character of anxiety did not end here. In *Draft E*, after presenting anxiety as a completely somatic illness, he returned to the absence of psychic elaboration as the factor inducing the transformation of somatic tension into anxiety. Among the causes of this absence he listed defence (CL 82). That is, Freud was not content with his notion of anxiety as an exclusively somatic phenomenon.

---

31 *Libido* is the term Freud used to refer to sexual energy. During this period, he sometimes distinguished somatic from psychic libido; during others, the term referred to both kinds.

I suggest that two factors motivated Freud's doubts. On the one hand, it was impossible to empirically deny the psychic character of anxiety. On the other, the explanation of anxiety as an entirely somatic phenomenon, suggested by the psycho-physiological model of sexuality, unequivocally led to the conclusion that every phenomenon is somatic, implying no significant difference between psychical and physical phenomena. Despite his fidelity to neurology, Freud did not want to adopt this extreme position.

The model of normal and pathological sexual functioning delineated by Freud to explain neuroses and psycho-neuroses clearly expresses a monist conception of the body-mind connection, a position raising some fundamental problems. If we agree with Freud's statement that ideas are expressions of cortical activity, it follows that ideas have no psychical features to distinguish them from physiological phenomena – at least until an explanation is found for how psychic phenomena emerge in the neuronal system. If such is the case, there is no reason to differentiate a neurosis resulting from the transformation of physical energy into anxiety and a psycho-neurosis (hysteria), produced by the transformation of psychic energy into somatic symptoms. However, if we assume that ideas contain non-physical facets, we are required to define the non-somatic aspects of ideas or, in Freud's terms, identify what gives physical energy its psychical character. In other words, what transforms physical into psychic energy? I argue that when stating that physical energy connects with ideas, Freud was only implying that this type of change occurs. He still had to identify which aspects of an idea's features enable it (like energy) to become psychic. Despite the fact that Freud did not treat the body-mind problem in his clinical papers, his texts show that he was deeply bothered by it. He would turn to this conundrum in the *Project*.

At this point, however, there began to appear in Freud's writings an element essential for understanding his later theorising: the parallel between defence and psyche-soma dualism, which he referred to as the '*alienation* between the somatic and the psychical sphere'.[32] By 'alienation' Freud meant the cortical resistance to the free passage

---

32 1894b, 3: 110; CL 82, 93.

of somatic energy and its transformation into psychic stimuli. Could Freud have been unintentionally hinting at a more general psychic defence against somatic sexual stimuli? According to his original conceptualization, alienation is completely normal and common to all. Only after many years did Freud propose an explanation for 'general alienation' (i.e., normal repression) while painting alienation as the product of historical processes and human culture (1913).

Freud's ideas in this period about alienation also had psychopathological significance. He proposed the presence of a defence that resembled the alienation between soma and psyche as the cause of psychotic disturbances.

Later, parallel to publication of his first paper on neurasthenia and anxiety neurosis (1894b), Freud tried to formulate a purely physiological explanation of melancholia. This explanation raised new problems, even more difficult than those associated with anxiety. To solve them, he expanded his psycho-physiological model; his efforts were fruitless and remained unpublished. Other than the fact that melancholia was then considered a nervous illness, we may venture that Freud had other reasons for trying to pass it through the psychophysiological sieve. As already pointed out, Freud had arrived at the conclusion that anxiety neurosis cannot develop in anaesthetic women. He then began to believe that a complete absence of sexual excitation may serve as the etiological basis for melancholia because melancholia was commonly thought to exhibit lower levels of excitation than did neurasthenia, and that sexual excitation may not always be present.

Melancholia

Among the actual neuroses that Freud tried to explain, melancholia was the most complicated. Stated simply, he viewed melancholia as a borderline case between purely somatic neuroses and psycho-neuroses. Due to its murkiness, *Draft G*, the main text in which Freud dwelt on this illness, is very difficult to decipher. This document is nevertheless of paramount importance for its being additional evidence of Freud's entanglement with the soma-psyche distinction.[33]

---

33 The *Draft* is undated. The editors of the *Anfangen* thought that it belongs to an envelope dated January 7, 1895, *Anf* 111.

Freud's starting point in his elaboration of melancholia (Paragraph II) was his view that *'melancholia consists in mourning over the loss of libido'* (CL 99). By this, Freud was referring to two aspects of melancholia: the symptoms of weakness and tiredness, together with strong feelings of sadness, longing and needing love. This description was very problematic from a psycho-physiological perspective because it implies that the illness has two contradictory features: on the one hand, decrease (loss of somatic and psychic libido); on the other, increase (mourning, pain and longing) in psychic energy (see *Drafts E* and *G*). Not just that, the respective increase results from a decrease of energy. This dichotomy led Freud to a fuller exposition of the psycho-physiological conception of sexuality. And yet, it appears that he did not publish this text because he was unable to resolve the contrasts with psycho-physiological thinking.

Freud apparently found it simple to explain the decrease of psychic energy in melancholia, which he did it in a manner similar to his explanation of neurasthenia. With respect to melancholia, Freud referred first to the two different situations in which the excitation of psychic sexual ideas declines (Paragraph III):

1) When the production of sexual somatic excitation drops or ceases: Once production halts, *genuine severe* (periodic or cyclical) melancholia appears. Production of somatic sexual excitation drops in cases of exaggerated masturbation. This leads to a prolonged decrease in somatic excitation and weakening of psychic sexual ideas (neurasthenic melancholia). In these two cases, the decrease of sexual tension is greater than what occurs in neurasthenia. Importantly, although in this context Freud revealed a specific cause that may explain typical melancholia -- complete cessation of the production of somatic sexual excitation -- he had not yet fully developed the idea. He initially preferred to explain melancholia as the outcome of an increase in the detrimental conditions of neurasthenia and anxiety neurosis.

2) When somatic sexual excitation is diverted from psychic sexual ideas: In this case, so long as the accumulation of sexual excitation is normal, energy is diverted from the group of psychic ideas and used elsewhere. Freud pointed out that this explanation is identical to that of anxiety neurosis and consequently named it anxiety melancholia, a hybrid form.

In his explanation of anxiety melancholia, not one element appears to explain the feelings of melancholic mourning because the condition allows for no reason to mourn: libido is not lost but diverted. Another amazing feature of this explanation is that Freud does not indicate what differentiates between the two illnesses. The discriminating factor may nonetheless appear in an obscure phrase -- 'at the boundary'-- written after stating that energy would be diverted elsewhere (CL 99). If his intention was that the respective energy is directed to the boundary between soma and psyche, we can conclude that Freud meant to distinguish between melancholia and anxiety neurosis by proposing that in the latter, energy is discharged in sub-cortical levels while in the former, it is discharged in higher but still not cortical levels. Admittedly, this is a very forced explanation, leading to the packing of numerous elements of his model at the boundary between psyche and soma. Because Freud was apparently dissatisfied with this explanation of mourning in melancholia (the increase of energy), he subsequently offered another explanation, one that connected melancholia with sexual anaesthesia (see Paragraphs IV and V of *Draft G*, discussed below).

Although it was clear to Freud from the outset that there are cases where anaesthesia does not cause melancholia, he was interested in seeing whether the physiology of sexual anaesthesia might clarify, even a bit, the existence of the two polar features in melancholia. Although this attempt also failed, it led Freud to dwell on a more detailed description of normal and pathological sexual functioning, which he captured in a sketch that he named *Schematic Diagram of Sexuality* (CL 100):

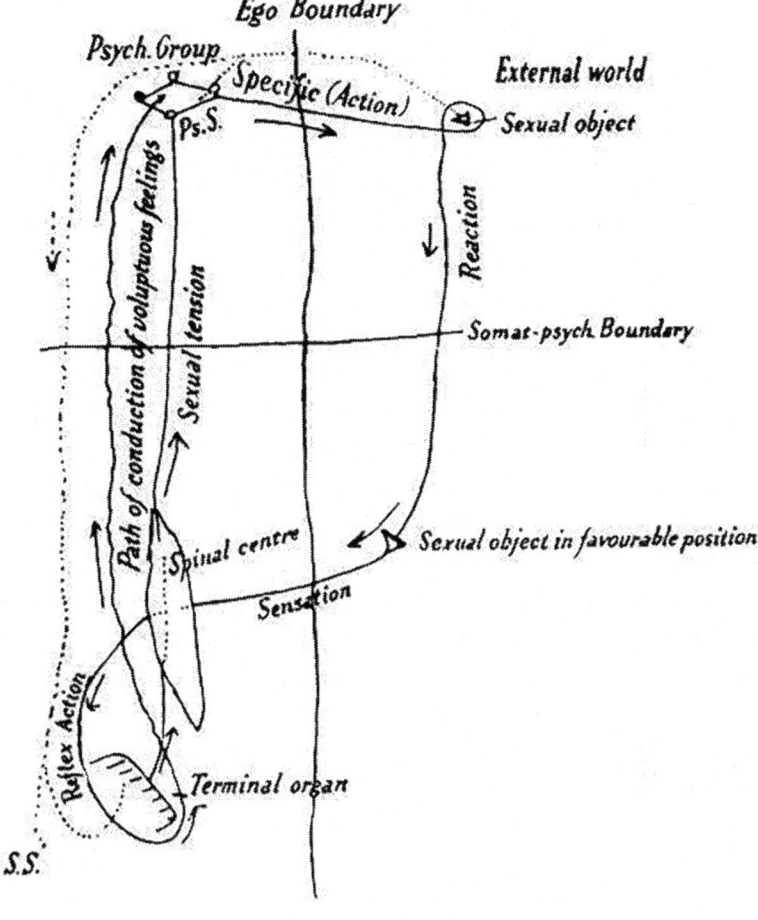

Figure 1. Schematic Diagram of Sexuality. [In the original, all the arrows are drawn in red, excluding the dotted one at the extreme left.]

What is important here is Freud's distinction between the sexual energy that reaches the psycho-neuronal system from the spine's sexual centre and that coming from the sexual organ (which Freud referred as the 'end organ') following coitus. Freud defined anaesthesia at this point as the absence of voluptuous feelings, normally conducted to the psychic group of sexual ideas subsequent to the unloading of accumulated energy by means of a reflex action in the end organ. He thus came to consider disturbance of the reflex discharge after the sexual act to be the specific cause of anaesthesia.

Freud's exploration of the possibility that sexual anaesthesia could serve as the source of melancholia, had a dual aim. First, he had to find a way to distinguish melancholia from neurasthenia because his descriptions of these conditions were very similar if not identical. Sexual anaesthesia, as the total loss of sexual sensibility, seemed an appropriate cause of melancholia, which exhibits an immense impoverishment of drive and functioning. Neurasthenia, like melancholia, was characterized as exhibiting a major energy decrease in the psycho-neuronal system as well as being an outcome of sexual weakness.

Second, the phenomenon of sexual anaesthesia allowed Freud to delve into the contradictory features of melancholia. This effort led him, I suggest, to refer to the difference between (1) the somatic sexual (s. S.) energy that is periodically transferred to the psychic sexual group and (2) the somatic sexual energy (V) that the psyche receives in the wake of the reflexive discharge accompanying normal intercourse. In the latter case, that of discharge following intercourse, the decrease of somatic energy produces an increase in pleasure on the level of psychic energy. This was to be contrasted to the instinctual energy continuously flowing from the sub-cortical sexual centre to the psycho-neuronal system. However, from a physiological perspective, there is no difference between the energy increase following intercourse and the energy increase in melancholia. The only difference is *qualitative*, that is, psychic, consisting in the difference between the pleasure felt after intercourse and the sense of mourning accompanying melancholia. It thus appears that the similarity between the two processes brought Freud to stress discharge after intercourse and to examine the consequences of disturbance of this discharge (what he defined anaesthesia) for the aetiology of melancholia.

In Paragraph IV of *Draft G*, Freud identified and examined three varieties of anaesthesia:

1) **Frigidity:** When the end organ is insufficiently loaded. In this case, discharge and the intensity of voluptuous post-coital feelings (V) are low. Here, anaesthesia is not the cause but only the sign of a predisposition to melancholia. Freud therefore assumed that anaesthesia

and melancholia result from the same cause -- the low loading of the end organ -- with anaesthesia an early indication of the melancholia that appears only if the harmful cause persists. This condition is similar to the one where the accumulation of somatic sexual (s. S.) excitation ceases. As in Paragraph III, Freud neither examines nor develops the aetiology of melancholia when rooted in this cause.

2) **Anaesthesia:** Consequence of masturbation and *coitus interruptus*. In such cases, because the path from sensation to reflex action is damaged, the action is insufficiently powerful, resulting in small discharges and little voluptuousness. In these cases, anaesthesia produces melancholia because the psychic sexual group weakens together with the voluptuous feelings (see diagram, above).[34] Within his diagram, the causes of neurasthenia and anxiety neurosis appear in the space between sensation and the reflex action while anaesthesia appears as a disturbance in the section containing voluptuous feelings. Freud's problem here is that he did not provide an explicit cause of melancholia while transforming anaesthesia and melancholia into phenomena accompanying neurasthenia and anxiety neurosis.

3) ***Hysterical anaesthesia:*** In Freud's nosography, this condition exhibits no disturbance in the production of somatic sexual energy (s. S.). Rather, it results from voluptuous feelings blocked from admission to the psychic sexual group. Freud did not develop this explanation further because he was apparently uninterested in anaesthesia of a psychic origin.

---

34 Freud's explanation strengthens my argument that he tended to view anaesthesia as the specific cause of melancholia. This explanation verily repeats his explanation of neurasthenic and anxiety melancholia, with the only difference being that melancholia does not directly result from the strengthening of the factors (masturbation, *coitus interruptus*) that disturb development of the somatic sensations leading to satisfaction but from disturbance of the reflex action following intercourse.

Based on his comparison of the three types of anaesthesia, Freud concluded that anaesthesia can appear in the absence of melancholia; that melancholia is related solely to the absence of somatic sexual excitation (s. S.), and that anaesthesia is related to the absence of voluptuous feelings, functioning only as a sign of or a preparation for melancholia since the psychic sexual group is weakened in the absence of voluptuous feelings as well as somatic sexual excitation. Freud's attempt to connect melancholia with a specific cause had thus failed; he consequently became convinced that the cause of melancholia was identical to that of other neuroses: disturbance of somatic sexual excitation.

But Freud did not give up easily. In Paragraph V of *Draft G*, he presented new evidence to prove that anaesthesia causes melancholia. This attempt, as the previous one, was grounded in the idea that melancholia results from a lack of somatic sexual energy. Freud now proposed that anaesthesia was primarily a female condition while exploring the implications of this 'fact' for the psycho-physiological explanation of melancholia. He was convinced that anaesthesia is more common among women on account of their passive role in intercourse. Anaesthetic men, he believed, would simply stop having sex. Contrary to men, women became more easily anaesthetic for two reasons: their education and their approach to marriage as well as the sexual act -- without love -- meaning with less somatic sexual tension and lower levels of excitation in the end organ. If so, they were frigid before as well as after marriage.

Freud went on to broadly explain how education produced anaesthesia in women. He thought that their entire upbringing was directed toward depressing somatic sexual excitation and transforming that excitation into psychic sexual stimuli (that is, they employed this mechanism to prevent themselves from wanting to have intercourse). In terms of his diagram, all somatic sexual excitation aroused by the sexual object is directed to the group of psychic ideas preventing women, contrary to men, from approaching their sexual object and from participating in the sexual act. Furthermore, Freud argued, women were educated to seduce men, that is, to direct their sexual energy to sexual representations and not to direct satisfaction of somatic sexual energy. Somatic sexual tension was thus maintained at low levels, with the psychic sexual group satisfied by seductive actions alone. Freud continued that in this situation, where a small amount of excitation remains in the end organ (and in the representations leading to direct discharge), the psychic group remains in a state of longing and women readily become melancholic. His analysis of this 'fact' reinforced his idea that a low level of excitation in the end organ is the main condition marking melancholia. Hence, whereas potent individuals easily acquire anxiety neurosis, impotent individuals are inclined toward melancholia.

This explanation has two weak points. First, there is no essential difference between it and that of neurasthenia. I thus return and rephrase my earlier question: Why does the decrease of somatic sexual tension in neurasthenia not produce anaesthesia and melancholia once it further declines? In terms of this explanation, could the two illness be identical?

Freud was aware of this problematic and he openly mentioned it (CL 104-105). He attempted to resolve it by creating a mixed subgroup, neurasthenic melancholia, and proposing that the energetic decrease is greater in melancholia, up to the energy's complete disappearance. Freud's failure to offer a clear and distinctive psycho-physiological aetiology for melancholia appears to be one of the reasons for his abandoning his efforts to explain the illness. Clear support for this argument is found at the end of *Draft G*, where Freud writes that this explanation is similar to that of neurasthenia. The only difference between them, he states, is that in neurasthenia, the impoverishment of sexual energy is somatic while in melancholia, it is psychic. He subsequently indicated that neurasthenic impoverishment may nevertheless reach the psychic domain.

The second problem with his explanation lies in his attempt to solve the main difficulty plaguing the psycho-physiological conception of melancholia, as indicated previously: the presence of two contradictory characteristics, that is, the simultaneous decrease and increase in energy levels. From within the psycho-physiological framework, Freud initially explained mourning as 'longing for something lost' (CL 99). This is a simple description from a psychological but not from a physiological perspective. Moreover, this explanation did not satisfy him because it referred only to the increase in feelings of longing. I therefore suggest that Freud had originally intended to explain how feelings of mourning increased in direct response to decreased somatic energy rather than the transformation of one psychic quality into another.

Also in Paragraph VI we find Freud's attempt to repair this lacuna by revealing his assumptions on how decreases of somatic sexual energy produce increases of psychic energy. He first defines melancholia as a *'psychic inhibition with instinctual impoverishment and pain concerning it [sic]' (CL 102)*. In his attempt to paraphrase this psychological description in psycho-physiological terms, he argued that when there is an especially large loss of energy in the psychic sexual group, an in-drawing [sic] immediately appears within the psychic sphere that sucks out all attendant amounts of excitation. The associated neurones then surrender their energy, an action that produces pain. Freud offered a physical analogy to this process by proposing that in the psycho-neuronal system, an *internal haemorrhage* develops that operates as a wound, producing depletion of excitation while impairing the other drives and functions. However, Freud apparently completely rejected this psycho-physiological formulation at a later stage. We find evidence for this conclusion in the *Project*, where he proposes a new and entirely different explanation for psychic pain, a phenomenon difficult to elucidate in psycho-physiological terms. This failure was thus added to the long list of problems with which Freud had to cope due to his unyielding desire to apply the psycho-physiological explanatory model to psychic illnesses.

The psycho-neuroses of defence

As stated, at the same time that he was completing his psycho-physiological explanation of hysteria, Freud began to investigate whether it was possible to extend the model to neuroses of a sexual aetiology. Sometime later, he succeeded in doing so for the psycho-neuroses as well as the psychoses of *defence*. The literature nonetheless provides a faulty portrayal of Freud's efforts in this direction. I therefore stress that Freud did not try to ground explanation of psycho-neuroses in the same sexual causes identified in connection with neuroses. It is also important to note the interesting fact that until his completion of the *Project*, Freud continued to explain psycho-neuroses exactly as he had explained hysteria. He did not develop his description of the defence mechanism beyond what he perceived as necessary for adapting it to other psycho-neuroses and psychoses (purely psychic illnesses). His achievement in explaining hysteria according to a psycho-physiological model veritably marked the end of one period and the beginning of another.

Only one factor separates the psycho-physiological explanation of hysteria suggested in the *Preliminary Communication* and a lecture given on January 11, 1893 from the later explanation, on which I dwell here. That factor consists in the crucial place of defence as a cause of hysteria and of psycho-neuroses in general. Although Freud had previously described the illness as resulting from patients' efforts to repress traumatic memories, he did not stress the importance of this act at the time and focused instead on energy displacement. The explanation proposed in his earlier papers was based on the harm done by delaying the discharge of accumulated energy. In his first paper on the psycho-neuroses, this explanation was associated with retentive hysteria, which is one of a trilogy of hysterias: hypnoid, retentive and defensive. Freud clearly hinted there that the first two hysterias could be treated like the third, defence, and probably did not exist at all.

The psycho-physiological explanation of defence neuroses as emerging from hysteria is straightforward. These neuroses share a common element: repression of a sexual idea from consciousness. Such repression is effected by depriving the idea of its energy (1894a, 3: 48-49, 58). The problem raised before the psycho-neuronal system by this process is that energy cannot remain in limbo, neither used nor discharged; it must find an alternative objective. The difference in the direction of discharge is what distinguishes the various defence neuroses:

1) In hysteria, energy is transformed into a somatic symptom. Freud named this process *conversion*. Contrary to anxiety neurosis, in which the transformed energy is completely somatic, the hysterical symptom has a psychic meaning and symbolizes the repressed idea. In hysteria, then, psychic energy is transformed into somatic energy.

2) In obsessions and phobias, the freed energy remains on the psychic level and attaches itself to other ideas, actions or drives that do not menace consciousness. Here, affect appears *dislodged* or *transposed* (1894a, 3: 54). He called this mechanism *transposition* in his paper '*The Neuropsychoses of Defence*', and *substitution* in his *Obsessions and Phobias* (1894c, 3: 79). This change in designation, I suggest, reflects the fact that Freud discussed this energy's destination in the first paper and the replacement of a repressed by an obsessive idea in the second.

Between these two papers, Freud greatly revised his conception of phobias (Strachey 1962b, 3: 83-84). In his first paper, he treated phobias as obsessions without differentiating between the two illnesses. In his second paper (published eight months later), Freud noted two distinctions, first, that the emotion accompanying the idea always entails anxiety whereas in obsessions, other feelings – doubt, remorse, anger – may appear (3: 74). This difference in the anxiety related to phobias and that associated with obsessions found expression in his paper 'Obsessions and Phobias', in two different names, *angoisse* and *anxieté*, respectively. Second, Freud described the mechanism driving phobias as completely different from that motivating obsession. He argued that in phobias, no substitution of ideas occurs; hence, a psychological analysis does not reveal any repressed ideas. He went on to explain that anxiety 'selects' the idea appropriate to the specific phobia. By means of this explanation, Freud intimated that those ideas are not true psychological phenomena; they are purely physiological in nature (i.e., neuroses). Phobias, he continued, belong to the category of anxiety neuroses.

As mentioned previously, this radical change in Freud's conception of phobias, which transpired over just a few months, speaks to the enormous difficulties he had in implementing his psychophysiological model but also of the essence of those difficulties. His weak explanation of phobias, where he tried to explain that phobic ideas lost their importance even though they still constituted the phobias' content, manifests Freud's core problem: his inability to explain psychological phenomena (ideas) in physiological terms. The clearest evidence of this problem is that shortly after he published his papers on obsessions, phobias and anxiety neurosis, Freud began writing the *Project*, in which he attempts to explain consciousness, the key psychological feature, along physiological lines.

Defence psychoses

Although psychoses did not constitute the focus of Freud's research in this period, they are impossible to ignore because the problems and themes arising greatly influenced his thought. The issues related to psychoses were among the main motivations leading him to write the *Project*. Here I refer only to his early writings on the subject, his first paper on the neuro-psychoses of defence (May-June 1894), but especially *Draft H* (January 1895), in which he discusses three types of psychoses.

1) Development of defence psychoses during neuroses

a) ***As the result of intensified obsessive symptoms:*** In his first paper on defence neuro-psychoses, Freud presented the case of a girl who obsessively criticized herself; for example, after reading about currency forgery in the newspaper, she thought that she had also committed this crime. Despite her clear awareness of the absurdity of her self-reproach, her guilt overcame her judgement and she began to accuse herself before her family and physician. Freud considered this behaviour to be a manifestation of a psychosis that had resulted from straightforward intensification, i.e., an overwhelming psychosis. He attributed its origins to the excessive masturbation that leads to self-reproach.

b) ***As an outcome of pathogenic factors associated with other neuroses:*** Although Freud did not develop this conception of psychoses, we should recall that in his first paper on defence psycho-neurosis, he had pointed out that the development of a defence psychosis or a hybrid neurosis was far from rare. To illustrate, he provided ample descriptions of the hallucinations and deliria experienced by Emmy, one of his patients, in his *Studies on Hysteria*.

2) Hallucinatory confusion

Freud considered this illness to be a consequence of very strong defences, stronger than that of psycho-neurosis. While the idea becomes separated from the affect in the latter, with patients in a state of confusion, the ego rejects the inappropriate idea, together with its energy, and behaves as if the idea did not exist at all. The result of this process is hallucination, the prominence of an appropriate idea; that is, an idea accepted by one's consciousness. As the inadequate idea is associated with reality, defence leads to dissociation of the ego from the portion of reality connected with the rejected idea. That is, the ego defends itself through flight into psychosis (1894a, 3: 58-60).

3) Paranoia

Although Freud published his ideas on paranoia in his second paper on psycho-neuroses (1896b), he provided a complete sketch of this illness's mechanism earlier, in *Draft H* (CL 107, January 24, 1895). In this draft, Freud criticized psychiatry's perception of paranoia and obsession solely as intellectual disturbances (hence, they were called *psychoses* as distinct from *neuroses*, which were considered neurological illnesses). Freud argued that paranoia, and delusions in general, as obsessions, result from affective and defensive conflicts. He also attempted to describe paranoia's characteristic mechanism, which led to the description of the element held in common by neuroses and psychoses: repression of an idea that the patient's consciousness is unable to accept. Paranoia is very similar to obsession with respect to the content of the repressed idea, which is always negative and self-critical. In his second paper on neuro-psychoses, Freud identified this content as 'the primary symptom of repression' (1896b, 3: 184).

The factor distinguishing paranoia from obsession is the patient's attribution of the repressed idea to others, meaning that the patient 'projects' the idea onto the external world. Repression, he realized, is similar to obsessive substitution: while the content is the same in the two syndromes, reproach is internal in obsession but external in paranoia. Freud further stated that the key issue in paranoia is the shifting location of the troublesome idea: the disturbance appears because the repressed idea can shift from one place to another. He also stated that this mechanism, while explaining the different forms of paranoia, likewise explains normal as well as pathological phenomena: the litigious paranoid cannot accept that he was wrong, the great nation cannot accept its defeat in war, the alcoholic, unable to view himself as impotent because of his addiction, accuses his wife, the hypochondriac is happy that his illness is physical, the official believes that he was not promoted due to some conspiracy against him.

What is striking about these examples is that they manifest Freud's tendency to eradicate the differences between the normal and the abnormal. Here, this tendency is expressed in a direction opposite to that indicated in my book *Freud and Psychiatry* (2010), where I described his approach to his patients' narratives as one in which pathological phenomena become normal and understandable. What Freud describes now is how to treat normal phenomena as pathologies. The dissolution of inherent differences between the normal and the abnormal found expression in *Draft H*, within Freud's response to the question: *How is a transposition of this kind brought about?* (CL 109). His answer: This mechanism implies exaggeration of normal transposition or projection. Projection takes place when there is an internal change that can be interpreted as originating in either an internal or external cause. If prevented from assuming that its cause is internal, we can consider that cause external. Furthermore, the fact that we regularly betray ourselves through our feelings helps us understand the normal delusions embodied by observation and projection. The difference between pathological and normal delusions and projection rests in our awareness that the change is internal. If we are unaware of this process, paranoia appear, accompanied by over-valuation of what others know and what they do to us. Freud added that substitution is also a normal mechanism, and that obsessive ideas appear because of substitution's exaggerated use.

This evolving categorization of psychoses and neuroses presages a tendency that will become more dominant in Freud's later work: his reorganization and reclassification of the objects studied in the human sciences.

We can now summarize the three main conundrums appearing in Freud's analysis of psychoses: a) what distinguishes an hallucination from a perception, what is their relationship and what gives hallucination its pathological character; b) what characterizes the relationship between the external and the internal world; where does the thin boundary between reality and fantasy lie, and the problem of the notion of perception as projection, intrinsically identical to paranoid projection; and c) the similarities between pathological and normal phenomena. Another problematic issue requiring resolution involved the close relationship of hallucinations to dreams, to which Freud would dedicate most of his time after abandoning the *Project*. These and other issues, especially the general problem of the mind-body relationship, led Freud to his intense efforts to obtain their resolution in the summer of 1895, the period I review next.

PART 2: Attempts to Solve the Brain-Mind Problem

Contrary to its name, the *Project* entails much more than an attempt to ground psychology on neurological, seemingly scientific explanations.[35] Instead, this work's authentic aim was to solve theoretical as well as practical difficulties through severe reduction of the broad spectrum of psychological and psycho-pathological phenomena to quantitative neuronal processes. From my perspective, the *Project* likewise reflects Freud's efforts to solve, by means of the most advanced knowledge of his time, the philosophical issues surrounding the relationship between the body (brain) and the psyche (mind) on the way to obtaining a comprehensive, reductive explanation.[36]

From the date of its belated publication in 1950, the *Project* has provoked disagreement as to why Freud himself did not attempt to publish it. Researchers have proposed different explanations for what led Freud to abandon the manuscript before its completion. These researchers are commonly divided into two groups even though both viewed the *Project* as a neuro-physiological document for some time, irrespective of Strachey's comment that it contains two models, one physiological, the other evolutionary (SE I: 305, note 3). For those trying to defend the independent scientific status of psychoanalysis, Freud is thought to have abandoned physiology the moment he turned to the construction of a pure, autonomous psychology, free of any roots in external biological explanations. For them, the *Project* constitutes the last vestige of his need to neurologize.[37] Opposed to them are others who view psychoanalysis as a sub-sector of

---

35 Now as then, the fact that neurology is a scientific discipline and that we need the brain (and body) to act is considered enough to imply that this discipline can explain human phenomena and behaviour. In this book I demonstrate those beliefs to be mistaken but also a huge obstacle to the development of the scientific study of human phenomena. This I do by showing the great advances Freud made in this direction once abandoning these beliefs in his practice though not always in his theories.

36 I consider that Freud, differently from neuro-psychologists then and now, tried to give explicit expression to the assertion, implicit in neurological explanations of psychology, that this is the solution to mind-brain dualism.

37 See Kris 1950, 1954; Cassirer Bernfeld, 1955; Jones 1972: Ch. 17; Sirkin and Fleming, 1982.

biology. They argue that although Freud abandoned the reduction of psychology to neurones, he did not forsake the *Project*'s general approach, implying that he tried to ground psychology in biology throughout his life. This text was, therefore, simply an early and failed attempt to do so.

An interesting change has taken place in the latter group's position over the years. The first researchers[38] to study the *Project* emphasized its physiological and mechanical[39] character; they even tried to validate and adapt its physiological assumptions in the light of neuro-physiological advances. Later, researchers were prepared to relinquish the idea that the *Project* was mainly a neuro-physiological document in favour of a broader biological stance. Frank Sulloway, the most important proponent of this view, suggested that the *Project* presents two different biological models: one neuro-physiological, the other evolutionary; or, as Freud labelled them, the mechanical and the biological, respectively (1979: 122). Sulloway argued that during its writing, Freud abandoned the psycho-mechanical approach in preference for the biological one. This change in direction, he continues, is the key to understanding the elder Freud.

There is still a third group, comprised of psychologistic and physiologistic interpreters, that considers the *Project* an inherently psychological work. They tend to overstate their point of view, arguing that the *Project* contains no more than clinical and psychological generalizations. They also claim that interpreting this work as neuro-physiological in character is incorrect and that Freud's neuro-anatomical model was influenced not by neurological discoveries but by abstract clinical and meta-psychological notions.[40] In other words, some consider Freud's refusal to publish the *Project* an expression of a complete withdrawal from his reductionist program while others consider it the failure of one reductionist approach but not of his basic reductionist program.

---

38 Amacher, 1965; Holt, 1962, 1965; Pribram, 1962, 1965; Fancher, 1973; Solomon, 1974.

39 I will use the term mechanical as Freud did throughout the *Project*, even though 'mechanistic' may seem more appropriate according to the current lexicon.

40 Kanzer, 1973; Sulloway, 1979; Friedman and Alexander, 1983; Mancia, 1983; Solms and Saling, 1986.

Karl Pribram and Martin Gill, the only researchers who analysed the *Project* a bit more closely, were attentive to its evolutionary aspects while ignoring Freud's integration of the biological with the mechanical model (1976). Sulloway, who stressed the importance of the biological model, argued that Freud abandoned it because he was unable to provide a pure mechanical explanation of normal as well as pathological defence; hence, he was coerced(!) into offering a combined mechanical/ biological-evolutionary explanation (1979: 125-126). That is, Sulloway also thought that the *Project* was mechanical in essence. However, the main argument on which Sulloway grounded his interpretation of Freud's late thinking is not supported by any Freudian texts. Sulloway attempted to endow his arguments with some credibility by eschewing the relevant texts entirely or relating to them very superficially.

The structure of Sulloway's arguments was among the factors motivating me to stress the necessity of precisely analysing Freud's texts from this period. Contrary to Sulloway, and without ignoring the difficulties he revealed, I argue that Freud was well-aware of the impossibility of providing a reductive model resting solely on neurons and mechanical (physiological) explanations. Hence, we find that already in the first paragraph of the *Project*, Freud explicitly rested on evolutionary explanations of psycho-neuronal structures and their functioning. He wanted, from the beginning, to provide an integrated evolutionary-mechanical explanation; the three groups of arguments just cited are therefore incapable of explaining what lurked behind his decision not to publish the *Project*. As I will show, Freud was immersed at this time in evolutionary concepts; he would not have rejected any premise just because it was evolutionary in character. [41]

I also strongly oppose the common view that the *Project*'s aim was to solve only clinical and psycho-pathological issues[42] and argue that this text is a comprehensive psychological document, one in which Freud sought to solve general psychological issues. However, his paramount aim, as he wrote to Fliess, was to develop a normal psychology that enjoyed the heuristic benefits of psycho-

---

41 Ritvo, 1965, 1972, 1974, 1990.
42 Kanzer, 1973; Sulloway, 1979: Ch. 4; Knight, 1984.

pathology (CL 129). It appears to me that Freud's clear statement at the beginning of the second part of the *Project* should lay to rest the whole question of the role of psycho-pathology in his thinking:

> This second part seeks to infer from the analysis of pathological processes some further determinants of the system founded on the basic hypothesis; a third part will hope to construct from the two preceding ones the characteristics of the normal passage of psychical events (347; *Anf* 427).

My objective, therefore, is to present as full and exacting a description of Freud's thought as possible, especially regarding his impressive confrontation with the relationship between the brain and the psyche. I argue that the *Project* provides psycho-physiological explanations within the broader framework of evolutionary and developmental concepts and theories. I am convinced that the adoption of this perspective will greatly further our understanding of the *Project*'s special structure, the problems Freud confronted, the solutions he proposed, and the failures he could not overcome.

This framework is nonetheless insufficient for understanding the full scope of this work. Its paramount importance lies in Freud's effort to rid the human sciences of the mind-body problem but also in revealing the revolutionary turn he took after abandoning the manuscript. I would likewise stress that Freud gradually attempted to formulate an explanation of 'the normal passage of psychical events', events that he conceived as linguistic in character. He formulated his thinking on these linguistic phenomena in terms of the psychic elements (sensations, perceptions, and memories) as identified by the philosophical analysis of human phenomena. This analysis had already been accepted by traditional psychology and, unfortunately, by psychoanalysis. In other words, Freud remained intent throughout the *Project* on synthesizing real, objective, empirical linguistic phenomena (sounds, syllables, words, sentences, stories) by employing the elements philosophy and psychology had incorrectly considered as their components. When this attempt failed, Freud took a step impressive in its simplicity: rather than trying to reconstruct these phenomena, he began to study them directly, as he encountered them in reality. This yearning to directly investigate objective phenomena rather than viewing them through philosophical and psychological lenses derived from Freud's scientific spirit, from a deep belief in exacting scientific research, so different from the approaches taken then and now by philosophers and psychologists.

3

The Project for a Scientific Psychology for Neurologists[1] (1895)

Over all, the *Project* is comprised of four primary tiers or stages, each of which is meant to shed light on the preceding stages. Throughout major segments of the *Project*, these stages are often only alluded to, a fact greatly complicating its interpretation, as is the fact that Freud often assigned different meanings to the same terms. The first stage introduces the specific empirical phenomena that Freud wanted to explain: the narratives composed by human beings and, even at this early stage, dreams. The second stage, which describes the initial segment of his explanatory mechanism, expresses Freud's attempt to ground those phenomena within the traditional framework of the psychological functions – perception, sensation, awareness, memory, emotion, thought, and so forth – said to be controlled by the ego. The ego, as a concept, had become widely accepted by then although it acquired a special meaning within the Freudian system.

I should note in this regard that Freudian scholars belonging to all theoretical schools, when turning to the reductionism that dominated

---

1 Freud did not assign any title to the original manuscript of this work because he never intended to publish it. This task was completed by his publisher, who decided on: *Entwurf einer Psychologie*. James Strachey selected *Project for a Scientific Psychology* as the title of his translation. In a letter to Fliess dated 27 April 1895, Freud referred to his psychology as a *'Psychologie für den Neurologen'* (*Briefe* 129). I have chosen to combine the three titles of Freud's outstanding work (or *Project*, in brief).

this period of his thought, have tended to stress its neurological, psycho-physical and physiological aspects in isolation from the ideational aspect of that same reductionism. They treat Freud's use of the concept *representation* as obvious and understood. Here, however, I offer a different approach, having weighty implications for our understanding Freud's thinking. As I see it, Freud's perception of the elements comprising a story or narrative as representations is itself reductionist. That is, during this period, Freud's reductionism has an initial and very important stage, in which narratives are reduced to psychological phenomena, to representations.

The third stage involves an attempt to ground the complex of these psychological functions within psycho-neurological mechanisms driven by the flow of energy within and between different types of nervous or neuronal (the term used by Strachey) subsystems. The fourth and final stage captures Freud's attempt to formulate an evolutionary account for the origin of these nervous mechanisms.

As I will show in the following pages, Freud encountered problems in all three of the reductionist directions he took: the mechanical, the evolutionary, and the psychological. Each issue gnawed away at his formulations, making it impossible for us to establish which was most influential or fateful for his abandonment of the *Project*. Freud's failure cannot, therefore, be conceived simply as a lack of success in solving any particular psycho-pathological problem. Rather, his true failure lies in not arriving at a solution for the psycho-physical conundrum, associated with the body's links with the mind, and in not providing any material foundations for his psychology as demanded by psycho-physiology, the grounding of psychological processes in neuro-physiological and neuro-evolutionary processes.

The *Project's* Structure

The first feature to be discussed here is the *Project*'s unique structure, a feature that can help us understand just how much Freud was influenced by evolutionary–developmental thinking even before he began writing. Within the *Project*'s framework he describes, stage by stage, the genesis of the nervous system's elements as well as the gradual development of the various layers of the ego, the psycho-energetic mechanism that controls the system's functioning from its initial appearance until the apex of its development. Freud likewise delineates the various psychological functions (sensation, memory, consciousness, will, feeling, and thinking) by their level of development, from the simplest to the most complex. It is important to stress this aspect of Freud's work because his presentation complies with the model employed by those evolutionary scholars who accepted Darwin's preliminary outlines of psychic development. Darwin, we should recall, wrote that the new psychology would reflect the gradual acquisition of mental functions and capacities.[2]

Although Freud does offer a full, detailed portrait of the ego's development, his descriptions and explanations of the nervous systems' evolution – including the most highly developed mechanism found in human beings – are fragmentary, often only intimated. Still, Freud's text does provide a very firm, broad basis for the reconstruction of the implicit evolutionary hypotheses that directed his thought. Should we ignore them, our comprehension of the *Project* in all its complexity, together with our precise positioning of this work within Freud's theoretical, clinical and scientific development, will be impaired. My approach to the *Project*'s analysis will therefore help us understand how Freud constructed his text as well as what tools he used to differentiate among at least four (and perhaps five) major developmental stages, as follows:

1) Sections 1 through 8: In these opening paragraphs Freud describes the formation of the nervous system together with its anatomical and functional features. Although Freud applied an overtly evolutionary approach in his description, a good portion of his explanations at this stage are embryonic. He also ignored several of the problems raised by his evolutionary approach at this point.

---

[2] See Darwin, 1988 [1859]: 346; 1877: 285; see also Haeckel, (1906 [1874]); Preyer, 1882; Romanes 1883, 1888.

2) Sections 9 through 14: Here Freud describes the beginnings of the ego mechanism's development within the nervous system. In his discussion of the ego's function — coping with the endogenous stimuli — he dwells on organisms more highly developed than those mentioned up to section 9.

3) In section 15, Freud divides psycho-energetic processes into two major groups: the primary and the secondary. Following section 15, Freud dwells on developmental mechanical explanations of the psychological processes emerging in the wake of the ego's organisation.

4) Sections 16 through 18: Freud devotes these sections to an explanation of primary thought processes and initiation of secondary thought processes.

5) In the midst of his description of the development of thought processes, Freud presented his reduction of selected primary processes. In sections 19 through 21, he described dreams, normal primary processes; in the second part of the *Project,* he explained pathological primary thought processes. We should view this sections' contents not in reference to an additional developmental stage but as a depiction of several of the issues associated with various stages of development.

6) In the third part of the *Project*, Freud focuses on his explanation of the most-advanced secondary thought processes in conjunction with the conditions enabling their appearance.

Basic psycho-neurological principles and creation of the neuronal system

In his efforts toward establishing a materialist psychology as a natural science, Freud grounded his work in two main concepts: quantity and neurones. He was hopeful of presenting psychic processes as quantitative states of specific material, i.e., neurological particles (295; *Anf* 379).

The idea of quantity was based on the notion that neuronal activity results from the quantities of energy (Q)[3] that flow inside the nervous system. The flow of energy was regulated by two principles: inertia and constancy. According to the principle of inertia, neurones naturally tend to divest themselves, reflexively, of any quantity of energy reaching them from whatever source. Freud referred to this natural discharge as the *primary function* of nervous systems, with constancy as the *secondary function* (296; Anf 381). The latter principle marked the accumulation of energy targeted at fulfilment of the neuronal system's various functions.

Freud's neuronal construct was based on the most up-to-date histological discoveries.[4] These pointed to a conception of the nervous system as constructed of discrete neurones, having a similar structure and connected one with the other by a 'foreign substance'. Neurones were thought to have pre-established conduction routes for receiving energy through dendrites and discharging it through axons. By combining this notion with quantity theory, it was possible to conceive of occupied (*besetzed*) or charged neurones, some of which are full while others are empty (as far as possible) of energy. The principle of inertia was represented as a flow passing from dendrites to axons. As to the accumulation, Freud posited the existence of barriers between neurones that resist, to differing degrees, energy's free passage and immediate discharge. Freud theorized, using Santiago Ramón y Cajal's theory of the neurone, that these barriers are present at contact points, and consequently named them *contact barriers*. Their function is regulation of neuronal energy's passage, its accumulation as well as discharge.

It is very difficult to understand why so many scholars of the *Project* relate to these two ideas solely as quantitative and mechanical, while ignoring Freud's explicit stipulations regarding the evolutionary nature of these principles. To the best of my knowledge, no researcher has yet stated that Freud presented a short but clearly evolutionary outline of the two principles and their diverse stages during the development of neuronal systems from the simplest, ruled by the

---

3 Freud used different symbols to denote each type of flow and neurone. For the complete list see Strachey's introduction (294).

4 Bernfeld, 1949; Brazier, 1959; Centonze et al., 2004; see Koppe, 1983 for an especially enlightening article.

principle of inertia, to the most complex, ruled by the principle of constancy (paragraph 1). Nor has any researcher suggested an interpretation of Freud's broad discussion of the evolutionary issues related to the presence of contact barriers or to his questions regarding whether those barriers are anatomical devices, characteristic of the types of neurones that had survived because they were needed, or whether they were to be found in all neurones but active in only one type and not in others (paragraph 4).

The principle of inertia as an evolutionary principle

Indicative of the evolutionary character of the *Project* is Freud's statement, in the very first section, that the principle of inertia explains internal neuronal activity in addition to the basic structure and formation of different kinds of neurones. Immediately after his presentation of this principle, he states:

> On this basis the structure and development as well as the functions [of neurones] are to be understood. (296; *Anf* 380)

That is, the principle of inertia explains the evolution of neuronal systems. Hence, it is a physical-physiological but also physical-evolutionary principle.

This explanation integrating structure and function precisely reflects Ernest Haeckel's evolutionary program. This renowned Darwinist had ascertained that the two areas of research – on the evolution of organs and on the evolution of functions -- are identical and that it is impossible to separate them (1906 [1874]): 7). Haeckel did not confine himself to a general theory on the close relationship between the two. He presented his ideas by means of examples, the most outstanding being that of the neuronal system, 'of which the psychic or soul-life is the physiological function' (id, p. 8). A comparison between Haeckel's and Freud's texts clearly shows that Freud tried to apply Haeckel's program, suggested twenty years earlier. Freud also gave no indications of even minimally distancing himself from the physiological and mechanical evolutionary ideas held by his teachers.[5]

---

5 See Bernfeld, 1949; Ritvo, 1965, 1974.

The principle of inertia: Development of primary neuronal systems as an adaptive response to the physical environment

Immediately after presenting the principle of inertia, Freud describes its evolutionary significance:

> In the first place, the principle of inertia explains the structural dichotomy [of neurones] into motor and sensory as a contrivance for neutralizing the reception of Qη by giving it off. (296; *Anf* 380)

The inertia that explains neuronal structure evidently rules more than internal mechanisms; it also directs the formation of neurones into the two kinds of cells that had survived and developed during adaptation to their environment. This environment, Freud's teachers had taught, is all 'masses in motion' (296; Brücke, 1874). The division into two kinds of neurones can thus be conceptualized as a biological device to aid organisms in their response to their quantitative environments. Based on this logic, I apply the term 'physico-evolutionary' to Freud's approach.

Ontogeny reproduces phylogeny and phylogeny explains ontogenesis (Haeckel's biogenetic law)[6]

According to the biogenetic evolutionary hypothesis, the main features of more-primitive systems and organisms reappear in compact form as they develop into more advanced systems. In paragraph 1, where Freud explains primary neuronal systems, a fragment appears that is impossible to understand without acknowledging his reliance on Haeckel's biogenetic law regarding the phylogenetic origins of these systems. When describing the primary function and the inertia principle as evolutionary factors, Freud wrote:

> If we go further back from here, we can in the first instance link the nervous system, as inheritor of the general irritability of the protoplasm, with the irritable external surface [of an organism] which is interrupted by considerable stretches of non-irritable surface. (296; *Anf* 380-381)

---

6 Gould, 1977: 76-85.

If we assume that Freud was interested in describing nervous mechanisms alone, what this statement is doing in the midst of an explanation of reflex movements remains a mystery. What led Freud to present an earlier developmental stage after having presented the division of neurones into two types?

We can only conclude that when Freud wrote 'further back', he was referring to the most primary stage in nervous system development. At this stage, a very primitive organism having only irritable and non-irritable external surfaces could not house a neuronal system. As Freud did not indicate how this surface discharges the absorbed energy, the only possibility remaining is that Freud wrote 'surface' when referring to the skin. We may also deduce that he viewed the nervous system as inherited from organisms whose skin had served as a sensory system. It is astounding to learn that Haeckel wrote that the nervous system originates in the skin, citing his source as Karl Ernst von Baer (1874: 267). Freud's references to the 'external surface' therefore provide additional evidence of the crucial influence exerted by Haeckel and his biogenetic law on Freud's evolutionary model.

This influence is also evident in Freud's explanation of the reflex arc, the nervous system's primary function, with respect to its tendency to discharge energy:

> A primary nervous system makes use of this $Q\eta$ which it has thus acquired, by giving it off through a connecting path to the muscular mechanisms, and in that way keeps itself free from stimulus. This discharge represents the primary function of the nervous system. (296; *Anf* 381)

Here, Freud describes the primary function of developed systems in terms of a primary nervous system. Freud's argumentation indicates that his mode of explanation was not by analogy but by incorporation of the implicit assumption guiding Haeckel's hypothesis: ontogeny recapitulates phylogeny; hence, a primary function is recapitulated in more-developed (secondary) nervous systems.

Neuronal system development, the secondary function and evolutionary theory

The important difference between primary and secondary neuronal systems lies in the latter's need and capacity to accumulate energy. From an evolutionary perspective, endogenous stimuli replace exogenous stimuli, with the former becoming the dominant evolutionary force directing the neuronal system's development.

Before progressing to secondary system development, Freud described still another preliminary stage. His description was based on the premise that the secondary function is anticipated in primary systems, in which flight from exogenous stimuli evolves as the preferred response among the discharge routes possible. Neuronal quantities are then discharged in the direction of the motor mechanisms, the effort needed to escape the stimulus being proportional to the intensity of the stimulus, as dictated by the principle of inertia (296). That is, neuronal systems that use the received energy to 'fly' from stimuli represent initial expressions of the secondary function, evidenced by the delay required for discharge (as opposed to storing) of energy. The system is still primary because, as Freud stated, flying from the stimulus is still only one of the discharge routes available. The principle of inertia is transgressed once a new situation arises: as the organism becomes more complex, its neuronal system begins to receive stimuli originating within the organism itself. These endogenous stimuli are crucial physiological needs: hunger, respiration, sexuality.

At this, later, point, the organism is unable to utilize the energy received to fly from the stimuli. Within this process, stimulation ceases only when special conditions materialize in the external world (e.g., the appearance of food). To respond to these conditions (e.g., acquisition of food), the organism must perform specific actions. This effort generally requires energy in quantities beyond those endogenously available. The system must then depart from its primary tendency for discharge and learn to accumulate energy sufficient to satisfy its biological needs. The trend toward inertia is, however, sustained by the new principle, constancy, according to which the system strives to keep energy at a level low enough to satisfy its somatic needs but not beyond.[7]

---

[7] Freud also referred to the principle of constancy as the 'first theorem'.

This description of the development of secondary functions and systems fully complies with the basics of Darwin's theory. For Freud, however, the dominant force driving evolution is not some physical principle but the difficulties organisms face when attempting to respond to *life's exigencies*, meaning to survive and satisfy their biological needs (297; *Anf* 381). To be able to do so, neuronal systems must store energy. Although Freud does not explicitly say so, his argument rests on the premise that for this ability to develop, organisms must struggle with the natural tendency of any neuronal system to discharge energy immediately upon its reception. Organisms that develop neuronal systems capable of storing energy will therefore survive, with the quality of that survival dependent on the quantities of energy these organisms can retain. This conflict between the two opposing forces regarding the tendency toward inertia and the need to store energy, engenders constancy, the principle henceforth dominating neuronal functioning. Constancy is thus the compromise emerging from the struggle between the two biological forces.

As to the secondary function, Freud based his explanation of this process on Haeckel's hierarchical conceptualization of advanced neuronal systems as containing vestiges of more primitive neuronal systems. These, he proposed, followed the path of the organism's phylogenetic development. Freud did not preoccupy himself with every stage but appeared to focus only on six of the stages preserved in the developed system:

a) Most primitive: protoplasm with an irritable external surface separated by large non-irritable surfaces.

b) Primary neuronal systems controlled solely by inertia and discharging energy through a reflex mechanism.

c) Primary neuronal systems exhibiting initial expressions of the secondary function: discharge of quantity in flight from external stimuli.

d) Secondary neuronal systems exhibiting full development of the secondary function.

e) Secondary neuronal systems exhibiting a newly developed function: consciousness.[8]

f) The most advanced human neuronal systems, housing the developed ego.

I also contend that Freud's integration of a psycho-physical with a biological-organismic approach when explaining the neuronal system's evolution is one source of the failure of his mechanical explanation of the ego's functioning. At this point, Freud was unable to free himself of physicalism and continued to feel that he must assign a decisive place to external stimuli in his evolutionary explanations. This attitude underlies his statement that the primary function is adequate to the task of handling endogenous stimuli, parallel to his position that these same stimuli induced development of the secondary function. This same attitude inspired his postulate that the conduction paths for energy discharge in neurones were fixed in the earliest stage of neuronal phylogenesis and that these pathways would be preserved in later stages. No mechanism developed later would contradict this postulate, with the *Project* indeed claiming to offer a modular presentation of an advanced neuronal system capable of fulfilling the primary and the secondary function. But, as we shall see in the discussion of ego functioning, Freud found it difficult to conceive of a mechanical explanation for integration, especially in light of his physico-evolutionary conceptualization of their conduction pathways.

Contact barriers, perception and memory

Freud's description of neuronal system development, the secondary function and how those systems perform remained incomplete. He still had to explain how neuronal systems store energy for later use. To solve this lacuna, Freud formulated a second theorem, mentioned previously: neurones exhibit *contact barriers* that resist the free passage of energy. These barriers enable neurones to store the

---

8 Although one might reject my assumption of the presence of a new stage and assume that consciousness exists from the beginning, it does seem that Freud did not leave room for any other interpretation when he postulated that new kinds of neurones developed after the appearance of those neurones responsible for the secondary function.

energy needed to accomplish the secondary function (297; *Anf* 382). He further stated that energy passes through the undifferentiated protoplasm found at the points of contact between neurones whereas the differentiated protoplasm remains within the neurone. This allows for improved conduction.

Freud was aware of the evolutionary significance of the existence of very delicate yet complex neurones fulfilling diverse functions:

> Under the compulsion of the exigencies of life, the nervous system was obliged to lay up a store of Qŋ. This necessitated an increase in the number of its neurones and these had to be impermeable. (301; *Anf* 385)

That is, impermeable neurones and barriers developed when neuronal systems began to store energy in order to complete specific actions. These new neurones, different from the original perceptual and motor neurones, signalled a more-advanced stage of evolution.

This is not the only evolutionary assumption found in Freud's description of the contact barriers. Other important notions also appear there that connect Freud with scientists (Haeckel, Romanes, Preyer) who had tried to formulate an evolutionary account for the appearance and development of the psyche as well as for psychological functions. The related premises provided Freud with the foundations for an explanation of the psychological functions of perception and memory in terms of contact barriers (paragraphs 3 and 4).

I paraphrase Freud's proposed explanation as follows: One of the main features of nervous tissue is the capacity for memory, what any meaningful psychological theory must explain. Memory can be viewed, therefore, as the ability of nervous tissue to permanently retain changes in the wake of each passage of energy. An integrated explanation of memory and perception would explain how neurones change permanently under such conditions. That theory would likewise have to describe the conditions for the reception of new excitations, all within the framework of Freud's dictate that the perception of external objects within this process, will be objective. Freud resolved the issue of two contradictory features by positing that there are two classes of neurones, perceptual and mnemic, which he labelled *phi (Φ)* and *psi (Ψ)*, respectively. Phi neurones allow the passage of energy as if no contact barrier existed, meaning that these neurones remain unchanged despite the passage of energy. Because these neurones are permeable, they are able to offer the same conditions when receiving any new stimulus. Alternatively, psi, the mnemic neurones, have active contact barriers that allow only the partial passage of energy. As impermeable neurones, they change after every passage of energy.

I should note here that Freud considered his premise regarding the existence of two different kinds of neurones (paragraph 4) as problematic. His rejection of a 'Darwinian line of thought' (303; *Anf* 388) to explain resistance was based on his lack of any histological proof of the presence of either permeable or impermeable neurones. What he subsequently proposed was that the contact barriers in the psi neurones become more amenable to transmitting energy, that is, more permeable and thus given to change after each passage of energy. These neurones thus evidence differing degrees of 'facilitation' (after Sigmund Exner, 1984: 76-82). He also advanced other physiological premises to explain the range of memory (or mnemic) features, such as the possibility that psi neurones were diversely facilitated, having different contact barriers as well as conduction paths to connect them with other neurones. Hence, the specific degree of facilitation depended on the number and intensity of passages, with each barrier's state of facilitation independent of that exhibited by the other barriers located in the same neurone.

In relation to his use of the terms 'mechanical' and 'biological' in this context, Strachey writes that Freud intended the first to mean phenomena determined by contemporary physical events whereas 'biological' was meant to indicate genetic determination, implying some survival value for the species (305, note 3). I agree with Strachey's clarifications in principle but have reservations about his sharp distinction between the two terms. Freud's text is not very clear on the subject:

> We should like to know whether the two classes of neurones can have had a different significance biologically and, if so, by what mechanism they may have developed characteristics so different as permeability and impermeability. What would be most satisfactory, of course, would be if the mechanism we are in search of should itself arise out of the primitive biological part played [by the two classes];.... (302; *Anf* 387)

For Freud, biological-evolutionary explanations, like physiological explanations, were mechanical in nature. This characterization fully corresponds to those of Darwin and Haeckel with respect to the evolution of organs and functions (Ghiselin, 1973: 967). When Freud states that the most satisfying solution to the issue would be an account rooted in the primitive biological functions of the two kinds of neurones, he meant to say that if we could identify these functions, we would be able to understand the mechanism driving their development as well as their specific functioning. As I have already shown, this conception is straightforwardly evolutionary in character.

In his initial responses to the question of the division of neurones into two kinds, Freud again referred to his model of the nervous system's development (302; *Anf* 387), which he followed with some anatomical justifications (due to the absence of histological evidence). Freud noted that anatomical research had identified two nervous systems: the first, comprised of the grey matter found in the spinal cord, is 'responsive' to the external world; the second, meaning the grey matter in the brain, is anatomically positioned above the first, and lacks any relationship to the body's periphery. The development of the neuronal system and all psychological functions occurs in this second system (psi), which is connected to endogenous conduction paths.

After this anatomical justification, Freud deliberated over how psi (Ψ) acquired impermeability while phi (Φ) contact barriers remained inactive (303; *Anf* 388). It should be stressed that Freud did not reject Darwinian thinking; he argued that Darwin's line of thought was worth adopting: impermeable neurones are needed and because of that, they survive (303; *Anf* 388). What Freud did reject was the existence of anatomical distinctions between the contact barriers belonging to the phi and psi neurones.

Other than that, Freud assumed no difference between the two. In principle, all were impermeable, able to resist the passage of energy and given to facilitation (304; *Anf* 389). Their variation resulted solely from their different location. Phi neurones were completely permeable because they received external stimuli, which are the most intense. In contrast, psi neurones received the filtered stimuli that phi neurones transferred to them, but also endogenous stimuli, which are of low intensity. Freud stressed that this description preserved the 'essential sameness' of phi and psi by 'biologically and mechanically' elucidating their different permeabilities (305; *Anf* 390). This solution, grounded in location as said, was no less evolutionary than any other of Freud's proposals and did not contradict his earlier premise regarding the presence of contact barriers only in neurones belonging to the complex organisms that require energy storage to satisfy life's exigencies.

Biogenetic influences are also felt in Freud's explanation of memory by facilitation. After proposing that energy and facilitations are interchangeable (in the presence of deep facilitation, a smaller quantity of energy is needed to raise the registered memory), Freud deviates from his circumscribed physiological explanation to state that facilitation serves the primary function of neuronal systems: preventing neurones from filling with energy (301; *Anf* 385). That is, in developmental stages evidencing important anatomical progressions (e.g., impermeable neurones), facilitation (as a functional, not anatomical, element) had survived from its primary nervous system origins. Once more, Freud combined an evolutionary with a physiological explanation while sharply shifting between them but without feeling any need to explain his approach.

We can summarize Freud's evolutionary description of the nervous system's development as well as the appearance of perceptual and mnemic neurones as follows: Consequent to the struggle for survival and the accompanying need to store energy, contact barriers, perceptual and mnemic neurones as well as psychological functions (perception and memory) developed. Physiologically, the crucial accomplishment at this stage was the capacity to store energy; psychologically, memory was the evolutionary achievement. And yet, the appearance of memory and the capacity to store energy were not accompanied by suppression of the primary function, which nonetheless became less and less relevant as the secondary function developed.

The neuro-physiological explanation of consciousness and its (failed) evolutionary explanation (paragraphs 5, 7 and 8)

In his depiction of the nervous system's formation, Freud identified an additional issue, more difficult than that of memory. After describing the two sub-systems, he felt it necessary to explain how the received physical and biological quantities were transformed into conscious phenomena. As the origin of consciousness (i.e., quality) lies neither in the external world nor in phi and psi, he posited the presence of a new kind of neurone, omega (Ω), whose function it was to create consciousness from quantity, as I explain in the following. Again, he grounded his explanation in evolutionary theories.

Freud was well aware of the difficulties of his proposal; he therefore took the precaution of summarizing the bio-energetic principles that direct nervous sub-system development and functioning in his introduction to the omega neurone. In paragraph 5, he argued that the nervous system's development is directed by an increasing tendency to 'keep off' [sic] or block the entry of quantity (306; *Anf* 391). In paragraph 7, in which Freud treated the appearance of quality and consciousness, he returned to the structure of the sub-systems, from the sensation organs up to the omega system, with the same arguments used to explain the increasing protection from energy-intense flows. Freud now proposed a further stage in nervous system development: a new kind of neurone, which had survived evolution, capable of transforming external quantities into qualities, that is, consciousness (309; *Anf* 394). Qualities, he continued, are sensations, differentiated according to their relations with the external world. These differences are expressed in series, similarities, etc., but nothing quantitative (308; *Anf* 393).

The issue of consciousness was especially problematic for Freud (as for others). According to his text, consciousness is the psychic function that produces qualities. To resolve the issue, Freud integrated two proposals. First, that omega neurones exhibit the highest resistance of all neurones; hence, the quantities that pass through them are the smallest in the nervous system. These neurones receive quantities only from psi, not having any direct contact with phi. Though Freud did not explicitly say so, the reason for this separation is clear: the quantities in phi are too energy-intensive for omega neurones to accept. He did not, however, consider this explanation as conclusive because omega neurones would have to be even more impermeable than psi neurones. High-level impermeability is inappropriate for omega neurones because they must evidence high mutability and ease in linking simultaneously perceived qualities. Such functioning requires extensive permeability and the capacity to return to the neurone's initial state subsequent to excitation. Omega must therefore behave like phi if qualities are to be received.

Freud thus was forced to offer another solution to the problem of consciousness, as follows: the transfer of quantities in neurones is temporal, similar to mass motion as conceived by physics, which moves according to different *periods*. In this construction, contact barriers do not oppose the passage of periods; they only oppose the passage of quantities. Freud also offered a complementary premise: the origins of different types of periods lies in the sense organs, which not only reduce quantities, they also act as sieves allowing the passage of a stimulus according to its specific periodicity (its quality). The various periods then pass on to phi, where diverse neuronal flows (specific energies)[9] are produced and then travel through psi on to omega. Omega's excitation by the periodic neuronal flows 'generates conscious sensations of qualities' (310; *Anf* 395) that are, as stated, conditional on the presence of very small quantities of energy. In addition, Freud was obliged to explain another series of sensations, that of pleasure and unpleasure.[10] In doing so he simply stated that the increase of quantity in psi is felt as a sensation of unpleasure, with its discharge producing a sensation of pleasure in omega (312; *Anf* 397).

It therefore appears that Freud assumed that in the course of the nervous system's development, a unique kind of neurone, inherently different from the others, had survived. Termed omega, this neurone was capable of transforming energy and periods into qualities, which it did without need of any quantity (see below). At first glance, this

---

9 Freud adopted J. Müller's theory of specific energies, according to which each nerve transmits only one kind of quality: visual nerves transmit only visual sensations, audio nerves auditory sensations, etc. See Boring, 1950: 80-95; Brett, 1953: 607.

10 'Unpleasure' is the term used by Strachey; I retain it as opposed to the more commonly employed 'displeasure'.

premise openly contradicts the *Project*'s mechanical-quantitative framework.

To understand this new direction in his theorizing, we should recall that Freud's description of the nervous system as a 'power plant' transforming physical and biological energy into consciousness represents his attempt to solve the psycho-physical problem. Freud nevertheless preferred not to make his objective explicit, perhaps for reasons of academic politics, or to avoid criticism. Then as now, to speak in terms of a solution to the mind-body problem rather than assuming a monist or dualist stance was unacceptable within the scientific and philosophical discourse. His implicit solution, which permeates the *Project,* can be summarized as follows: After the lengthy development of living matter and nervous systems, including increasingly successful and more complex results, the only neurones surviving were those able to function solely with qualitative inputs. A nervous system able to miraculously transform quantity into quality in omega neurones, working with minute quantities of energy, eventually evolved. Hence, once omega neurones appeared in the course of evolution, physiological processes functioned as conscious processes as well.

As might be anticipated from any exercise in reductionism, just when Freud reached his explanation of the advent of psychic processes, he was unable to culminate his efforts with a theoretical climax. His difficulties in explaining consciousness on quantitative grounds increasingly grew due to his understandable inability to conclusively decide whether omega neurones worked with or without quantities. At the end of paragraph 7, the contradiction becomes explicit. On the one hand, omega neurones cannot receive energy; on the other, to function at all they need a minimal quantity of that energy (310; *Anf* 395). In paragraph 8, Freud declares this theoretical impasse:

> No attempt, of course, can be made to explain how it is that excitatory processes in the omega neurones bring consciousness along with them. (311; *Anf* 396)

And so, at this very early stage, Freud renounced his attempt to reach a quantitative explanation of consciousness; he explicitly repudiated the *raison d'etre* of his *Project*.

We should return here to a core trait of Freud's scientific approach, one already hinted at. Contrary to the norm in contemporary philosophy, psychology and psycho-neurology, Freud, in the *Project* and in *On Aphasias*, verbalizes the conundrum faced in its most radical form. In the *Project*, he acknowledged the problem's insolubility. We may therefore ask why did Freud continue writing the *Project,* in the course of which he developed a comprehensive neurological vision of psychological processes?

My answer is three-pronged. First, in continuing an inconsistent line of argument he was merely following common philosophical and scientific practice. Second, he wanted to delineate all the problems resulting from reductionism, meaning all the issues surrounding the relationship between the physical and the psychic. Third, and more importantly in my opinion, Freud truly wanted, and felt that he was able, to solve the body-mind problem.

Hence, the previously quoted statement ('No attempt, ...[to] bring consciousness along with them') is vital for understanding the *Project*'s character. I am convinced that Freud's failure to formulate a reductionist explanation of consciousness is by far the main although not the sole reason for his decision to refrain from publishing this work. His open recognition of the impossibility of reducing consciousness to neurology and matter is the main factor separating him from all the reductionist researchers (psycho-physiologists, neuro-physiologists, psychiatrists, etc.), then and now, who remain resolved in this effort. In Chapter 5 I return to this issue and elaborate the reasons why I view the body (brain)-mind project to be a collective epistemic malady, ill-conceived and tending to bias efforts to acquire true knowledge in the human sciences.

The nervous system and ego development: The reflex mechanism (paragraph 9)

The Functioning of the Apparatus, the title of paragraph 9, was assigned not by Freud but by the *Project*'s editors. Freud had, in fact, detached paragraph 9 from its predecessors, indicated by his adding the partition *Second Part* before the paragraph. For some reason, this partition was omitted in the work's German publication and English translation.[11] By ignoring Freud's intention to isolate this from the preceding paragraphs, the editors' inadvertently distracted us from the text's purpose. The original title, I maintain, indicates that Freud wanted to distinguish the evolution of the human nervous system from the emergence of its functions.

Paragraph 9 delivers a summarized account of the nervous system's mechanical characteristics, described in the *Project*'s first eight paragraphs. This summary served Freud as a preamble to his description of a new evolutionary stage, that of nervous system development and ego organization. In this paragraph, Freud described the neuronal system's basic functioning, and how it coped primarily with external stimuli, in terms of reflex mechanisms and the principle of inertia, which can be paraphrased as follows: external quantities reach the phi system's nerve endings (sense organs). The latter have a dual function: one, to provide a threshold allowing only the reception of medium quantities of energy. That is, if a stimulus is too strong (i.e., the quantity is too large), the nerve endings divide it into smaller quantities; if the quantity is too small, it is not absorbed at all. And two, they (the nerve endings) act as sieves, receiving stimuli of only certain periods. Due to these dual operations, the quantities reaching psi are of a lower intensity than the quantities existing in the external world; they also have a unique period (a quality).

A quality passes straight through phi, with no obstacles, to go on to psi and omega, where it produces sensations that are consciously perceived. This period is brief, after which it disappears in the direction of the motor mechanisms without leaving any memory traces. Quantities reaching phi are subsequently discharged in two directions: directly to the motor apparatus, or transferred to those

---

11 See Strachey's note 2, p. 312.

psi neurones connected with phi. Should the quantities in phi still exhibit intensities too high for psi to absorb, phi channels them along highly ramified conduction paths capable of reducing those intensities to a manageable intercellular magnitude. This process enables the quantities reaching phi to be received by numerous psi neurones. Quantity in phi is therefore expressed by psi's complexity whereas quality is expressed by topography, given that each sense organ is anatomically connected only to specific neurones (315; *Anf* 399). The circuit along which quantity passes closes when the diminished quantity moves from psi to omega; there, together with the period, conscious sensations are produced. These sensations are then discharged into the external world by means of motor innervation.

Freud's description of the reflex mechanism for coping with external excitation is startling, especially if the *Project* is examined from a mechanical perspective. This description reads like a withdrawal from the obtained theoretical achievements. We thus need to respond to a series of questions: Why did Freud return to the reflex mechanism, presented in paragraph 1, after completing his description of the ΦΨΩ system? Why did he present the nervous system's functioning only in terms of exogenous energy despite previously attributing its development to the presence of endogenous stimuli and the need to satisfy biological needs? And why did he not describe the work of this apparatus as a combination of the two classes of energy, physical and biological, from the onset?

My response is that Freud meant to sketch the nervous system's earliest stages, observed immediately after it appeared in its entirety along the evolutionary continuum (see above). By conceiving a developed nervous system as functioning reflexively (i.e., in response to an external stimulus), Freud applied the approach accepted by the associationist psycho-physiology of his time, which considered the sensation-motor paradigm of reflex actions to be adequate for describing all neuronal activity, even on its most developed levels. This approach was most fully developed by Meynert and Jackson, which provided Freud with the foundations of his own version.[12]

---

12 Amacher, 1964; Young, 1990: 204-210.

The evolutionary approach, in which an early stage is described as a primary stage of a more developed stage, is crucial for our understanding of the *Project*, especially for Freud's outline of psychic function's development. It verily explains why the description of an evolved functional stage, together with its less-developed predecessor, may seem inadequate.

But Freud's seemingly superfluous description of psychic development in paragraph 9 is significant in a different sense. I suggest that in this paragraph, Freud refers to the initial helplessness of the child as parallel or analogous to the first stages of the secondary neuronal system's development, when the latter is insufficient to defend itself and its carrier, a human being, from the external world. At this early stage, the psychic apparatus functions only by reflex, which leaves it exposed to the physical world. We should likewise draw attention to the fact that although one of the *Project*'s core aims was to explain how neuronal systems cope with major biological needs (e.g., hunger, sexuality and respiration), the text was highly influenced by the physicalist approach of Freud's teachers. Only in subsequent paragraphs did Freud begin to integrate endogenous biological stimuli into his mechanical explanations and to cope with issues related to their integration.

Amacher has pointed out that the main limitation of the psycho-physical models advanced by Meynert, Brücke and Exner, Freud's teachers, emanated from their supposition that the main objectives of the psyche, like the nervous system, were to cope with external stimuli and acquaintance with the physical world. They therefore concluded that the exogenous physical stimuli received by afferent nerve fibres constituted the source of all psycho-neuronal activity (Amacher, 1965: 45). Although this notion greatly influenced Freud, he now began shifting his analytic gaze to endogenous stimuli.

Primary processes and the development of the ego mechanism

In Freud's model, the aim of the secondary mechanism (described in paragraphs 10 to 15) is to contend with endogenous stimuli. This mechanism is much more complex than the reflex mechanism because the respective stimuli are internal. As Freud conceived the process, some of the quantities flowing in psi must become organized before they can control other parts of the system. Freud called the ensuing organization the 'ego'. When presenting its development, he made use of paradigmatic descriptions of two experiences, both produced after storing endogenous quantities.

Regarding the integration of internal with external stimuli, Freud distinguished between psi's *mantle* or *pallium* neurones, which receive quantities from the external world through phi, and psi's *nuclear* or *kern* neurones, which receive quantities from endogenous sources.[13] External excitations are very intense; internal excitations are not. The latter are permanent in nature; once accumulated and able to trespass psi barriers, they act as psychic stimuli. At this point, the system's functioning depends on internal quantities, which produce impulses, the cornerstones of all psychic (psi) activity. Freud added: 'We know this power as the will -- the derivative of the instincts' (317; *Anf* 402).

Various authors have stated that the translation of the term *Trieb*, into the French and English 'instinct', as used here by Freud, is unsuccessful. Laplanche and Pontalis, for example, argue that this translation confuses the Freudian theory of *Trieb* with psychological conceptions of animal instincts, thus obscuring the originality of the former. Nevertheless, with the notion *Trieb*, Freud sought to clearly differentiate between instincts and impulses (or drives).[14] Instincts are fixed behaviours, genetically established. They are present in organisms characterized by primary nervous systems, reflexive actions, and the lowest forms of secondary nervous systems. Impulses, coming from endogenous sources, appear only in more-developed organisms and systems. When referring to '*Triebe und Triebschicksale*' (1915), Mills (2004) stresses that Strachey's translation of the term '*Trieb*' as 'instincts' has mislead generations of English readers about Freud's true intentions and the deep interpersonal and relational character of the concept.

Freud also distinguished between *Trieb* (impulse) and its advanced derivative, will. With this term, he suggests a further developmental stage. He first implicitly distinguished between a purely

---

13 According to Meynert, 1892: 85. See 315, notes 3 and 4.

14 See Lacan, Lecture 13 in his Seminar 11 on the four fundamental concepts of psychoanalysis (1981); Laplanche and Pontalis, 1973, entry Instinct (or Drive).

biological phenomenon, instinct, and a relatively developed psychic phenomenon, *Trieb*, which he depicted as the transformation of endogenous energy into psychic phenomena once that energy reaches psi. Freud now turned to will, a progressive derivative of the secondary process *Trieb*, which appears only after the ego has developed.

The assumption that endogenous excitation sets the psycho-neuronal system in motion constitutes a fundamental change from the psycho-physical model that the neuronal system's primary aim to be cognition of the physical world and coping with external quantities. How does the psycho-neuronal system work with endogenous quantities? Freud offered a paradigmatic description of the quantities accumulated in psi, with the process open to a range of experiences, primarily satisfaction and pain. Accumulation of experience thus became for him the core of his bio-mechanical view of ego functioning.

The experience of satisfaction (paragraph 11)

In paragraph 11, Freud's describes the experience of satisfaction as resulting from the saturation of nuclear neurones with endogenous quantities, what produces pressure for discharge along the motor conduction paths. Discharge begins with internal changes (e.g., screaming) which do not interfere with the production of internal quantities. By taking actions in the external world (e.g., eating, increasing proximity to the sexual object), neurones temporarily stop the release of internal quantities. Freud argues that in their earliest stages of development, human beings are unable to complete these actions alone. Children thus require external help, a situation where primary conduction paths (for example, discharge through crying) motivate acquisition of a secondary function, communication. Freud considered this process as the origin of morality.[15] That is, when someone assists the organism in completing an action, it halts the internal stimulus by means of reflex mechanisms. This experience of satisfaction (i.e., soothing the internal stimulus) has important

---

15 These short sentences, which Freud introduced here, provide clear evidence of his social view of psychological processes from the very beginning of life. This aspect has been entirely ignored by postmodern and relational American approaches as well as by Freud's neuro-psychoanalytic interpreters.

implications for the development of psychological functions in light of the three important processes that then take place in psi:

1) A lasting discharge that stops the impulse (*Trieb*) producing unpleasure in omega.
2) Cathexis of one or more mantle neurones, involving perception of the satisfying object.
3) Other points of the mantle receive information regarding the discharge of the satisfying reflex movement.

Taken together, the three result in facilitation of the mnemic image of the wished-for object, the reflex movement and the charging of nuclear neurones when the impulse arises. The strong resistance of the psi neurones involved is thereby partially neutralized.

At this point, Freud's discussion of psi development (318; *Anf* 403) hints at an implicit assumption according to which psi functioning develops consequent to repeated experiences that create new or strengthen older facilitations. These facilitations are very important for pure psi activity (reproductive thinking). When a quantity charges one of the respective neurones, it is simultaneously transferred to other neurones, which are then activated, a process captured in the basic psycho-neuronal law of *association by simultaneity*.

States of urgency or wishing (when energy is accumulated and overcomes the resistance of contact barriers) take place when the cathexes that reach the nuclear kern neurones pass to the two memories (mnemic complexes) embedded in the mantle and refresh them. A hallucination, which resembles a perception, is produced (319; *Anf* 404). If the hallucination activates the reflex mechanism, the result will be disappointment. That is, if in the presence of a wishful cathexis the system behaves according to the reflex model, this behaviour will result in unpleasure.

The experience of pain (paragraphs 6 and 12)

Freud treated pain in two different paragraphs, 6 and 12; just why he separated his discussion in this way is still unknown. In the following, after summarizing Freud's texts, I present my interpretation of these distinctions.

In paragraph 6, pain is discussed in isolation from the omega system, which is responsible for consciousness. Though psi neurones are involved, I would argue that Freud was thinking of a situation where organic pain results from external stimuli. He goes on to explain pain as the product of the system's failure. This phenomenon occurs in unusual (but not pathological) conditions, when large quantities of energy erupt into phi and psi. The state of pain leaves permanent facilitations within psi, an effect that nullifies the resistance produced by the contact barriers and creates conduction paths similar to those of phi. As the neuronal system has a powerful tendency to flee from pain, its experience awakens all phi and psi discharge paths.

In paragraph 12, Freud returns to the subject of pain, noting the three responses it triggers in psi:

1) A rise in the quantity level, felt as unpleasure in the omega system. The fact that Freud, diverging from paragraph 6, introduced the omega system into his description provides additional evidence of his developmental approach.
2) A tendency for psi to be discharged.
3) Facilitations connect this tendency and the painful object's mnemic image.

If any cathexis of the painful or uncomfortable mnemic image takes place as a result of a new perception, for example, a state resembling pain but not actual pain will result. This state of unpleasure arouses a tendency to discharge the cathexis attached to the mnemic image so as to free it of the painful perception. According to Freud, the source of the quantity producing unpleasure in this case is unknown. In the case of pain (treated in paragraph 6), the increase in psi is produced by intense or very high external quantities. As to the experience of pain, the only quantity added to the hostile object's memory comes from perception of that object. This perception is as intense as any perception not producing an increase in the general level of psi quantities. As Freud assumed that cathexis of memories releases unpleasure inside the body, to complete his explanation, he found himself forced to posit the presence of hypothetical 'secretory' neurones, the 'key-neurones' that 'secrete' unpleasure.[16] These neurones were to supply energy to the system when stimulated by an unpleasant mnemic image.

The treatment of pain in the two different paragraphs requires further explanation. I begin with the title of paragraph 6, which is 'pain', whereas the title of paragraph 12 is the 'experience of pain'. Only if we understand Freud's view about the evolutionary character of neuronal development is it possible to explain this textual dissociation. My reading of the text indicates that in paragraph 6, Freud's intention was to describe organic rather than psychic pain, which he considered produced at more-advanced states of neuronal development. His description in paragraph 6 thus serves as a 'draft' for his formulation of the experience of pain, continued after his discussion of consciousness. This distinction between organic and conscious psychic pain therefore parallels the distinction between organic and psychological memory previously presented. Later, in paragraph 13, Freud writes that the residues of the two experiences are wishful states and affects, respectively. This distinction is, again, important from the perspective of psychic development.

In paragraph 12, Freud elaborated his distinction between pain and its residues while pointing out how experiences of pain are distinguished from affect. In this paragraph, he argues that pain is produced by an eruption of an external quantity that increases the energy level in psi. In contrast, affect (as a more elaborate experience of pain) results from the endogenous release of a quantity by key-neurones.[17]

That is, Freud distinguished three different phenomena: pain, experience of pain and affect. I understand these terms as amenable to arrangement in two series, one quantitative, the other evolutionary and qualitative.[18] Pain (organic) is produced by very strong external quantities, characteristic of an evolutionary stage in which

---

16 On the combined chemical and electrical explanation of neuronal processes, see Wundt, 1969, Ch. 3; Glick, 1966, 94-97.

17 See also paragraph 19.

18 Preyer hinted at this arrangement in terms of different degrees of intensity and development but without distinguishing any clear stages, 1882: 146-152.

undeveloped organisms are unable to deploy adequate defences and thereby elude external stimuli. This phylogenetic stage is expressed in children's helplessness immediately after birth, when they are exposed to maximum pain. Pain, when accompanied by consciousness (that is, the experience of pain), is weaker and produced by an external quantity when associated with the perception of a hostile object. In this case, because individuals are sufficiently developed, the perception of a hostile external object serves as a signal activating the tendency for flight, thus avoiding physical injury.

Affect is a more-delicate phenomenon. It is produced primarily by internal cathexis of the hostile object's memory. The organism's capacity to cathect hostile memories with internal quantities is a crucial evolutionary achievement, one enabling organisms to avoid situations that may produce pain or experiences of pain with a minimum of effort and energy.

Freud's description of the two basic experiences of satisfaction and pain is followed by his sketch of psi's functioning, which can be divided into two stages: that of the primary ego (paragraphs 13 and 14) and that of the secondary ego (paragraph 15).

The primary ego (paragraphs 13 and 14)

As stated, the experiences of satisfaction and pain leave strong facilitations among the respective psi neurones, easing the absorption of additional quantities when new experiences take place. In the case of affect, increases result from a sudden release of key-neurones, whereas in wishful states, we witness the gradual accumulation of endogenous energy. These states are compulsory for the passage of energy. The wishful state attracts cathexes to the wished-for object's mnemic image, while the experience of pain results in resistance to cathexis of the hostile mnemic image. Primary attraction and primary defence are the residues left in psi by these experiences.

Wishful attraction can be readily explained, Freud states, because cathexis of the satisfaction memory is stronger than cathexis of a simple perception. Wishful states exhibit especially good facilitations between nuclear and mantle neurones. More difficult to explain is primary defence or repression:

...the fact that a hostile mnemic image is regularly abandoned by its cathexis as soon as possible (322; *Anf* 406).

To understand the problem of primary defence and its two dimensions, the mechanical and the evolutionary, we must refer to Freud's difficulty in explaining the origin of the ego mechanism, which he treated in the third part of the *Project*. There, he begins to develop his biological-evolutionary solution to the problem of defence.

Freud, we should recall, believed that the difficulty in explaining primary defence arose from the fact that cathexis quickly abandons the hostile mnemic image. The mechanical difficulty Freud confronted was that of explaining how neurones remain totally uncathected or minimally cathected either at a stage when the ego has yet to develop or when the ego malfunctions (such as in the presence of strong emotional trauma). When explaining primary defence (i.e., the rapid release of cathexis) Freud combines an evolutionary with a mechanical hypothesis: initial pain experiences end in reflex defences (322; *Anf* 406). That is, he proposed that reflex defences appear prior to any primary defence. There is no hint in the *Project* that Freud felt it necessary to explain reflex defence. This was so, I maintain, because his explanation was well-anchored in the widely held view of the nervous system as functioning reflexively. Given the concept's explanatory power among his colleagues, Freud was undoubtedly confident in writing that initial pain experiences ended with initiation of a reflex defence; the emergence of a new object to replace the painful object indicates that the original pain experience was over. Later, the psi system, which learns from biological experience, will attempt to reconstruct the event that indicated conclusion of the painful experience.

Contrary to Sulloway, I argue that Freud was content with his own developmental assumption:

> With the expression *taught biologically* we have introduced a new basis of explanation, which should have independent validity, even though it does not exclude, but rather calls for, a recourse to mechanical principles (quantitative factors). (322; *Anf* 406)

Although this statement seems clear, we should note that the 'new basis of explanation' is 'new' only in the context of his explanation of psi system functioning. Freud made use of biological explanations from the very beginning of the *Project*. What he did here was complement his biological with a mechanical explanation, done by assuming that the increase in quantity, which always occurs during cathexis of an unpleasant object, leads to an increase in discharge activity and a flow of that energy away from the respective memory (322; *Anf* 406). That is, after presenting his difficult biological problem and its solution, Freud closes with a simple mechanical response, grounded in the principle of inertia, according to which energy is discharged once neurones are full. From here on, Freud assumes that on the basis of its biological experience, the neuronal system gradually learns to discharge hostile mnemic images as quickly as possible.

Pribram and Gill, who advocated a neuro-psychological approach, have argued that even though Freud declared that he did not know how to provide a mechanical description of primary defence (370; *Anf* 450),[19] he in effect demonstrated ample understanding of this mechanism (1976: 74). We should also stress, that Freud's mechanical explanation is much more detailed than those of his teachers or colleagues. Whereas others were content to describe different components of the nervous system without probing into how they worked, Freud tried to be comprehensive in his description of their functioning. Pribram and Gill likewise note that Freud distinguished between different stages in the development of defence -- reflex, primary and secondary -- while stressing the developmental character of his descriptions. Freud's pessimistic comment about the mechanical explanation, they say, must thus be taken with a grain of salt, a view with which I agree.

Turning to the subject of learning from biological experience, Freud often mentions such learning in the third part of the *Project*, whenever he tries to reduce normal psi processes. There, it becomes clear that Freud's most difficult challenge in this context was not mechanical but evolutionary: how to explain the ego's origins. This

---

19 Sulloway, while ignoring Pribram and Gill's statements, uses this sentence to justify his argument that Freud did not have a mechanical explanation for primary defence.

was the cause of the mechanical problems he encountered when describing the ego's functioning. However, it is crucial to stress once more that Freud's greatest hardship in completing the *Project* was to explain consciousness, an adversity he did not overcome.

In what follows I summarize Freud's description of the formation and operation of the ego mechanism, which includes the activity of the different defences (reflex, primary and secondary), attention and indications of reality.

Freud theorized that wishful attraction and inclinations for repression both assumed the existence of the psi mechanism, which interferes with the free passage of the quantities accompanying satisfaction and pain. Freud readily explained the ego in terms of the repeated and facilitating reception of endogenous quantities in the nuclear neurones, a process that creates a network of constantly cathected neurones. The ego, he continued, consists of all the cathexes present at any one moment within psi neurones. In this structure, permanent and variable elements can be distinguished. The permanent storage of quantities allows the ego to fulfil its two most important functions: impeding the development of primary processes and activating secondary processes.

To explain the ego's actions, Freud assumed the presence of another powerful factor, alongside cathexes, the strength of facilitations and the opposition of contact barriers: the cathexis of neurones contiguous to the neurone receiving the new quantity. In this case, there is temporary facilitation of the contact barriers of the two neurones, causing changes in the flow's direction; if no such facilitation occurs, the flow continues in the path defined by previous facilitations. That is, a 'side-cathexis' acts as an inhibitor (Exner, 1894: 69-76).[20] This is the primary defence.

Freud imagined the ego as a network of cathected neurones, connected by effective facilitations, as seen from this illustration found in Freud's original draft (324; *Anf* 408):

---

[20] For a comparison between Freud and Exner's conceptions of facilitation and inhibition, see Koppe, 1983: 10.

If we follow the direction of the arrows in the illustration, we discover that a quantity moving from phi to neurone a continues on to b if it is not influenced by the side cathexis α, which allows neurone a to transmit a small quantity of energy at most to neurone b. In this manner, the ego prevents primary processes. This inhibitory mechanism has great advantages, especially when a hostile memory is present in neurone a and b acts as a key-neurone. The ego, after noticing the cathexis of a hostile mnemic image, inhibits the passage of quantity from the mnemic image to the discharge of unpleasure by neurone b. Freud also theorized that if the ego receives an initial discharge of unpleasure, that discharge may constitute the source of the ego's side cathexes. If this occurs, the intensity of the primary defence depends on the intensity of unpleasure.

The secondary ego (paragraph 15)

Although Freud did not explicitly divide ego development into two stages, it soon becomes clear that he envisioned the ego as resting on an additional mechanism, one that would help it distinguish whether the wished-for, or the hostile, object is truly present in external reality. He therefore conceived of a new stage, one where secondary processes and mechanisms begin to develop. The secondary defence, the secondary ego and other more-developed psi processes appear when the ego learns to use another resource: indications of quality and reality (higher-level quality indications). When considering that quality indications are provided by omega neurones that work with minimal energy, this achievement is momentous. Now the system can defend itself against the most minor cathexis of hostile mnemic images.

From a cognitive point of view, indications of reality are crucial for the functioning of psi neurones. The ability to pay attention to reality indications allows thinking to emerge. Once the system is able to perceive, register and examine stimuli, it can compare their registrations, that is, think.

However, soon after delineating the three stages in this system's development – (1) the ability to register received stimuli (memory) and cause contact barriers to appear[21]; (2) neuronal processes achieve consciousness and become psychological, initiated by the appearance of omega, a new kind of neurone; (3) thought processes become capable of identifying reality indications, which enables the ego to distinguish between fantasy and reality -- Freud's theoretical progress stalled once more. During his efforts to explain reality indications and distinguish them from consciousness,[22] Freud discovered a new, purely mechanical quandary, one he did not try to solve at all.

The function of reality indications is to provide the ego with information about the object, wished for or hostile, including whether the object is present in reality or only in fantasy, as a representation. The absence of any reality indication can result in two detrimental situations for the ego: cathexis of the mnemic image of the wished-for object, or cathexis of the hostile object. Cathexis of the wished-for object's mnemic image is damaging when it is excessive. The discharge of unpleasure is always damaging when the source of the hostile image's cathexis lies in psi rather than in the external world. To prevent injury, the ego must halt the quantity increases in the wished-for image as well as stop cathexis of the hostile image.

As previously stated, the ego, with the help of (primary) defence and attention, initiates the actions that avoid arousal of primary processes. In both cases, the ego requires further assistance. In the first case, that of an overcharged wished-for image, the ego must apply a

---

21 With the second stage, psychological processes also appear. This follows from Freud's newly developing conception of the unconscious character of most psychological processes.

22 Contrary to Sulloway's claims regarding Freud's theory of repression.

criterion to aid it in distinguishing between a perception (the object exists in reality) and a representation (the idea of the object). In the second, cathexis of the hostile image, the ego requires an indication to direct its attention to that image. With the help of this indication, psi is able to avoid the release of unpleasure by activating a side cathexis to divert that quantity away from the hostile image. But from where will the ego receive the assistance needed to activate repression (i.e., inhibition by a side cathexis) and transform primary into secondary processes? Freud proposed that perceptual neurones (here he meant omega) provide the reality (quality) indications that assist the ego in discriminating between perception and representation, fantasy and fact.

Freud nonetheless remained sceptical regarding this model. I would suggest that his uncertainty originated in the immense difficulties he confronted when trying to elaborate how omega functions with respect to quality (that is, provision of consciousness) and when activating reality indications.

These difficulties undermined Freud's attempt to achieve an integrated evolutionary and mechanical explanation of psycho-neuronal processes. As part of this effort, Freud was forced to distinguish between the different qualities and to provide a quantitative-mechanical explanation for their distinctiveness. These challenges perhaps explain the text's increasing murkiness. In an attempt to extricate himself from this impasse, Freud proposed that in the case of external perceptions, a qualitative stimulus appears in omega. At first, though conscious, this excitation has no significance for psi. However, after the energy causing excitation in omega is discharged, information of the discharge reaches psi and becomes relevant to the system. For psi, this information becomes an indication of quality or reality (325; *Anf* 410).

I will try to clarify this step. Freud argued that in its first stage, qualitative excitation (i.e., the period of excitation) is irrelevant to psi. That is, psi is not implicated at the beginning, when the neuronal system first becomes conscious of external stimuli. Only after omega discharges the minimal energy it received from the perception, does psi receive information about the discharge, which now constitutes an indication of reality. But how does psi obtain this information? Freud assumed that omega neurones are connected to the conduction paths of the sense organs that discharge energy in the direction of the motor mechanisms to which they are connected; information of this discharge is then transferred to psi.

Although Freud left his description unfinished, I build on the material available to suggest that he entertained the idea that the energy discharged through motor mechanisms results in actual movements, these being perceived by the sense organs that transfer new quality indications to psi. The new indications now constitute reality indications, true information that psi is able to use.

Despite his awareness of the intricacies of formulating the nature of reality indications, Freud did not abstain from using the concept in his description of ego functioning and secondary defence. He first described the functioning of indications in the cathexis of the mnemic image of a wished-for object. In situations of very strong cathexis, reality indications are activated in a hallucinatory manner, that is, before the ego can distinguish between fantasy and reality, and before it can inhibit the passage of energy. In this case, the reality criterion fails. Otherwise, if the cathexis is completely inhibited by the ego, the reality indication does not appear at all or remains dormant. In the case of external perceptions, quality indications always appear, irrespective of their intensity. The reality indication originating in psi, needed to determine if the image perceived corresponds to an external object or is only a representation, appears only in cases when the ego inhibits strong cathexis, thus reducing its intensity to make it available for use (326; *Anf* 410). That is, the reality criterion distinguishing between perception and representation will take effect once the ego learns to inhibit the hallucinatory cathexis.

In this mechanical formulation, the issue of the ego's origins and its functioning arises once more. Freud now appears to have believed that for reality indications to appear, the ego must be active, whereas he previously believed that these indications are required for initiation of ego activity. Freud's solution was to claim that biological experience 'teaches' the neuronal system not to initiate discharge prior to reception of the reality indications that the ego gradually learns to use.

Another issue embedded in Freud's definition of reality indications is his use of the term 'information' with respect to the omega discharge signals transmitted to psi. The version of this concept as used within the *Project*'s framework is too abstract. The attempt to define information in mechanical terms led Freud to suggest a mechanism combining quantitative-mechanical and qualitative components. Just as Freud had failed to explain the simple primary consciousness accompanying external perceptions, he was also unable to provide a mechanical explanation of secondary consciousness (see the letter to Fliess dated January 1, 1896). All he could do, as he himself declared after acknowledging his failure to offer a quantitative explanation of consciousness in paragraph 8, was to integrate the characteristics of consciousness (in this case, of reality indications) into psi and omega processes, but nothing beyond.

Other issues also continued to interfere with Freud's efforts to explain reality indications. While he did not refer to them in the *Project*, it is difficult to believe that he was unaware of them or of his inability to offer a comprehensive, coherent formula for the reduction of all psychological functions to mechanical processes. The letter to Fliess written some months after the *Project* provides clear evidence that Freud remained deeply troubled by the problems of relating quantities to qualities as well as how to discern primary as opposed to secondary consciousness. As Freud noted in that same letter, he was intent on correcting the mechanical model underlying the *Project*, in all its directions. We return to his solutions later.

Reduction of High-level Psycho-neurological Processes: Thought

After completing his description of the psycho-neurological system (in section 15), Freud turns to the reduction of thinking, an activity employing all the most highly developed of psychological processes (from section 16 through the conclusion). His explanations range from the simple to the very complex. Along the way, he attempts to explain dreams as well as pathological thinking, processes characterised by the disruption of logical connections. Freud integrates his reductive explanations with a renewed treatment of mechanical, evolutionary issues, which will become increasingly relevant to his work. As part of his progress, Freud turns to a description of the more-advanced stages of ego development together with its auxiliary mechanisms, especially attention and indications of reality.

Freud completed section 15 with a highly preliminary and generalized definition of the primary and secondary psychological processes that underlie his reductive explanation. These processes are divided into two categories: *wishful cathexis*, which can induce hallucinations, and *complete discharge of unpleasure*, responsible for activating *defence mechanisms*. He conceives these secondary mechanisms as weaker versions of primary mechanisms; they appear only in situations where the ego is well-cathected. A necessary condition for the existence of these secondary processes is the correct use of the reality indications that make possible the ego's inhibition.

This definition is, however, far from clear. Its interpretation is highly problematic, with Freud doing little to solve or at least shed some light on its intricacies. First, identifications of these processes in terms of some quantitative-energetic attribute sometimes interferes with their precise classification as primary or secondary mechanisms, especially when referring to processes in which the ego's strength is equal to that of the flow of energy. Such is the case of what Freud dubbed *primary judging* (333, *Anf* 417), despite his description of judging, and thinking in general, as subject to the ego's dominance (328, *Anf* 413). The problems with such a definition become less severe when the process occurs at one of the two poles of the quantitative continuum extending between primary and secondary processes; in other words, in cases where either primary (large quantities of energy accompanied by a weak ego) or secondary (small quantities of energy accompanied by a strong ego) clearly dominate. However, despite Freud's comment that proper functioning of reality indications is necessary for secondary processes to occur, he illustrates his argument with examples where this condition materializes as primary processes (yet together with the ego's complete control), such as thinking aimed at achieving identity with external perceptions.

These issues resolve themselves once we recognise the implicit scheme framing the developmental stages of reality indications. That is, in order to arrive at an improved version of Freud's definition of thought processes, we need to stress, next to their secondary quantitative character, the proper functioning of reality indications. This stipulation is crucial because numerous Freudian scholars have ignored the obstacles Freud encountered in his efforts to formulate quantitative explanations of qualities; they seem to have preferred to dwell on the quantitative elements in his definition (Pribram and Gill, 1976: 87). Some, such as Levin (1978), for example, have not concerned themselves at all with reality indications, or the problem of consciousness, when discussing secondary processes (Levin, 1978: 153-183). In their work, the place of reality indications in Freud's evolutionary, mechanical explanations vanishes. This lack of attention prevents us from accurately understanding Freudian psychopathology, but especially his psychology, as well as the way in which he contended with the respective issues as they emerged.

A bit prior to beginning his work on the *Project*, and throughout its writing, Freud formulated the view that no human being can determine whether a perception relates to an external object or is itself an hallucination. In a letter sent to Fliess dated 25 May 1895, Freud mentions that he had taken two of his core ideas from the book *The Function of Judgment* (*Die Urteilsfunktion*), authored by the evolutionary philosopher Wilhelm Jerusalem.[23] One of these ideas is that: 'internal perception cannot claim to be 'evidence' (CL 129; *Anf* 130). I believe that Freud had intended to say that internal perceptions, in and of themselves, lacked certainty; that is, they themselves provide no 'evidence' or 'proof' of their reality. Jerusalem's discussion of internal perceptions revolves around this issue of their certainty, the source of their truth (or our belief in their truth; see Jerusalem 1895: 194-217). He also argues that all perceptions, including fantasies, implicitly contain the idea of their own existence but not of our conscious knowledge of them (1895: 207, 210).

For Freud, identification and explanation of the component that endows internal perceptions with certainty were crucial to

---

[23] The truth is that Freud was inspired by numerous ideas in Jerusalem's book, among them the difference between practical and theoretical thinking, the distinction between verbal and nonverbal thinking, the sources of thinking in conscious (as well as unconscious) desire. With respect to his analysis of superior (primary and secondary) thought processes, Freud adopted a developmental model that was, in principle, identical to that suggested by Jerusalem (Jerusalem, 1895: 13-21).

his theorizing. He had previously argued that internal perceptions do not provide a criterion for differentiating between them and hallucinations; as his research on hallucinations and paranoia had taught him (Draft H, CL 107-112, *Anf* 118-124), there is no fundamental difference between perceptions and hallucinations. Furthermore, due to their indistinguishability, and a human being's incapability to ascertain whether the object of concern is real on the basis of perceptions alone, Freud found it necessary (when still intent on salvaging psycho-physics) to hypothesize the existence of an independent factor that allows cognition of perceptions. Freud became convinced that the source of this independent factor is always an exogenous stimulus.[24] This issue, of the exact relationships between reality and fantasy, perception and hallucination, internal and external reality, preoccupied Freud throughout his creative life, far beyond the period of his work on the *Project*.

We now turn to Freud's descriptions of reality indications, which were made in reference to the three major stages of ego development. In the first or reflex stage, psi processes are conscious even though the ego remains incapable of grasping reality (conditions pointing to the difference between representation and perception); that is, psi processes occur in the absence of any reality indications. Furthermore, the ego, which at this stage is only just beginning to organise, lacks the power to activate inhibition; it thus has no choice but to defend itself by maximal activation of its reflex defence capacity, a process initiated only after the appearance of a strong cathexis of unpleasure.

The second stage appears after the ego becomes capable of grasping reality indications and consequently takes part in tangible thinking. At this stage, the person learns to differentiate between representation and reality; he thus can start to think. This implies that in the first stage, the ego's capacity to think is non-existent because it is unable to pay attention to reality indications. In the second stage, however, with the perceptual reality indications being the sole reality indications the person (meaning a baby) is capable of cognizing, thinking remains only partially developed. Only now does the infant begin to differentiate between fantasy and reality. We should also stress

---

24 Jerusalem had conceived of a similar idea (Jerusalem, 1895: 209-210).

that at this stage, thinking is non-verbal. I therefore suggest employing the term *primary thought* exclusively for these processes, conducted on the basis of perceptual reality indications even though from a purely mechanical point of view, these are incontestably secondary processes even if controlled by an incompletely developed ego.

The third, most developed stage formulated by Freud is that of thinking with words. At this stage, the ego functions on the basis of verbal reality indications (the child starts to speak). Thought is most advanced here, entailing mature secondary processes, with thinking conducted exclusively on the basis of memories, free of reliance on external perceptions.

Rather than an energy-based description of the differences between primary and secondary processes,[25] with qualitative factors considered of no more than subsidiary value, I offer a definition of thought processes based on Freud's developmental view of consciousness. At its initial stage of development, the ego is capable of paying attention solely to perceptual indications of reality while thought processes tend to establish an identity between perceptions and external objects (Freud termed this identity *perceptual identity*). Afterwards, the child becomes capable of discerning more-developed, complex reality indications, specifically, verbal indications, which support thought on the basis of mnemic images (*internal perceptions*). At this stage, the aim of thought is to establish an identity with mnemic images, that is, *thought identity* (1900: 535). My suggested definition is based on the type of reality indications referred to. Within this framework, the fundamental goal of primary processes is establishment of an identity with external perceptions, just as the fundamental aim of secondary processes is establishing an identity with mnemic images (internal perceptions). The less-important features of primary processes include: associative flows of large quantities of energy, rapid discharge of energy, and weak cathexis of the ego. In contrast, within secondary processes, we find narrow streams of energy together with postponement, or even absence, of discharge and strong cathexis of the ego. Moreover, in contrast to the specific

---

25 See Holt, 1962: 481-491; Pribram, 1962: 444; Jones, 1972: 427-428; Laplanche & Pontalis, 1973: 339.

qualitative element by which I differentiate between these processes, all the pertinent quantitative factors are relative. The ego's strength, like the primariness or secondariness of energetic processes, is not determined on the basis of energetic strength alone but according to the relations holding between (wishful, or hostile) energetic charges and the ego's cathexis. We can therefore position each of these charges along an axis extending between two ideal poles: the primary and the secondary. At the primary pole, budding secondary features are found, whereas at the secondary pole, remnants of primary elements appear although in highly weakened states.

To better understand Freud's account, we must assume an ego constituted of diverse levels, resting one on the other within the psi system. These levels are remnants of different developmental stages, with each new (or higher) level embodying the secondary function's progressive achievements. We can therefore conceive of these levels as forming a developmental continuum, extending from primary to increasingly secondary stages. In consequence, according to Freud, the ego can be viewed as a tower constructed of different stories, with the highest belonging to the most developed secondary stages. At each level, the nervous system functions in a more-primary, or more-secondary mode, based on the relative strength of the quantities of energy engaged. Adoption of an integrated mechanical-developmental perspective allows for a more precise understanding of Freud's explanations of the secondary processes functioning in a primary mode, such as primary thought processes (330-332; *Anf* 417-418).

Freud adamantly stood by the evolutionary character of his program. In the first part of the *Project* he described the thought processes taking place in the presence only of sensory reality indications; in the third part he turned to the most complex, advanced thought processes, those involving verbal reality indications. His theoretical journey thus marked Freud as a participant in the most meaningful debate held at the time, that over thinking with and without words.[26] Concurrently, Freud turned his attention to two further phenomena -- dreams and neurotic symptoms -- which he viewed as residuals of earlier developmental processes, elements he

---

26 See Kleinpaul, 1888; Preyer, 1890, v. 2: 3-33; Jerusalem, 1895: 95-106.

hoped would assist him in explaining 'the normal passage of psychic events' (347, *Anf* 427). Based on this insight into the character of the *Project*, I divide the remainder of my analysis into the following parts: primary thought processes without words (sections 16-18); the reduction of selected primary processes, dreams, a normal primary thought process (sections 19 – 21); hysteria, a pathological primary thought process (Part II); and the explanation of verbal secondary thinking processes (Part III).

Primary Thought Processes

Once the ego's organisation is fixed, thought processes develop based on the capacity to pay attention to reality indications, and to recognise whether the desired object is real. Freud described thought processes by means of illustrative situations of increasing complexity, with each new situation demanding advances in the ego's development. His depiction of these processes, found in paragraphs 16-18, is very difficult to decipher given the short, sometimes fragmentary descriptions. In addition, despite his overtly developmental orientation, Freud did not clearly delineate the various developmental stages, nor did he clarify what distinguished thought at each stage of its development. However, the main difficulty impeding the text's interpretation pertains to Freud's wish to relate primary thinking to judgment (or cognition) and secondary processes to reproduction (the term he used to refer to memory).

As part of their attempt to clarify the plethora of concepts Freud employs when defining these processes, Pribram and Gil suggest that we concentrate on the two main distinctions that, they believe, Freud employed for purposes of differentiation. The first distinction is that between thinking for the purpose of examining external perceptions as well as thinking based on memories. In their opinion, Freud termed the first form of thinking *observant* or *judgmental*, and the second *reproductive* or *reflective* (1976: 111-112), with the second distinction based on the idea that some portion of thought is guided by a 'wishful aim' (1976: 112), what can be called 'practical" as opposed to critical or theoretical thinking. Pribram and Gil do not explain what guided theoretical thinking (1976: 112). Instead, they discuss two other distinctions Freud makes: in observant thinking, the reproduced associations 'are experiences of the subject's own body'; in reproductive thinking, the reproduced associations entail memories of the organism's experiences in its interactions with the external world. 'An external experience is also called a "psychic" experience in contradistinction to a "body" or somatic experience' (1976: 114). In any case, Pribram and Gil fail to identify the contradictions that Freud encountered when linking judgmental thinking with earlier physical processes, as well as relating memory with those other experiences he termed 'psychic'. At the bottom, his intentions regarding the nature of these distinctions remain unclear. Freud may perhaps have referred to the notion that at the beginning of life, the baby learns to know the world through his movements.

Pribram and Gil, aware of the contradictory character of the Freudian text, confess to their suggestions' inability to resolve all the interpretive conundrums (1976: 111). In order to narrow the gaps separating Freud's from their own descriptions, they suggest viewing all thought processes as varying combinations of the two types of distinctions they had proposed (1976: 112). Their failure to present precise definitions of the processes Freud described, together with their unsuccessful attempt to compensate for his lack of precision are not the only problems marking their interpretation. Pribram and Gil also err in their unwrapping of the processes Freud did elaborate. Their first distinction takes into account neither the judgmental examination of mnemic images (itself both judgmental and reproductive) nor the importance of reproductive thinking for examining external perceptions, as Freud explicitly noted (according to Pribram and Gil, scrutiny of external perceptions is inherently judgmental, not reproductive). They are also unable to grasp that despite Freud's allusions to judgment's identity with primary processes and reproduction's identity with secondary processes, his position was inconsistent, as I later show. Furthermore, Pribram and Gil do not distinguish between the two separate meanings of reproduction found in Freud's work. An analysis of these two meanings can significantly contribute to the accuracy with which we understand Freud's text.

When speaking of reproduction, Freud referred, on the one hand, to the recollection of memories as integral to the judgment of the object perceived and thought about. In this instance, memories are recollected for the purpose of comparing the awakened mnemic image with the object of thought. Throughout this process, as stated, judgmental as well as reproductive thinking participate in dialectic collaboration. Judgmental thinking cannot, therefore, take place without memory (cognition of the external object is treated in paragraph 16, under the heading *Das Erkennen und Reproduzierende Denken* [cognition and reproductive thought]).[27] On the other hand, Freud uses the term reproduction in a very specific way, in relation to more developed stages of thinking. He does so without explicitly differentiating this from its previous use. These more-developed stages of thinking are characterised by the transformation of mnemic images themselves into objects of thought. That is, he posits two types of thought objects: external and internal perceptions, otherwise referred to as perceptions and memories, respectively.

This latter type of advanced reproductive thinking is inherently verbal in character. Verbal associations enable the transformation of mnemic images into thought objects. Such a development is achieved only after an interim stage (between thinking without and thinking with words) in which a perceptual identity is established without any attendant motor discharges, while thinking becomes increasingly based on the judgment of memories (cognition of mnemic thought objects is treated in paragraph 17, under the heading *Das Erinneren und das Urteilen* [remembering and judging]). In sum, reproduction in its first sense (with memories being awakened for the purpose of knowing the external perception) occurs at every stage of thought's development. In contrast, reproduction in its second sense (when a memory is the object of knowledge) transpires only at thought's most advanced stage of development: verbal thinking.

I am therefore convinced that Pribram and Gil were unsuccessful in illuminating Freud's murky text because they did not recognise the true scope of Freud's evolutionary program. Their descriptions are occasionally cloudier than those of Freud himself. And yet, I can hardly condemn them; as stated, the portion of the text they dwelt on is one of the most difficult to decipher in the entire *Project*. Contrary to

---

27 For these and other names of thought process, see S.E. 1: 327, note 1.

these authors, I suggest treating Freud's evolutionary approach as the background against which he formulated his proposals; recognition of this background makes it possible to accurately grasp all the distinctions, quandaries, and contradictions in Freud's elaborations, together with his internal logic.

Freud delineated his basic reductive model of thinking at the beginning of paragraph 16: '...during the process of wishing, inhibition of the ego brings about a moderate cathexis of the object wished-for, which allows it to be cognised as not real' (327; *Anf* 411). If, under these conditions, perception of the external object also occurs simultaneously, the ego starts to think. This process is demanded if gratification of biological needs is to take place: it is by thinking that the ego examines the external object as well as the memories associated with the desired object, all in order to ascertain their similarity. Put simply, thought's purpose is to ascertain the similarities and differences between the desired object and the immediately perceived object. The first possibility results from the absolute identification of the perception with the mnemic image of the desired object. However, even though the two cathected objects may be identical, the ego is unable to take advantage of this situation until some reality indication appears. Afterwards, the cathexis will be successfully discharged. This is the simplest of all possible situations.

The second situation possible is very interesting in terms of our understanding of thinking. In this instance, only a partial identity is established between the perception and the desired object's mnemic image. But suppose, as Freud wrote, that in this situation, the perceptual item is comprised of the perceptual neurons $a+c$ whereas the desired object's mnemic neurons are comprised of $a+b$. Freud cites biological experience, which teaches that a neuronal discharge will be delayed until an identity between the two entities is established. This identity is achieved by comparing the different neuronal complexes.

Analysis of the perceptual event also reveals its two parts: a permanent segment that contains all the object's intrinsic elements, and a variable segment. Freud argues that language will later assign the term 'judgment' (*urteil*) to this assessment, which will reveal the similarity between the ego's core, the *kern* neurones, and the permanent perceptual segment; and between the variable perceptual element and the *mantle*'s changing cathexis. In this model, neuron *a* is the thing itself (*das Ding*), the object, and neurone *b* its activity or characteristic, the thing's predicate (328; *das Prädikat*, *Anf* 413).

Freud was especially interested in identifying the specific stages in the development of thought functions. His description of thinking, accomplished through the analysis of diverse, progressively more difficult situations, is based on one underlying assumption: a person's capacity to solve increasingly more complex situations is subject to the evolution of his ego together with his capacity for thought. He also posited the presence of a truly hypothetical stage, perhaps parallel to the ego's reflex defences, at which judgmental thinking assesses perceptual neurons while ignoring mnemic neurons. At this, the most preliminary stage of thought's development, the purpose of judgment is to recognise whether the perceptual complex matches the wished-for mnemic object. Freud termed this type of judgment 'cognition' (*Erkennen*), a process we can describe as a 'reflex examination', meant to establish a match. Memory's participation in this process is limited to ensuring the presence of the desired object's mnemic image as long as thinking continues. Freud termed this type (or stage) of memory 'reproductive thought' (*Reproduzirende Denken*). That is, when judgment and memory are insufficiently developed, judgment is defined as a psi process that exists only in the presence of the ego's inhibition, which begins with the minimal differentiation between a mnemic image's wished-for cathexis and a similar perceptual image's cathexis. Recognition of the (absolute) identity between the two charges provides the biological signal indicating the conclusion of judgmental thinking and the onset of cathectic discharge. That is, the difference between the two cathexes motivates thought, which concludes with the establishment of an identity.

At this stage, judgment is fed by a mix of exogenous and endogenous energy, provided by the desired object's mnemic image, absent the collaboration of ego energy during the examination. This process differs from that of Freud's later description of judgment, which occurs on the basis of external together with ego cathexis, described above. In the initial stages, the ego exerts little influence. Whatever influence is exerted can be summarised as the prevention of the accumulation of cathexes of the desired object's mnemic image and thus of its immediate discharge, accomplished in a hallucinatory manner. Freud's description of this situation resembles that of babies who, during the first days of life, are unable to search for an object capable of meeting their needs; all they can do is accept or reject whatever their mother offers. This implies that in the absence of any possibility to alter the situation, babies differentiate only between pleasure and unpleasure, and respond accordingly.

In the course of paragraph 16, Freud describes the second, reproductive, aspect of thinking's initial stage of development. As stated, neurone a is identical in the two cathexes (perception and memory), but now, neurone c is perceived in place of neurone b. Once this happens, the ego examines neurone c's connections prior to motivating the attachment of new cathexes until some route to the missing neurone b is found. Freud stated that under normal circumstances (for this early stage), 'the image of a movement' (*Bewegungsbild*) appears between neurone c and neurone b. When this motor image is activated by some real physical movement, neurone b's perception is loaded and the desired identity is achieved. This reproductive act allows babies to establish the desired identity.

This analysis appears to rest on Freud's assumption that mnemic motor images do exist in a baby's memory. Hence, at this stage, as in the most primary stage, cathexes travel when the desired object's memory image (neurone b) is first cathected, which then direct the examination of all neurone c's connections. The difference between the two stages rests on the fact that in the earlier stage, only desired objects are cathected, with no cathexis of mnemic images, a consequence, I submit, of the baby's meagre experience. In other words, the baby's memory has yet to store a sufficient number of perceptual memories (experiences with the external world, which Freud termed '*psychic*'). Freud described the development of this reproductive process in terms of motor experiences; by doing so he, may inadvertently complicate his initial premise that judgment is characterised by motor experiences.

Freud concluded this section with a description of the relatively developed ego activity that evolves in response to many judgmental and reproductive experiences, which culminate in what we can envision as a 'treasury' of memories. At this stage, where the ego is somewhat more developed, each act of search among facilitated neurones is controlled by the ego and directed not by facilitations but by a goal: to return to the missing neurone b and to release the identity. This aim is reached through exploratory movements, employing fluctuating levels of energy. The amount of energy required to achieve this aim depends, however, on the ability to utilise existing facilitations.

Mnemic images of pain experiences fulfil an important role in the examination of associative connections. If they encounter a mnemic image capable of releasing unpleasure during the transmission of cathexes launched by the ego for the purpose of examining neurone c's connections, this event unequivocally signals that neurone b will not be found by this route. The energy flow turns to search for alternative routes.

Freud adds here a sentence worthy of careful attention in this connection: 'The struggle between established facilitations and the changing cathexes is characteristic of the secondary process of reproductive thought, in contrast to the primary sequence of association' (329; *Anf* 414). This sentence is confusing because it seemingly equates reproduction with secondary processes. I argue that the true source of this confusion is the urgency with which Freud wrote down his ideas, a condition determining the *Project*'s summary character. It may well be that Freud already sought to describe more-highly advanced secondary stages. I nonetheless suggest that the main reasons for his connecting reproduction with secondary processes were two, first, his assumption that the accumulation of memories provides the foundations for those processes' gradual development, and second, Jerusalem's idea that judgment is preliminary to all other thought activities (see below).

This interpretation is reinforced by paragraph 17, which begins with a summary of reproductive thinking as described in paragraph 16. Here Freud argues that the purpose of this type of thinking is practical and biological: to transfer the cathexis from the unwanted, superfluous perception to the wished-for yet absent neurone b. An identity is thereby established between the desired object's mnemic image and its perception, a process enabling thinking to fulfil a practical function: discharge of cathexes in the wake of reality indications received from neurone b. That is, the aim of reproductive thought at this stage is to achieve identity between the mnemic image and the perception of a desired object, that is, a perceptual identity (332; *Anf* 416-417). Another characteristic is reliance on motor images to activate real movements for the sake of establishing perceptual identities. These features indicate the primary nature of this thought stage.

As stated, Freud had intended to draw a modular blueprint of primary and secondary processes in paragraphs 16 and 17 although he described, in effect, only the primary and secondary stages of primary thinking. I base this conclusion on the fact that Freud did not actually describe the verbal reality indications essential for establishing the identity marking the most developed secondary processes in these paragraphs.

The search for perceptual identity also characterises another sub-stage in the development of nonverbal thinking, one distinct from the practical thinking described in section 17. Freud argued that thinking can free itself from the tendency toward discharge and aspire identity alone. He termed this process 'a pure act of thought' (*reinen Denkakt*). Even though he did not explicitly describe how pure thinking emerges, I conclude that he assumed that as children mature, their treasury of memories and their ability to delay gratification enlarge. Thanks to this accumulation, the child's capacity to use memories constantly increases. The way in which this new, more-developed thinking operates follows the basic model of thinking described at the beginning of paragraph 16. Hence, the main difference between the two thinking stages (the practical and the pure) is the added strength that ego now enjoys, so necessary for postponing gratification of the desired object through inhibition, which directs the cathexes toward further examination of external perceptions.

The ego's cathexis of perceptions, what Freud termed *hypercathexis* (Überbesetzung), represents the beginning of other, more-developed judgmental, reproductive processes. Thinking is now aimed at establishing perceptual identities without discharge of the desired object's cathexes (330-331; *Anf* 414-415). This type of thinking occurs in the absence of any movement transpiring in the external world. However, despite this being an act of pure thinking, what Freud termed *theoretical thinking*, it can later be applied to practical uses (331; *Anf* 415). Researchers nonetheless commonly treat Freud's conceptualisation of theoretical thinking as a secondary process. Instead, I suggest we call this process *primary theoretical thinking* given that it aims at establishing the perceptual identity characteristic of primary processes.

Freud described this new development by analysing a third situation, potentially occurring during cathexis of a desired object's mnemic image. It occurs when, in the presence of a wishful cathexis, a perception appears that is totally unlike the desired object's mnemic image. Under such conditions, a new perception is to be cognised (*erkennen*) in order to locate some route to the cathected mnemic image. The ego then 're-cathects' the entire perception just as it had earlier cathected only one of its parts (neurone c). That perception now reaches a state of hyper-cathexis. If that perception is not totally new, it will recall a similar mnemic image. For reasons of clarity, it should be stressed that this mnemic image (i.e., the image recalled through the perception's hyper-cathexis) is not the desired object's mnemic image but a mnemic image that, while similar to the perception being examined, differs completely from the wished-for object's mnemic image. Cathexis of the (initially neutral) mnemic image by the hyper-cathected perception activates thought.

Freud added here that thought is undertaken 'to some extent without the *aim* which was afforded previously by the cathected wishful idea' (331; *Anf* 415; italics in the original) I will try to clarify this sentence. As I have suggested, 'pure acts of thought' are initiated for the sole purpose of establishing identities. When Freud wrote that thought is undertaken without the previous aim, he meant that at this point, thought transpires solely for the purpose of establishing an identity between the perception and its associated mnemic image, without inducing need gratification and discharge of the cathexis associated with a desired object's mnemic image. This implies that thinking can transpire, at least temporarily, independently of gratification and discharge, without being freed from the goal of establishing a perceptual identity between the mnemic image and the perception inducing its cathexis.

In this third situation, only some parts of the perception will resemble the mnemic image cathected by means of the ego's hyper-cathexis. Later, this process will come to resemble the previous instance, which was framed by cathexis of the desired object's memory image. This implies that in the presence of similar elements, thought remains dormant. Dissimilar elements, however, do arouse one of the two modes of thinking: If the examination (cathexis of the ego) focuses on stored memories, aimless memory activity (reproductive thinking) ensues; should cathexis be directed toward new elements, somewhat aimless judgmental acts ensue.[28]

Freud demonstrated aimless thinking through an example: cognition of another person. Theoretical interest in '*a fellow human-being*' (331, *Anf* 415; italics in the English translation;) is explained, he argued, 'by the fact that an object like this was simultaneously' the initial gratifying object, the first threatening object and the only source of assistance (i.e., help). These motives (mentioned but left unexplained) incite a person to learn how to cognise by comparisons with another human being[29]. By means of this pivotal yet sketchy account, Freud substantially subverts the psycho-physiological program.

But why did he begin his exposition of thought with the simplest, most common perceptions of physical objects rather than the complex situation of relationships with others? From my perspective, Freud became aware of the import of this insight into the learning process only as he wrote. Freud's declaration that '...it is in relation to a fellow human-being that a human-being learns to cognise' (331; *Anf* 415) is highly meaningful. This statement represents a denial of the entire philosophical tradition that pays no heed to the types of objects subjected to knowledge acquisition. This philosophical tradition treats human objects of knowledge in an abstract manner, similar to its approach to physical objects, which is based on the study of elemental abstract components. In contrast to this tradition, Freud argues that cognition of the human other provides the foundations of knowledge in general. In just one step, he effectively dismisses all he had previously written on the subject.

---

28 I am convinced that Freud, in these descriptions, intended to delineate preliminary, preparatory thinking that, should the need arise, would be activated for the purpose of need gratification.

29 Lacan developed a similar thesis in lessons 3, 4 and 5 of his seventh seminar on the ethics of psychoanalysis (1992).

In completing his argument, he turns to judgmental thinking, which likewise divides perception of the person's complexity into two parts, one comprised of new (and unique) elements not given to comparison (e.g., facial features), with the other comprised of fixed elements (e.g., hand movements, or crying) that match the memories of the visual perceptions of bodily movements, in this case, painful movements or experiences. Another person's complexity can therefore be categorised into two components as well: the first – the thing (*das Ding*) – is constant in form; the second, inconstant and given to understanding by means of mnemic activity, assesses stored knowledge about the human body. Again, Freud conceived of judgmental and reproductive thinking as two simultaneous yet complementary activities.

To reiterate, the two main, comprehensive categories of thought suggested by Freud are thinking with perceptual images but without verbal associations, and thinking with verbal associations or verbal thinking. All the thought processes examined in paragraphs 16-18 belong to the first category. Verbal associations provide the reality indications facilitating more-advanced thinking. At the primary, non-verbal stage of thinking, reality indications are limited to perceptual indications. The object of thought is an external perception that stimulates perceptual neurons; with thinking meant to establish perceptual identity.

Because the examination of mnemic images plays an important role here as well, we should differentiate between the examination of mnemic images within the framework of primary thinking and that conducted in the secondary stage, when mnemic images are themselves transformed into objects of thought. Thought here is aimed at establishing an identity between two mnemic images (thought identity). As to the energy required, thinking during the primary stage occurs in the presence of a mixture of exogenous and endogenous energy. In contrast, the most-advanced secondary thought transpire by means of endogenous energy alone.

Freud's explanation becomes clearer when we distinguish between situations in which perceptual and mnemic neurones represent the cognitive object (the empirical reference) and situations where those same neurones indicate the location where thought takes place.

This distinction differentiates primary reproductive thinking from a later stage, when mnemic images are transformed into the examined objects. As stated, Freud did not explicitly differentiate between the two stages; he also often confused the two. However, by means of this distinction, we can distinguish the complete set of secondary processes from primary and transitional primary-secondary processes.

Freud then divided nonverbal cognitive processes with external perceptions as objects into two stages: a primary stage involving practical thinking (paragraph 16), and a secondary stage, involving pure thinking (paragraph 17). Despite the fact that most pure, nonverbal thinking takes place within the realm of mnemic images, the respective images have yet to become objects of thought; rather, they provide the sites where much thinking takes place. In order to reconstruct Freud's analytic course, we should consider this stage as bridging between primary and fully developed pure thinking. We can even view it as the last stage of primary thinking or the initial stage of verbal thinking. Within this context it is worth repeating the two basic modes that Freud conceived as parts of every thought process: The cognitive (judgmental) mode, which examines external as well as internal reality while analysing thought objects (external and internal perceptions); and the reproductive mode, which provides the memories employed when thinking.

As he progressed, Freud was confronted with a problem in his treatment of those reproductive processes, which he referred to as secondary processes even though they take part in the examination of external reality (primary processes). This was complicated by his argument that judgment 'is not a primary function' (332; *Anf* 416). Our quandary: How can he discuss primary judgment (333, *Anf* 417) while simultaneously positing that judgment is not a primary function?

I maintain that the fuzziness characterising these paragraphs resulted from Freud's eagerness to attribute an evolutionary meaning to these thought functions before he had fully explored this approach's implications for his hypothesis regarding reality indications. He had intended to formulate a model in which judgment developed prior to reproduction: 'Judgmental thought operates in advance of reproductive thought by furnishing it with ready-made facilitations for further associative traveling' (332-333; *Anf* 417).

It is difficult to unravel why Freud was convinced that judgment precedes memory. It may be suggested that his loyalty to the principles of associationist psychology and psycho-physics forced him to maintain his belief that knowledge of the external world is antecedent to memory (or the accumulation of memories). He nonetheless began developing an approach where endogenous needs operated as the initial motivations or triggers for the creation of mnemic images and for any actions to be undertaken. I suggest that this conundrum is solved once we take another of his assumptions into account. As previously stated, Freud mentioned Jerusalem's work as providing the source of two of his main ideas in the letter to Fliess dated 25 May 1895. One of these relates to internal perceptions; the other to judgment, which Freud conceived as 'transference into the motoric sphere' (CL 129). In response to the psychological school that viewed acquisition of knowledge of the world as a passive act, with the person submissively receiving impressions of the world based on ideas registered in memory, Jerusalem theorised that judgment, rather than memory, plays a central role in knowledge acquisition. That is, Jerusalem considered judgment in terms of action, during which all other functions (perception, memory, etc.) are activated. In addition, Jerusalem stressed that perception is likewise an active act while simultaneously pointing to the central role of bodily experiences and motor mechanisms in thinking as well as knowledge (Jerusalem, 1895: 85-86, 93-95). This led to his deduction that experience is importantly involved in knowledge of the world. Freud adopted his views regarding the salience of bodily experiences, in contradiction to the traditional approach stressing perceptual knowledge.

Jerusalem's approach met another, developed by Jackson, which Freud apparently also adopted. Jackson conceived of the nervous system as a motor organ housing neural arrangements representing sensations and movements but not ideas. Jackson's aims were varied. He wanted to eliminate the confusion found in the physiological literature between physiological and mental concepts so as to neutralise psychology's influence on physiology in an effort to establish physiology on material foundations (Young, 1990: 204-210). His approach fit Freud's with respect to the primary stages of human development, characterised by large-scale motor discharges in the absence of advanced thinking. As motor experience and development precede theoretical thinking, we can understand why Freud came to assume that judgment precedes reproduction.

However, although human motor development occurs in advance of cognitive development, this sequence does not require the prior development of judgment. In the respective paragraphs, Freud himself deviates from this timeline for judgment's development. Instead, he adopts a dialectic view of thinking, according to which there is no judgment without reproduction and vice versa, with the two functions developing in parallel. His entire approach is based on a clear but insufficiently elaborated view that differentiates between thought processes according to how and when mnemic images are transformed into thought objects. Such a development is feasible only once the baby learns to talk and use verbal associations as reality indications of mnemic images. Throughout all developmental stages, the two thought functions work dialectically.

It is impossible to ignore the contradictions that arise from Freud's (forced) attempts to develop definitions of judgmental and reproductive processes parallel to his efforts to implement the ideas elaborated by Jerusalem and Jackson:

> 'Cognitive or judging thought seeks an identity with a bodily cathexis, reproductive thought seeks it with a psychical cathexis of one's own (an experience of one's own)' (332; *Anf* 417).

Freud's notions 'bodily cathexis' and 'psychical cathexis' nonetheless remain cloudy.

If we assume that by 'bodily cathexis' Freud was referring to cathexis of the mnemic motor images accompanied by bodily movements, it becomes impossible to define the secondary theoretical judgment emerging upon cathexis of those mnemic images when accompanied by motor innervations but not by bodily movements. Alternatively, if we assume that Freud was referring to the cathexis of motor images unaccompanied by actual movement, it becomes fairly impossible to define primary, more practical judgment. Stated differently, the notion 'bodily cathexis' cannot be employed to differentiate between judgment and reproduction. Moreover, the notion 'psychical cathexis', as the cathexis of experiences, cannot be used to differentiate between cognition and reproduction because these experiences involve mnemic images of the perceptions and movements associated with them.

My conclusion is that the use of these two notions, bodily cathexis and psychic cathexis, for distinguishing cognition from reproduction, is inappropriate. For example, an inconsistency arises when identifying judgmental thinking with bodily cathexis because cathexis of bodily images is a reproductive process (328-329, 331; *Anf* 412-413, 415-416). Similarly, reproduction, which Freud often identifies with thinking, is conducted on the basis of neuronal clusters containing bodily cathexes, such as those retained in the wake of an experience. As Freud himself later commented, as I will show, the differences between the various thought processes resulted from the strength and level of motor discharge but not from their content (334; *Anf* 418).

In paragraph 18, Freud describes the onset of thought (judgment) from the perspective of somatic development. His underlying premise is that bodily experiences, that is, sensations and motor images, are necessary for the development of thought, for making people capable of understanding changes in perceptual complexes. In the absence of such experiences, it is possible to recall the perceptual complex but not to understand it or to apply it when thinking (333; *Anf* 417). This premise underlies Freud's complicated assumption regarding sexual development, described somewhat later in the *Project*. By means of this premise he attempts to explain why repression of sexual contents exclusively initiates pathological outcomes. His proposed explanation states that early sexual experiences are incapable of causing any outcome if the person has no sexual feelings, that is, prior to the onset of physiological sexual maturity.

Freud also broadened his description of primary bodily processes, which he once more divided into two parts according to the type of associations and their strength, aroused during the establishment of perceptual identities: (a) During instances of perception that include movement in that perception's changing parts, movements are repeated. To fix identity in such cases, strong cathexis of the motor image leading to movement is initiated. Here, perception has 'imitation value'. (b) When the perception recalls pain sensations, with the associated unpleasure, an appropriate defensive act is begun. Here, perception has 'sympathy value'. Freud argues that the primary process in both instances should be viewed in relation to judgment, with all ensuing secondary judgment based on the weakening of pure associative processes. From my perspective, it would be preferable to substitute the word 'judgment' for the word 'thinking'.

Later in the text, Freud describes the quantitative differences between (secondary) thinking and the primary process in greater detail. He uses these terms as antitheses for the first time, in place of judgment/reproduction. He describes thinking as cathexis of psi neurones by the ego's collateral cathexis, an act that changes their existing facilitations. He mentions that thinking can also involve motor innervations should motor mnemic images be cathected. Hence, thought introduces savings in energy because only a small fraction of the total energy available needs to travel through the existing facilitations with the strength of the cathected flow always regulated by the ego's cathexes. Otherwise, all the loadings required for final discharge would be dissolved by the motor mechanisms in the course of thinking. *'Thus the secondary process is a repetition of the original ψ passage* [of quantity]*, at a lower level, with smaller quantities'* (334, *Anf* 418, italics in the original).

At the conclusion of this section Freud mentions two of the issues arising from his elaboration, to which he would devote a great deal of space in the *Project*'s third part. First, he thought it would be exceptionally difficult to explain the fact that secondary processes transpire by means of smaller quantities of energy than those generally flowing through psi neurons. These small charges never acquire the strength needed to open passages throughout psi, despite facilitation of the respective neurones. In the same section, Freud intimates the solution he would develop in the third part: When side cathexes are available, quantities smaller than those ordinarily required are able to flow through the facilitations. This occurs because side cathexes bind some of the energy flowing through the neurones. In order to enlarge upon his solution, Freud broadens his account of the ego's organisation and its mechanisms.

The second, more crucial issue emerged from the conditions that thought processes are obligated to fulfil: These must not alter the facilitations created by primary processes; if they do, impressions of reality will be falsified. As Freud argued, we can assume that the small cathexes flowing during thought are powerless to alter the facilitations imprinted under the influence of stronger cathexes. However, he added, there is no doubt that thought leaves permanent imprints; new rounds of thinking thus expend less energy. Hence, we should assume the presence of special residues that constitute indications of thought processes, enable their fixation in memory, and differ from the indications of reality with which we had familiarised ourselves until that point.

Freud next turned to an analysis of exceptional thought processes, those occurring either free of the ego's control or in response to the impairment of that control.

Primary processes absent ego control: dreams and hysteria
Dreams (paragraphs 19-21)

Freud begins his explanation of dreams by discussing sleep (paragraph 19). The main condition enabling sleep is need satisfaction in the absence of external stimuli. In Freud's psycho-physiological terms, this condition involves *'a lowering of the endogenous load in the Ψ nucleus'* (336, *Anf* 420, italics in the original), an action that halts secondary activity. Unloading of the ego is generally incomplete, which induces sleep's characteristics: motor paralysis and withdrawal of cathexis from mantle neurones (those involved in perception), that is, a pause in attention. When mantle neurones are not cathected, they cannot excite omega; perception consequently occurs without quality indications, a state allowing us to dream.

In paragraph 20, Freud explains these characteristics:

1) Dreams are *devoid of motor discharge*.
2) The associations found in dreams may be nonsensical, 'feeble- minded', meaningless, strange, or even crazy. Freud ascribes these events to the compulsion to associate. In the absence of a loaded ego, simultaneous charges can be associated, with some of the cathexes not withdrawn and remaining within psi, perhaps moving to

contiguous facilitations while others possibly moving to proximate charges. That is, we dream because the ego is not fully unloaded.

3) A dream's most important feature is the hallucinatory character of the ideas aroused, that is, the fact that they awaken consciousness. Freud suggested two alternative explanations for this phenomenon. One, hallucinatory perceptions are caused by a retrogressive flow from psi to phi. As stated, the cathexis of phi causes the excitation in omega that induces consciousness of perceptions. Reversal of the process avoids psi motor discharges. Hallucinatory perceptions, if devoid of motor discharge, are not dangerous, a characteristic that allows retrogressive discharge to phi. In waking life, the retrogressive cathexis of phi and the ensuing appearance of consciousness is avoided by the current's flow toward motility. Neuronal activity as conceptualized according to the reflex model does not allow for movement in any other direction. Freud's solution therefore does not deviate from that model, which states that dreams appear because the first memory of a perception, registered in psi, is always hallucinatory. Only inhibition, as a learning mechanism, prevents stimulus of a perception so as to avoid a retrogressive energy transfer from psi to phi. Freud also writes that the flow from phi to psi is smoother than the flow in the inverse direction. Continuing in this vein, he notes that a psi cathexis[30] of a neurone does not produce a retrogressive flow even in cases where this cathexis is much higher than the perceptual (external) cathexis of the same neurone.

4) A dream's aim and significance lie in wish fulfilment. This aim is not easily recognized because pleasure discharge in dreams is slight, taking place with almost no energy and concluding in no action.

---

30 Though Freud does not explicitly say so, I assume he is referring to an endogenous cathexis.

5) Freud also relates to two other dream-related phenomena: (a) Most dreams are forgotten; and (b) Dreams produce little damage in comparison to other primary processes because a dream's cathexis follows old facilitations without changing them. This results from the lack of discharge indications left by perceptions and consequent actions.

6) In this paragraph, Freud first hints at a theoretical explanation of the unconscious, a concept he had presented earlier, in the *Studies on Hysteria,* from a clinical perspective. Freud writes here that in dreams, consciousness appears as it does in waking life, proving that consciousness is not related to the ego although it may be attached to any psi process. To this notion he added an important qualification: primary processes are not to be identified with unconscious processes. That is, Freud thought that the primary or secondary character of a process does not offer any hints about its conscious, or unconscious, character. Another important quality is concealment of the unconscious meaning of a dream's conscious memories by psi-related processes, with the latter also operating in neuroses.

In paragraph 21, Freud's main proposition regarding consciousness in dreams relates to this state's discontinuity. He describes dreams as structured by separate, distinct points rather than a succession of associations. Connecting those points are unconscious relations that can be discovered when awake. In this Freud deviates from his previous aim of developing a model according to which psi processes, especially primary processes, represent movements, not ideas. Instead, he now applies a reductive formulation to explain a dream's conscious content as isolated ideas: Suppose that in a dream, two ideas, A and C, appear that exhibit no relationship either on the conscious level or from a logical point of view. In place of C, we expect B because A leads to B on the conscious level. B does not appear because C lies between B and D, a cathected unconscious idea.

As Freud continues, he turns to the contradictory aspects of his view of the discontinuous character of consciousness and tries to resolve them. He points out how strange it is that the intermediate element B and the deviating idea D do not appear in consciousness, that is, they remain unconscious even though they may be sufficiently strong to be conscious; only C, cathected from both sides, can reach the hallucinatory level characterizing dreams. This enigma, he notes, is likewise characteristic of waking life; the difference lies in the ease with which cathexes are displaced in dreams, illustrated by the replacement of B by the more-strongly cathected C.

A similar contradiction appears in relation to dream wishes. What appears in hallucinations, in the consciousness appearing in dreams, is fulfilment of a wish but not the wish itself. The relationship between a wish and the idea that fulfils it is unconscious and must be deduced. Wishes taking part in dreams do not develop qualitatively (342, *Anf* 425-426), that is, they do not become conscious. The subsequent contradiction is found in the impossibility of the cathected wishful idea to be stronger than the wish itself. To reconcile this contradiction, Freud writes that consciousness does not depend on quantity (342, *Anf* 426). These descriptions should therefore be considered as expressing Freud's continuing withdrawal from a reductive explanation of psychological processes.

Freud ends paragraph 21 by considering another contradiction inherent in dream consciousness. From one perspective, we can infer that consciousness appears during the passage of quantities rather than in the presence of a constant cathexis. Consciousness, however, becomes attached to the outcome of that energy's passage, that is, to a relatively constant cathexis.

Freud proposed viewing these contradictory features as results of retrogressive flows to phi, in opposition to the stronger flows to psi. As Freud assumed that the presence of a retrogressive current is one of the more-problematic aspects of his psycho-physiological *Project*, we anticipate this discussion (see Chapter 4, following) by stressing that current's central role in primary processes, normal and pathological, and in their differentiation from the secondary processes that do not deviate from the reflexive model.

Hysteria (Part 2)

Freud begins his reductive explanation of hysteria with a description of its features (paragraph 1). Hysterics suffer from highly intense compulsive ideas, ideas that can also appear in normal people. These ideas are strange, 'unintelligible', 'incapable of being resolved by the activity of thought', 'incongruous' (348, *Anf* 428). He goes on to explain: when a strong compulsive idea A is accompanied by crying, for example, we always discover that another, unknown idea, B, can readily explain the crying and make it understandable. What is special in the relationship between the two ideas is that when the person is about to remember B, A always appears in its place. A thus becomes a substitute for B, its symbol. The hysteric that weeps when A appears does not know that he cries as a result of the relation A-B because B does not exist in his conscious life: 'The symbol has...taken the place of the *thing*...' (349, *Anf* 429). Should B attempt to penetrate consciousness, A will necessarily appear in its place.

This explanation of hysterical symptoms led Freud to conclude that all compulsion is accompanied by repression and amnesia (350, *Anf* 429). He further proposed that the quantitative meaning of the term repression means to be emptied of energy, whereas the sum of compulsion and repression is equal to a normal quantity, taken from B (350, *Anf* 429). The difference between the two lies in the distribution of energy between A and B. The respective pathology entails *displacement*, a primary process also present in dreams. The idea B is not, however, like other mnemic images: as we approach it, resistance becomes stronger. This resistance receives its energy (the energy that had previously repressed B) from the compulsive idea A and is directed at avoiding any thought of B, even when B is partially conscious.

In trying to explain how this occurs and what distinguishes it from other normal, primary processes, Freud argues that repression is activated by sexual ideas, which produce unpleasure in the ego. He distinguishes between this pathologic process and psi's other primary processes by pointing out that the source of hysterical repression and compulsion is a defensive mechanism originating in the cathected ego. That is, a disturbance in ego functioning produces pathological processes.

At the beginning of his paragraph 3, Freud confesses that he was still far from providing a good explanation of pathological defence, and that it is impossible to explain such a defence by assigning its cause solely to unpleasant sensations. To repeat, hysterical differs from normal repression in that A appears in place of the repressed B, that is, in symbol formation. He further argues that it is also impossible to adequately explain excessive symbol formation by assigning its cause solely to a relatively intense defensive affect. Experience had taught him that even the most difficult memories are not necessarily repressed or replaced by symbols.

Freud subsequently suggests another condition to explain the formation of pathologic defence: the sexual content of repressed ideas. For the first time, he distinguishes between repression and the mechanisms guiding energy flows, a distinction absent from his earlier papers on neuroses. As a preliminary to his attempt to explain why only repression of sexual ideas induces pathologic phenomena, Freud situates the problem in the first segment of defence, that is, in the defensive action per se. As hysterical repression manifests itself through symbol formation, the displacement of energy and meaning to other neurones allows us to encapsulate the entire riddle of repression within the displacement process. And yet, the fact that in obsessive neurosis we find repression without symbolization, with repression and substitution chronologically separated, prompts Freud to conclude that repression still rested at the 'the core of the riddle'.[31] He therefore identifies the only difference between pathological and normal repression as being intensity, with the former 'performing more than its normal function' (353, *Anf* 432).

At this point we turn to explaining how the ego comes to display features that appear only in primary processes even though the ego's primary aim is to avoid those same primary processes. Freud assumed that the solution to this conundrum depended on his being able to explain the psychic characteristics of the abnormal process within the context of sexuality's plentiful characteristics.

---

31 Freud referred to repression as 'the core of the riddle' within this context exclusively. From this together with the following paragraph 4, we must conclude that his intention was not to state that the physiology of repression needs explanation but that its development does. In what followed, Freud proposed quite a good mechanical explanation for pathological repression.

In paragraph 4, Freud exemplifies how, after a person reaches sexual maturity, memories may awaken feelings that the original experiences did not. He coined the term *hysterical proton-pseudos* (false premises) to capture the character of these memories, explained by the fact that the biological changes experienced in puberty lead to a different understanding of memories. Later, new comprehension (or reinterpretation) of past sexual events leads to their repression if those events are experienced as traumatic when remembered. This response is known in the psychoanalytic literature as *Nachträglichkeit* (deferred action).[32]

The context in which sexual memories become traumatic is contrary to the manner in which other traumas occur, and rests on what Strachey calls the 'retardation of puberty' (paragraph 5). However, due to the generality of delayed sexual maturity and the consequent late interpretation of memories as sexual, other causes must be sought to explain why only a small number of persons become hysterical.

Freud thus suggests that the disconcerting factor in sexual trauma is the release of affect. He claims that experience has taught him that some hysterics became sexually excitable prematurely as a result of masturbation while others reached this state due to an innate disposition for premature sexual release. He viewed these two factors as quantitatively equivalent and given to reduction. Freud stressed the priority of premature sexual release as the main factor in repression; if every sexual release activated repression, pathological repression would become extremely widespread.

Freud goes on to offer a mechanical explanation of repression, based on a developmental solution (paragraph 6). To reiterate, the developmental factors on which Freud rooted his explanation refer to his assumed connection between sexual release and memory as well as to premature release. It is therefore important to note Freud's remark that these two factors are potentially present in normal people; his solution therefore abrogates any essential distinction between normal and abnormal repression. His analysis is more exceptional when we recall that at the time, hysterical patients were considered

---

32 See Laplanche and Pontalis, 1973.

hereditary degenerates, with a polar distance separating what was perceived as normal from what was perceived as pathological. There can be no doubt that Freud saw his notion of repression as nullifying that dichotomy.

By means of his mechanical explanation, Freud comments on the proximity between normal affective processes that delay normal thought, and uninhibited primary processes. He focused on two factors in his description of the normal: the release of affect that strengthens the released idea, and the principal functions of the cathected ego: avoidance of new affective processes and weakening of old affective facilitations. Freud describes the process as follows: at the beginning, cathexis of a painful experience releases unpleasure. This cathexis intensifies with the discharge of key neurones through facilitated pathways. After formation of a cathected ego, when the cathexis of those painful experiences is renewed, the ego's attention is directed at these experiences. This act inhibits the passages of quantities away from hostile perceptions by means of those side cathexes that limit the discharge of unpleasure. Side cathexes henceforth signal the ego to activate normal repression so as to avoid repetition of the painful experiences. The ego's ability to defend itself from the release of unpleasure is nonetheless limited. Beyond this limit, it allows primary passage of cathexes along early facilitations. The greater the quantity, the greater the difficulty of the ego in activating thinking, that is, in executing trial displacements of small quantities of energy.

Should an unpleasure-releasing cathexis escape attention, this lapse delays ego activity, as observed in hysterical proton-pseudos. Normally, attention is directed to perceptions because these, rather than memories, ordinarily release unpleasure. However, with proton-pseudos, the ego's delayed action results from the unexpected release of unpleasure by a memory. The primary process is activated just because the ego did not expect this action to occur.

Freud describes what happens in traumatic experiences by a comparison with normal memories, which can also arouse unpleasure. Although the ego already exists, initial memories of the trauma escape its attention. From the onset of these events, side cathexes gradually develop with every new release of unpleasure, thereby weakening the trauma's memory until it (the memory) is transformed into a signal directed at the ego. This process does not take place in the case of proton-pseudos because no ego inhibition transpired during the first unanticipated release of unpleasure, once the experience is remembered. The absence of ego inhibition thus allows the appearance of a traumatic primary affective experience. That is, a traumatic affect emerges out of delayed sexual maturity but also from deferred comprehension of memories.

It is important to stress once more that Freud, here as throughout the *Project*, described and explained normal and pathological functioning of the ego as well as affect by means of a combined developmental-mechanical approach, with his explanations falling neither in scope or complexity when compared to other mechanical explanations of his time; they even surpass them.

Secondary thought processes (verbal thinking)

In the third part of the *Project,* Freud presents a mechanical description of normal thought as comprised of secondary energy processes transpiring between ideas (neurones), phrased in the terms of associationist psycho-physiology. This effort should be understood in terms of his attempts to progress from elementary and discrete units (ideas) to complex empirical psychological phenomena, specifically, narrative-linguistic phenomena. Freud went from simple to more-complex thought processes according to an impressive developmental model. He consequently also mentions here a new objective: to explain philosophy, especially the principles of logic, on the basis of psycho-biological assumptions.[33]

I should admit here, once more, that despite the conceptual assistance provided by the hermeneutic principles previously outlined, the task of reading this part of the text is not at all easy. Freud's style gradually loosens and descriptions diminish in their precision. This decline may well reflect the complexity of the mechanical and especially evolutionary issues raised by his presentation of normal psychological processes. Freud himself acknowledged that although he had succeeded in resolving some issues, many others remained. Moreover, as he progressed in his writing, he came to

---

33 An explanation suggested by Jerusalem, 1895: 13-21.

recognize the presence of other, more general challenges, touching on psychological tenets that he had borrowed from his teachers' psycho-physical psychology. In the end, the reductionist issues raised by his analysis of normal psychic processes led to his abandonment of the *Project* (see his later letters to Fliess). With this history in mind, my descriptions of Freud's reasoning must be taken as rudimentary and preparatory, conducted to deepen our penetration of his complex thinking while avoiding the superficial interpretations current in the literature.

Part 3 of the *Project* can thus be viewed as an array of reductionism's core issues, which existed prior to and were fundamental for Freud's explanation of repression. These issues are for the most part intertwined because they constitute different aspects -- mechanical, evolutionary and psychological -- of the same subject. I begin with a summary of Freud's descriptions:

1) The *mechanical-localizationist problem*, an outcome of the contradictory conditions with which mnemic neurones must comply. On the one hand, initial facilitations cannot be changed so as not to alter traces of reality; on the other, all changes in affective and thought processes, such as forgetfulness and inclusion of the same mnemic images, transpire in these neurones.

2) The mechanics of the retrogressive discharge from psi to phi cannot be readily integrated into explanations of the normal hallucination found in dreams, or of the normal thought processes leading to unpleasure.

3) Evolutionary conundrums: (a) If the evolution of thought depends on two biological laws, attention and defence, it totally contradicts descriptions of the most-advanced, pure theoretical thinking. (b) Why are verbal quality indications important for ego functioning and why do they develop at all, considering the possibility that the ego may have learned to function without them.[34]

---

[34] We should recall that Freud grounded all his explanations of the most-advanced secondary processes on these indications.

4) Two psychological dilemmas: (a) Freud's conclusion in part 3 that most psychic processes, even the most developed, are unconscious, implies that consciousness is only a contingent and secondary feature of these processes opposes the centrality of consciousness in modern psychology and in the *Project* itself. (b) The idea that wishes influence the examination of perceptions opposed Freud's original and objectivist conceptions about knowledge. This idea matured from his premise that perception was facilitated by attention, a process based on endogenous cathexes.[35]

In what follows, while presenting Freud's description of the appearance and development of higher-level thought processes, I show how these issues became increasingly relevant. His text reveals new developments in his analysis of the ego mechanism, especially the pivotal ability to use verbal quality indications, to which we now turn.

Paragraph 1: Here, Freud begins describing the emerging ego developments that enable secondary processes to emerge. He starts with the developed ego mechanism, including a more-elaborate evolutionary description of attention, the mechanism allowing us to differentiate perception from hallucination. From a biological perspective, the absence of this distinction lead to maximal unpleasure. Freud therefore postulates that attention evolved in response to biological experience, which trained us not to confuse ideas with perceptions and to delay discharge until indications appear to confirm the reality of the respective ideas.[36]

Within the context of his discussion, a sentence appears that has apparently confused many interpreters and led them to think that Freud was intent on admitting to the failure of the physiological-mechanical aspect of his *Project*:

> 'I find it hard to give a mechanical (automatic) explanation of its origin' (360-361; *Anf* 439).

---

35 This is, of course, an epistemic problem as well.

36 I should stress that the crucial challenge embodied in the ability to distinguish between ideas and perceptions has no direct relation to defence.

However, I am convinced that Freud was referring not to the difficulty of providing a mechanical explanation of the (later, developed) attention mechanism but to its genesis.[37] The crux of his dilemma was how to explain this mechanism's appearance during the evolution of neuronal systems and how it worked thereafter. He subsequently offers a clear mechanical description of the mature attention mechanism. After suggesting diverse mechanical explanations, with each exhibiting increasing precision, Freud became satisfied with his conclusion that attention is the process by which the cathected ego tracks the associative passage of energy from the reality indication to the perception by way of facilitation (362, *Anf* 441). That is, Freud became convinced that he had provide a sound explanation of attention, rooted in biology.

Now we come to another, frequent interpretative error, made by Strachey among others. After citing Freud's expression of satisfaction with his explanation, Strachey refers the reader to page 360 (*Anf* 439), where Freud presents an initial description of the mechanism's operation in the presence of a more- or less-developed ego. This referral is incorrect. If we turn to the text's subsequent two pages, we find Freud progressively explaining the mechanism's formation and development, beginning at a stage devoid of an ego and of defence (361-362; *Anf* 440-441). Freud's solution to attention's mechanical issues is that the mechanism had survived throughout the biological evolution of psychic systems. When Freud mentions his difficulties in providing a 'mechanical explanation' of attention's origin, the term 'mechanical' alludes to evolutionary mechanics as described in the contemporary professional lexicon. Freud goes on to explain as follows:

> For that reason, I believe that it is biologically determined -- that is, that it has been left over in the course of psychical evolution because any other behaviour by ψ has been excluded owing to the generation of unpleasure (361, *Anf* 439).

This statement clearly indicates Freud's desire to provide a mechanical explanation of why and how this kind of mechanism

---

[37] Freud wrote *Entstehung*, which means genesis, coming into being, origin, emergence, and formation in German.

appeared. It is also implicitly Darwinian: In the course of evolution, some psychic systems appeared but did not survive; the only systems able to do so were those that functioned with the help of attention, the only psychic mechanism that prevents accumulation of unpleasure. His reasoning nevertheless raises another core question – Why does the attention mechanism exist at all? – one of the many awaiting resolution in the biological sciences, especially: Why is there life? How did life appear? Why did consciousness appear?

In paragraphs 16-18 of part 1, Freud discusses situations where a thought process is initiated when the ego finds it necessary to differentiate between similar perceptions and ideas. Beginning in part 1 and culminating in part 3, Freud develops his argument by pointing out the importance of also being attentive in situations where external perceptions and wishful cathexes (ideas) share nothing. Paying attention to every perception 'has in fact become important' (361, *Anf* 440; another developmental hint) because, he proposes, the wished-for object may lie somewhere in the space between perceptions. In what follows I therefore present some examples of how this occurs together with the related issues.

Freud first describes a situation in which an insufficiently developed ego ignores a perception accompanied by a quality indication. This indication nonetheless draws attention, which cathects the perceptual neurone with energy coming from psi. The next identical perception will consequently be examined more thoroughly because the now-cathected ego will conduct the examination (362).

Freud also emphasizes in this section the importance of endogenous energy in thought. The presence of endogenous energy creates mechanical difficulties stemming from the incorporation of two kinds of energy into one model. During his attempts to solve this dilemma, Freud becomes aware of a still more-essential psychological and epistemological issue, that of subjective (in mechanical terms: endogenous) influences on knowledge of the external world, the presence of which contradicts the objectivist psycho-physiological model (4b).

As Freud conceived mechanical psychic processes, if an external quantity reaches perceptual neurones that are not cathected by psi (ego-endogenous), that external energy associatively flows in the direction of existing facilitations. This flow ends very rapidly because the energy sub-divides and decreases along its course until it is unable to overcome the contact barriers. If the external energy fails to awaken attention, it will continue on its way unexamined. This represents attention-less perception. However, if the external stimulus appears in the presence of charged neurones and attention is directed to quality indications, their excitation will occur. Excitation then strengthens the existing perceptual cathexes by means of attention cathexes -- a process made possible by the fact that the ego has learned to follow the neurones' associative trail from quality indications to perception.

The subjectivity-objectivity issue attached to knowledge arises, once more, with Freud's remark that knowledge about the object (in his words, 'judgment on the quantitative characteristics of the object') is not altered as a result of attention (362). This is odd if we recall Freud's statement that examination of a perception depends on the ego's activation of attention and hyper-cathexis (attachment of endogenous energy). Contrary to this position and in accord with the objectivist stance, he declares that it is impossible to represent an external object's quantity with a psi quantity and that external quantity can be represented solely by facilitations (those traces remaining after the initial perceptions, which take place in the absence of endogenous quantities) (362).

By stressing that external energy cannot be represented by endogenous quantities and thus isolating knowledge about external perceptions from the influence of internal cathexes, Freud reached the apex of self-contradiction. This quandary would become increasingly convoluted as his work progressed. The problem was rooted in the contradictions that had arisen between his psycho-physical approach, which demanded absolute objective knowledge of the external world, and his theorizing, which led to his discovery of the central importance of endogenous energy for explaining psychic processes (he even concluded that it is impossible to examine a perception in the absence of attention and strong endogenous cathexis).

This confusion was exacerbated when mechanical ideas came into play: With regard to the idea of activity integrating external and internal energy, Freud postulated that the two energies would mix but did not explain how this was to come about. If endogenous cathexis is necessary for adequate knowledge of perceptions, and if perceptual energy can be combined with internal energy, this implies that knowledge of the physical world loses its objectivity once exposed to internal, biological and psychic influences. I cannot imagine that Freud was blind to the more general theoretical significance of his new ideas. Although he did not explicitly assert that significance at this point, his later works, grounded in the idea of unconscious determination of psychic processes, show that his revised conception of knowledge contributed to the decline and eventual abandonment of the objectivistic psycho-physiological tenet that perceptions and their original memory traces constitute an exact representation of external reality.

Freud's major aim in his meticulous description of the attention mechanism was to show how the psycho-neuronal system becomes fine-tuned as attention on mnemic images per se. In compliance with his goal, Freud further elaborated his notion of attention, based on the idea of hyper-cathexis of perceptual neurones. In this instance, the resulting mixture of internal and external energy may move in the direction of the best facilitations. Unlike exclusively external energy in the absence of attention, the presence of endogenous energy (attention) permits cathexis of more-distant neurones. The result of this process is that the associated mnemic images (363-364, *Anf* 442) appear in place of the perceptions despite the object's continued presence as an external perception. This transitional phase, he concluded, nurtures advanced thought processes, those focused only on mnemic images.[38]

This new, transitional phase thus takes place when energy passes on to a previously charged mnemic image, causing its hypercathexis. Renewed cathexis indicates that the ego is interested in examining this image. Attention is now diverted to the mnemic image rather than to the perception that incited its renewed cathexis.

Due to the convoluted nature of the text, I provide a streamlined version of Freud's description of the cognition of mnemic images. To begin with, among the preliminary conditions, production of a quality indication is required to prevent the image from becoming

---

38 To simplify a reading of the text, I here enumerate the respective stages of attention: (1) Unattended external perception; (2) Attention to the perception (hyper-cathexis); (3) Reproduction (cathexis) of mnemic images as part of the examination of perceptions; (4) Attention (hyper-cathexis) to mnemic images and verbal indications of quality.

hallucinatory, a situation resulting in early and undesirable discharge. Freud assumed that mnemic images were unable, by themselves, to produce quality indications; hence, they must acquire these indications from perceptions of motor discharges (we should recall that perceptions are the only phenomena containing quality indications). What then remains to be explained is how the passage of energy through mnemic images produces a perception and not a hallucination. A mechanism would have to exist that would allow mnemic images to be further cathected and able to discharge this hyper-cathexis to the motor pathways (364, *Anf* 443). As originally conceived, the passage of energy was not accompanied by motor discharges. This implies that motor discharges must be obtained elsewhere. In turn, perception of discharges provides information on their occurrence, that is, quality indications direct attention to the correct points at which cognition of the mnemic image can occur.

Here Freud presents one of the most important hypotheses to appear in the *Project*: speech associations are the phenomena that provide the small motor discharges and quality indications requisite for thinking about mnemic images, thus avoiding hallucination. If some of this energy passes from the mnemic image to verbal sounds and motor images, pursuant to the creation of good facilitations, the mnemic images will always be accompanied by information about the discharge of those motor images. Once the ego learns to charge verbal motor and sound images, it constructs a mechanism to maintain attention directed at the memories appearing during the passage of energy (364-365, *Anf* 443). The highest of thought processes can now begin to develop.

The label Freud attached to the verbal thought processes participating in the examination of memories was 'Observing thought' (*beobachtenden Denken*) or 'cognition' (*Erkennen*). This judgmental-cognitive processes examine memories while focusing on external perceptions (364, *Anf* 443). Thanks to speech associations, the psycho-neuronal system can also remember and cognize at this point the processes located only on mnemic images, which puts them on the same level with perceptual processes (366, *Anf* 444).

Freud then describes the biological development of verbal associations, beginning in the primary stage when the voice acts solely as a pathway for energy discharge, until the secondary stage, when it supports communication. Afterwards, he turns to two of the mechanical and evolutionary questions posed by his hypothesis on speech (verbal) associations. When writing within the framework of his mechanical explanation, Freud states that the psycho-neuronal system functions according to two contradictory features. Parallel to the enhanced development of thought processes, the ego and the attention mechanism strengthen, to become much more cathected. But, there is no doubt, he affirms, that during thinking, endogenous energy's passage must be weak (368, *Anf* 447). The joint presence of these two characteristics, strong cathexis and weak flow, forced Freud to explain how the ego works with such weak quantities, smaller even than those regularly travelling in neurones, given its simultaneous hyper-cathexis of the perceptions and memories needed for thought.

To comply with the two conditions, Freud depicts a situation in which the ego not only inhibits the free passage of cathexes, it also binds them. With the aid of this bounded energy, a fixed and completely cathected ego allows the passage of small quantities of energy for short periods, allowing it to charge and bind the perceptual and mnemic neurones involved in high-level thought processes. Binding of the neurones thus facilitates the combined passage of endogenous quantities of attention and exogenous quantities of perception.

Another issue to be confronted pertains to how a developed, bounded ego could assign small quantities for displacement while simultaneously binding new neurones with strong quantities. This quandary touches upon the most challenging of issues, that of the bounded ego's origin. Freud states that an evolutionary ('genetic') approach promised the most appropriate resolution (369, *Anf* 448), a position reaffirming his commitment to the evolutionary model as he nears the *Project*'s end.

In an earlier section of the *Project*, Freud had stated that the ego was originally composed of nuclear neurones that had received endogenous energy. The neurones' discharge of that energy along conduction paths produced internal changes (317, *Anf* 402). The consequent experience of satisfaction created a connection between those neurones, the wished-for perceptual image and information about the reflex movement of the action inducing satisfaction

(318, *Anf* 402-403). Furthermore, as stated, the ego developed on the basis of repeated wishful situations once two conditions were fulfilled: the ego has learned to avoid hypercathexis of the wishful idea so as to prevent hallucinations and subsequent cathexis of motor images and their discharge until a signal is received from the perceptions. The fulfilment of these conditions, accompanied by attention directed to new perceptions, allows the ego to achieve the wished-for satisfaction.

Freud theorized that the ego, as an organized system, is sustained by 1) conduction paths that uninterruptedly channel endogenous cathexes; 2) barriers preventing discharge into the motor mechanisms; 3) barriers to hyper-cathexis of wishful ideas; and 4) resistance to the passage of energy to distant neurones. If the energy level inside this energetic mass rises, the ego expands; if it declines, the ego shrinks. No opposition to the displacement of cathexes exists within this mass.

The issue then becomes one of explaining how two of those barriers – one that defends against hyper-cathexis of the wishful image (*attention*), and another that acts against cathexis of motor images (*primary defence*) – emerged. Freud tries to explain primary defence by means of the following scenario: prior to this barrier's existence, should a motor discharge combine with a wishful situation, unpleasure occurs instead of the anticipated pleasure. The threat of unpleasure, which accompanies all early discharge, thus constitutes the mentioned barrier. Under the rubric *primary defence*, Freud states that all the neuronal system's biological achievements can be interpreted as responses to the threat of unpleasure, inhibiting the charging of neurones. Although Freud admitted that he was unable to provide a mechanical representation of this process, he was not deterred from theorizing along this path. On the contrary, he henceforth stopped seeking mechanical descriptions of biological laws and became satisfied with the clear description of developmental processes as guided by the evolutionary model (370-371, *Anf* 450). He now found it sufficient to declare that the mechanisms described are important for neuronal functioning, while implying that neuronal systems not satisfying biological needs will not survive.

Freud also offered a similar explanation of attention: the origin of this mechanism lies in a biological law determining the control of ego cathexes while insisting that the appearance of reality indications leads to the hyper-cathexis of perceptions, thus avoiding hallucination, as previously noted. These two biological laws can be considered to underlie all of Freud's mechanical explanations thereafter (370-371; *Anf* 450-451).

Paragraph 2:

Here Freud elaborates more-advanced secondary thought processes. Before beginning the exposition, I stress the mechanical roots of his explanations because they intimate the range of issues subsequently arising.

The key to understanding Freud's mechanical descriptions is his contention that endogenous-psychical energy does not reflect external quantities and that the ego's alternating energy levels do not modify the facilitations upon which the picture of the external world is based (371-372, *Anf* 451). We can read this statement as Freud's admission of his intention to continue exploring other aspects of his general psychological problem (4b) as well as the localizationist-mechanical issues (1) that disturbed him. We therefore find him stating that the mechanical hypothesis of the bound ego is meant to explain the simultaneous presence of the large and small quantities that make it possible for small quantities to easily move throughout the system when energy levels in the ego are high (372). He thereby lays the groundwork for resolution of one of his two most difficult mechanical-localizational problems: (1) Do the perceptions registered in memory (facilitations) change after exposure to innumerable energy passages? Freud delves into this problem only in paragraph 3.

But before reaching a solution he would be required to solve yet another problem: Why did the most highly developed quality indications (linguistic/verbal indications) develop, and with them theoretical thinking, if they had no practical aim? Freud explicitly acknowledged that he was at a loss here. For us, however, the most interesting aspect of this problem (3b) is that it is purely evolutionary – rather than mechanical – in nature, as I show in what follows.

How, then, did Freud begin his mechanical description of developed secondary processes? This he did by first examining observation or cognition, which he distinguished from other cognitive processes, those based on expectation. In his investigation of the ego's examination of perceptions, nothing appears about wishful cathexes. He ignores them by examining only cognitive processes and secondary judgment (which precedes the more-developed judgment that focuses solely on mnemic images), free of practical objectives and momentarily unrelated to wish satisfaction or fulfilment. That is, in this cognitive process, reality indications direct attention to the perception to be cathected. The associative passage of exogenous energy transpires smoothly along previously cathected neurones and allows perceptual cognition, that is, the cognition of associations related to the initial perception. Due to the presence of a strong ego capable of binding the wishful cathexis, the external quantities, instead of rapidly disappearing, branch out according to the existent facilitations.

Freud then describes here what may be called a *transitional cognitive process*, still directed by perceptions and perceptual indications but involving mainly mnemic images and inklings of speech associations (verbal indications). Activation of speech associations during this process causes the passage of energy to become conscious and reproducible, that is, registered and memorized. Once the ego has reached this relatively developed stage, it can assess external as well as memory perceptions. Freud does not, however, explain how the two kinds of reality indications, the perceptual and the verbal, function together in the same cognitive process and why speech indications are activated only after perceptual quality indications.

After this introductory description, Freud surprises us by stating that we should question the usefulness of speech indications! Unpleasure, he notes, if resulting from ignored cognitions, is less important than ignoring external reality. He explains his position by referring to these indications' function – to cause the ego to more-intensely cathect an already cathected mnemic image that may appear during an associative passage – so as to cognize that image. As quality indications do not provide cathexes (they contribute miniscule energy at most), the ego may have learned how to set its cathexes in motion along the passage travelled by external quantities but without the help of any quality indications (372, *Anf* 452).

We therefore find that Freud's attempt to defend the status of quality indications triggered the emergence of three of the *Project*'s most profound dilemmas. The first of these is the second evolutionary issue, mentioned above (3b). Freud was unable to explain why speech (thought) indications, which differed from reality (perceptual) indications, developed at all. He explicitly admitted that he could provide no biological explanation for their appearance. He did expose his convoluted reasoning on this issue, which I briefly recapitulate.

Before detailing his two biological laws (371, *Anf* 451, end of paragraph 1), Freud indicates that the attention mechanism's functioning, with the assistance of all quality indications, may be superfluous because in situations of expectation, 'The ego might have learnt biologically itself to cathect the perceptual region...' (371, *Anf* 450), that is, the ego can act independently, without the help of attention to speech associations. In the course of his description, Freud repeats two arguments, discussed above, to justify the attention's development: First, the ego saves very large quantities of energy by cathecting the omega region, a space smaller than the perceptual area; second, speech indications are used to differentiate real perceptual from wishful cathexes.

To rationalize the prominent place of speech indications, Freud points out that the biological law of attention was 'abstracted' [sic] from perceptual processes, implying that the law originally related only to perceptual indications. Although discharge indications of speech associations also function as reality indications, they are in effect 'thought reality indications' (373, *Anf* 452 - *Denkrealität*), that is, they are not products of external reality. Freud also admits that no biological law exists to explain them and, in consequence, that he did not know why these indications and, it follows, language had developed.

Engrossed in this quandary as he appears to have been, Freud forsook provision of an evolutionary response. He paraphrased the evolutionary conundrum in these terms:

> ...and in their case [of speech-indications] a rule of this kind [the biological rule of attention] has not by any means come into effect,

because no constant threat of unpleasure would be attached to a breach of it. The unpleasure through neglecting cognition is not so glaring as that from ignoring the external world, though at bottom they are one and the same. (373, *Anf* 452)

Freud clearly has changed direction. He now states that his two biological laws, attention and defence against unpleasure, do not govern speech associations whereas he has previously assumed that they controlled all psychic development. If the development and functioning of speech indications were not subject to biological laws, why did they at all develop and according to what laws did they function? Later in this same paragraph 2, Freud firmly adds:

It has not been shown, biologically, that they are indispensable for the process [of thought]. (375, *Anf* 454)

This acknowledgement sounded the death knell to his entire evolutionary project.

It is generally accepted that he abandoned his mechanical reductionist project even though he suggested a precise description of the functioning of speech associations and attention. And yet, he also failed to provide an evolutionary explanation for the appearance of language. This failure, as I argue later, would lead Freud to significantly abandon the biological framework and dedicate himself to studying linguistic phenomena as they appear in reality, without offering any biological explanations for their form or appearance.

I now turn to the two other issues arising in paragraph 2. Although Freud forsook these issues, they continued to crucially influence his later work, especially his scientific revolution as it erupted in 1900.

The second (psychological 4a) of the three issues arose when discussing the significance of verbal quality indications during observation of thought processes. After stating that no great damage would arise from ignoring speech indications, he notes that verbal indications appear not at all or only sporadically in 'observing thought'. That is, the ego automatically follows thought's passage and its cathexes. This, ordinary, unconscious thinking, is the most common type of thought, one that exhibits casual or sporadic incursions into consciousness. Freud thus conceived of ordinary thinking as only partially conscious and, for the most, unconscious (373, *Anf* 452).

These new propositions regarding thinking instigated some very fundamental questions. First, Freud states that ordinary thinking takes place thanks to automatic ego activity, absent any or accompanied by only sporadic quality indications. If he was correct, why did he expend so much effort on the *Project,* a work explaining consciousness and its workings at all its developmental stages, as one of its fundamental aims?

Furthermore, and perhaps more crucially, if Freud now concludes that most ordinary thinking is unconscious, with 'occasional intrusions' into consciousness, we can only deduce that by the end of the *Project,* he had reached conclusions contradicting the premises he had borrowed from contemporary psychology and psycho-physiology, according to which consciousness is the signal characteristic of psychological phenomena because conscious knowledge directs psychic processes. Although unconscious processes had been described by others before Freud, his innovation rests in the shift from the conscious to the unconscious as characterizing most thinking, including high-level (i.e., abstract) thought. Furthermore, when Freud states that conscious content results from 'occasional intrusions' of unconscious thoughts, he anticipates his later ground-breaking idea that the explanation of any (normal and pathological) conscious process is to be found in unconscious processes. This text thus represents Freud's preliminary expression of one of his most important achievements: the explanation of human behaviour in terms of its unconscious contents.[39]

The third and last problem discussed here (psychological 4b) surfaces in his repeated attempts to confirm the centrality of quality indications. To reiterate, Freud had declared that attention's main task is to ensure objectivity during the associative passage of cathexis. Attention to quality indications therefore compensates for the difficulties encountered by the ego when examining external and internal reality, a situation caused by the constant presence of wishful cathexes. The presence of those cathexes during investigations of reality in effect influences the associative passages and creates false knowledge of

---

39 See footnote in *Anf* 452.

perceptions. Freud assumed that it is possible to avoid false knowledge by directing the ego's attention to the quality indications that strengthen free associative passage rather than wishful cathexes. This shift of attention to speech indications allows the ego to achieve the most advanced and secure form of cognition, that reflected in the impartial examination of all cathexes awaken by (external or internal) perceptions.

Although speech indications are also reality indications of perceptions, Freud's description remains very problematic. We may venture that he was unaware that his proposal does not truly solve the problem of objectivity. For his suggestion to work, he was required to posit that the ego could function without wishful (or purposeful) cathexes or, alternatively, that the influence of these cathexes was weak. Such a premise is, however, antithetical to the assumptions on which he described the ego's origin and development in experiences of satisfaction and pain, with their strength depending on continuous reception of endogenous (subjective) cathexes.

Freud, once more, remained uncommitted to his own solution, shown in his statement that the ego *almost always* (emphasis added) includes purposive or wishful cathexes (374, *Anf* 452). Later in the text he revises his remark by stating that the ego *always* (emphasis added) contains purposive cathexes (377, *Anf* 455-456). Here we should recall that Freud's central premise regarding the inscription of perceptions was that they take place during wish- and need-fulfilment, and that in the primary stages of development, wishful cathexes are very strong. If he was to avoid contradicting himself, Freud could not propose that the ego functions without wishful cathexes because the ego is verily a repository of old wishful cathexes. His fundamental goal of explaining objectivity thus remained unmet. But more: the problem of objectivity provides one expression of a much greater issue, one that will come to rest at the centre of Freudian psychoanalytical thought: Is it possible to assume the existence of thought processes neither influenced nor conditioned by unconscious wishes within the framework of his model?[40]

---

40 Various psychoanalytical schools are divided regarding the answer to this question. This lack of agreement provided Lacan with one of his main criticisms of American ego psychology, which maintains that conscious causes exist, independently of the unconscious.

Paragraph 3:

Paragraph 3 focuses on practical thought. It is here that Freud again confronts the change and permanence of memories. This issue – localizationist and mechanical in character – is yet another expression of Freud's doubts regarding the general psychological objectivity-subjectivity problem with respect to knowledge (psychological 4b).

Freud distinguishes practical from the 'disinterested'(376), objective (or purpose-less, presumably pure and objective) cognitive thought treated in his previous paragraph. In practical thought, a wishful cathexis is retained so long as attention focuses on a perceptual cathexis. Here, the process is not meant to discover where the perception can lead us in general but the avenues along which to release the retained wishful cathexis.

Freud begins his description of practical thought from the state of expectation, as previously discussed. In this situation, we find a strong wishful cathexis (V+) and a perception undergoing examination (W). When attention turns to the perception, an exogenous quantity passes first to a, the best facilitation, before continuing on to other facilitations. The passage of energy ceases should side cathexes appear. In mechanical terms, if the path leads, by degree of facilitation, from a to b, c and d (the last being the weakest facilitation), and d is near a wishful cathexis V+, the external quantity will pass on to d rather than the better facilitations, b or c. That is, the best path would be W-a-d-V+ (376-377, Anf 455-456). Discovery of this path complies with the aim of practical thought: achievement of an identity between the perception of the wished object and the wishful image, what leads to the discharge of a phi cathexis into the wishful cathexis, retained throughout the entire process. At this point, thought stops, followed by the complete discharge of cathexes in the specific action that satisfies the wishful image (378, Anf 456-457).

When relating to practical thought, Freud discovers yet another mechanical difficulty, belonging to his explanation of pure cognitive thought: the tension between perceptual facilitations and wishful cathexis. This struggle, which appears regularly in practical thought, explains the hardships characterizing the progression to pure cognitive thought, as follows. If, as previously stated, an exogenous quantity is not influenced by V+ energy, it will pass on to neurones a, b, c and *d*, and only thereafter to V+. However, under the influence of V+, quantity (phi) passes directly from *a* to *d*. To stress the importance of the conflict, Freud refers to another complication inherent in thought: wishful cathexes pass from V+ to other neurones to create a large wishful area. Hence, the passage of energy from W is now influenced not by one but by many wishful neurones.

During this description of ever more-complex practical thought (a similar stance is expressed in his description of `reproductive thought` (379-380, *Anf* 458)), Freud repeatedly counters his prior premise regarding the existence of purposeless thought. His declaration that the ego always contains wishful cathexes (377, *Anf* 455-456) raises the question of whether it is at all possible to assume the existence of theoretical, abstract, pure cognitive thought in the absence of some objective. And yet, he continues to maintain that the ego temporarily neutralizes wishful image cathexes by binding them, an act that enables investigation of perceptions and search for the appropriate path toward satisfaction without action and discharge. What he does not explain is how binding of the ego neutralizes its grounding wishful cathexes and avoidance of subjective directions of attention.

We should recall here that the ego's nucleus is itself built from memories of satisfaction experiences, a condition that makes neutralization of wishful cathexes problematic if not impossible; and that in the first paragraph of this part 3, Freud clearly states that the cathexes constantly arriving from the body are to be found among the cornerstones sustaining the ego. These reach the ego through memories of old satisfaction experiences. Although Freud does not explicitly say so, this outline hides an implicit assumption: the ego's contours and its development as well as functioning are conditioned by its history of wishes together with satisfaction and pain experiences. This history operates, if implicitly, every time the ego is activated. By claiming the ego's dependence on wishful cathexes, Freud testifies to his inability to explain objective, purely cognitive thought from an evolutionary as well as a mechanical perspective. He may possibly be tacitly questioning the existence of this kind of thought.

But the complications do not end here. Freud's premises contradict a basic demand of localizationist reductionism as maintained by his psycho-physiologically oriented teachers and colleagues, one he declared in the first part of the *Project*: to avoid falsifying registrations of perceptions, no energy passage is to alter earlier primary facilitations. His suggested quantitative solution for the problem -- passages transpiring during thinking lack the strength to change primary facilitations (335, *Anf* 419) -- contradicts his own previous position by stipulating that all thought processes leave lasting registrations. Freud nevertheless promises to formulate a new solution later, one rooted in the idea that thought does not modify registrations of perceptual reality because they leave distinctive traces, meaning thought memories (335, *Anf* 419).

In paragraph 3, after incisively rephrasing the conundrum, Freud provides his solution, based on ego functioning, speech indications and higher-level thought processes. He also returns to the idea that an original memory does not change when we think about it although we cannot deny that thoughts on a subject leave important traces and registrations, available for future reflection (378-379, *Anf* 457-458).

Freud's difficulty regarding this issue rests, in effect, on his belief in the existence of only one kind of facilitation (379, *Anf* 457). In other words, the facilitations Freud designates as remaining unchanged despite repeated passages of thought were the very same original perceptual facilitations affected during associative passages. As thought passages must also be registered somewhere, Freud proposes a new condition to protect the original facilitations: thought facilitations are created and reappear only in the presence of high levels of bound energy while primary associative facilitations reappear only when the conditions for the unbounded passage of energy are established (379, *Anf* 457).

According to the new solution, thinking does not alter perceptual traces because they occur at different energetic levels. Hence, memory of thoughts is physiological as opposed to anatomical. Although this solution may be reasonable in light of his evolutionary and mechanical theories of ego functioning, Freud admits:

> Accordingly, then, some possible effect by thought-facilitations upon associative facilitations is not to be denied. (379)

Freud concludes his treatment of memory change with this statement, which expresses doubt and admits to failure. But what disturbed him? He never said. I am firmly convinced that the source of his discontent is to be found in two of his basic premises: first, that the ego binds cathexis, and second, the need and existence of speech indications. The premise of bound energy assists Freud in explaining the hyper-cathexis of perceptual and mnemic neurones during thought yet without contradicting his proposition that mnemic registrations do not change even when the bound energy is very strong. As stated, this premise has another advantage: it allows for the movement of small quantities of energy in the presence of strong bounded cathexes, what enables thought and the examination of all the memories reproduced during associative energy passages of pure cognition. But even if we accept his description, this does not explain why the strong cathexis of the ego's bounded perceptual and mnemic neurones during thought does not alter its primary registrations.

This brings us to another important yet problematic element, speech indications, which allow for registration of thought memories at the ego's different levels. To reiterate, Freud eventually concluded that most thinking takes place in the absence of consciousness and either external or internal quality indications (373, *Anf* 452). Hence, as unconscious processes cannot be registered at new energetic levels due to the mentioned absence of internal quality (verbal) indications and of the bounded ego, we must conclude that they modify mnemic registrations; unconscious processes thus modify our perception of reality. As stated, Freud tried to save localizationism by means of a premise allowing for diverse perceptual and thought processes, arranged according to the degree of their complexity and development, functioning at different energy levels, with later cathexes unable to interfere with those traces already registered in memory. This idea, however, is inadequate as an explanation for even the simplest of everyday experiences, and certainly for the narrative phenomena that Freud studied during the same period. That research revealed that ideas and perceptions, being embedded in a narrative continuum, do not appear twice in the same form.

We cannot but be amazed at the increasing number of contradictions appearing in this paragraph. The impression obtained is of conceptual chaos, a product of the failure of fundamental evolutionary, mechanical and psychological ideas to explain normal (rather than pathological) mental processes. This may provide us with some insights into why Freud did not publish this work even though it provided him with a platform from which he could explore the contradictions he had discovered in the theoretical paradigms characterizing modern philosophical psychology and psycho-physiology.

End of paragraph 3 and paragraph 4

Before returning to the two major issues afflicting the end of paragraph 3, which symbolize the character of the entire text and illustrate the conceptual problems with which Freud was attempting to contend, I turn on to paragraph 4, where Freud continues his mechanical description of situations in which thought leads to either unpleasure or contradiction, a subject he began to explore in the last part of paragraph 3. I should stress here that his preoccupation with logical contradictions and errors was based on his belief that these factors produce unpleasure.

For Freud, unpleasure appears when thought encounters a memory of some painful experience, that is, memory produces unpleasure if the original perception had produced pain. Perceptions such as these are characterized by their relation to affect and defence; their mnemic images retain their sensorial qualities and continue to awaken unpleasure. And so, when a thought reaches an 'untamed' (i.e., painful) mnemic image, quality indications accompanied by unpleasure as well as tendencies toward discharge are likely to appear. Our train of thought halts at this point. Freud describes the 'taming' of painful memories as a lengthy process in which the ego is required to repeatedly bind those memories before balancing their strong facilitations.

In paragraph 4, Freud turns to another thought phenomenon causing unpleasure: errors. Writing in an almost telegraphic style, Freud divides errors into two groups: practical and theoretical. I will only point out that Freud's arguments were steered by the idea that theoretical as well as practical errors result from 'non-observance of *biological rules* for the passage of thought' (386, *Anf* 464, italics in the original). He also argues that biological rules are given to direct permutation into logical rules; hence, the unpleasure felt when a logical contradiction appears is proof of the existence of biological rules. Needless to say, this formulation contradicts a prior statement, made on the same page, where he writes that 'in theoretical thought unpleasure plays no part' (386, *Anf* 464).

Here I conclude my reading of paragraph 4 and leave to others the task of unravelling the remainder of Freud's text, in which he essentially reprises the contents of paragraphs 16-18 of part 1 although in expanded form. I consider that the most fruitful direction to take for this purpose is an investigation of the writings of those philosophers who were intent on demonstrating that transcendental realist metaphysics and rules of logic could not exist independently of either human biology, psychology or sociology.

Before closing my analysis of the *Project,* I would like to mention, as noted above, the two issues appearing at the end of paragraph 3 but left open for discussion. Freud's examination of unpleasure's arousal consequent to thought, part of his description of how the ego tames pain facilitations, is ultimately confusing. His discussion of whether original facilitations are changed or, alternatively, that registrations at higher energetic levels weaken them, remains unclear. Both solutions lead to a contradiction, based on his assertion that after thought facilitations subdue primary pain facilitations, the ego can cathect and bind pain memories, an act preventing the arousal of unpleasure (382, *Anf* 460).

A bit of elaboration is warranted here. Freud, we should recall, wrote that facilitations necessarily remain as they were formed during their first cathexis, a premise complemented by another, that the ego takes advantage of the first facilitations, without changing them, by creating new facilitations at higher energy levels. He further states that pain facilitations can be cathected without releasing pain. His intentions behind these claims are nonetheless unclear. If, by 'cathexis of the memory of pain' he means cathexis of a secondary pain memory, that is, thoughts about memories of pain, it becomes evident that a secondary pain memory will not release the same measure of unpleasure as that released by the painful primary facilitation. That is, the memory at stake is not of the pain experience but of a later registration, occurring after returning to that experience by thinking.

But can we be sure that Freud intended to suggest only one possible scenario? I am convinced that he was dissatisfied with his premise about subduing painful mnemic images by means of later thought facilitations, with the latter conceived as forming a kind of protective shell around the primary experience, one that prevents its recathexis. Freud may have striven to maintain the premise that primary pain facilitations can be altered, notwithstanding the clash produced with his previous premise regarding the unchangeability of primary facilitations. What he did manage to propose was that facilitations gradually decay (382, *Anf* 460) and that their disuse increases their resistance to the awakening of unpleasure. However, introduction of the idea that facilitations can decay raises, once more, the question of whether this process can alter primary perceptions of reality? If a later and renewed cathexis of the primary facilitation does not produce the identical intensity of affective response, does this imply that a change in the perception of reality has occurred?

Again, although we might argue that Freud was referring to the cathexis of later facilitations, to only those registered at high energy levels, I suggest that this direction would be mistaken. From my reading of the text, I can only conclude that Freud did not want to completely abandon the idea of change in the original facilitation.

In the same fragments, Freud describes the second mechanical problem (2) plaguing the *Project,* what I have referred to as 'the problem of retrogressive current', a notion Freud proposed to explain the 'hallucinatory' character of untamed memories of pain experiences. This concept was formulated in connection with the taming of pain experiences during his description of the unpleasure aroused by errors and contradictions (380ff, *Anf* 458ff). His previous explanation of hallucination had referred to a state resulting from an especially high cathexis and the superiority of primary over secondary processes. He now revised this description by adding two related ideas, that hallucination involves the retrogressive passage of energy to phi and omega and that hallucination, together with unpleasure, are common phenomena resulting from cathexes of ordinary intensity, similar to those appearing when thinking about old experiences of pain.

The issue of the direction of retrogressive current speaks to Freud's difficulties in remaining loyal to the mechanical approach. According to the reflex arc model, the appearance of a retrogressive discharge interferes with the regular direction of energy passages. A reversal of this kind does not appear even in cases of serious organic damage. However, cathexis of minimal unpleasure is essential for directing thought and activating the primary defences that prevent the passage of energy along paths arousing unpleasure. If unpleasure is aroused, identity with a wishful cathexis will not be found along this path (382, *Anf* 460-461). Stated differently, a situation permitting unpleasure is needed to direct thought. It thus appears that Freud considered unpleasure-producing cathexes to be universally characteristic of thinking, what implies that every thought leads, to one degree or another, to a retrogressive, hallucinatory discharge. It is therefore interesting to note that Freud made no mention of any issues associated with his idea of a retrogressive current moving from psi to phi and omega on the *Project*'s pages. He made his concerns explicit only in the revealing letter he sent to Fliess on January 1, 1896, examined in Chapter 4.

4

The Fate of the *'Project for a Scientific Psychology'*

After sending Fliess the two notebooks comprising the *Project*, Freud made only one attempt to solve some of the problems raised by his physiological explanations, which he describes in a letter dated January 1, 1896. This date effectively marks the beginning of the end of his attempts to elaborate a combined evolutionary neuro-physiological model of psychic functioning although the same ideas continued to influence his thought and writing throughout his life. The Fliess letter thus contains clear testimony of Freud's recognition that the most problematic parts of his project pertained to the explanation of general psychological phenomena. Freud sometimes wrote about these fundamental problems in a state of despair because he had come to understand their insolvability within the limits of the biological paradigm.

In the period between his letters dated October 8, 1895 and January 1, 1896, Freud continued to confront with what he called on different occasions 'the psychological construction'. One early letter (October 20, 1895) still finds Freud optimistic about the possibility of constructing a comprehensive psychological model along the lines of the *Project*. He writes to Fliess that the 'machine' (CL 146) appeared to work. However, repression is only one among the many psychological issues finding almost no place among the diverse topics he mentions. We find no trace of any change in his optimism until the letter dated November 8, in which Freud wrote that as result of further reflexion on psychological issues while trying to write on migraines, he had revolted against his 'tyrant', the same term he used in the letter of May 25, 1895 when referring to his psychology.

A turning point comes in a letter dated January 1, 1896, where Freud presents a new idea, on the basis of which his ΦΨΩ theories would require reformulation. The letter is difficult to decipher. Its ideas are only hinted at or telegraphically formulated and full of contradictions, similar to many other parts of his manuscript.

In this revised version, endogenous nerve endings do not awaken conscious sensations and psi no longer operates on omega. The nervous paths starting at sense organs and absorbing external stimuli no longer conduct quantity but only the quality specific to each stimulus, which they transfer to omega. Omega transfers neither quantity nor quality to psi; it only excites psi and establishes the paths along which free energy will travel. As noted earlier in the *Project*, omega neurones are capable of working solely with very small quantities.

This new outline reflects the issues Freud had encountered throughout the *Project*. In his revision, Freud indicates the new version's two main advantages: 1) the manner in which consciousness participates in the neuronal system's relations with external and internal stimuli; 2) a new elaboration of omega discharge and of psi backward discharge. Freud also argues that the new scheme contributes to the explanation of (a) normal and pathological defences, (b) the source of the energy that activates the system and (c) the release of unpleasure. We therefore find that as a result of omega's relocation, now between phi and psi, phi transfers quality to omega and omega limits itself to exciting psi. But how can omega excite psi without transferring either quantity or quality (CL 159-160)? Freud sidesteps this conundrum by adopting his colleagues' approach: continued theorization along the same lines while proposing new hypotheses on neuro-physiological functioning yet without treating the fundamental contradiction emerging from his attempt to explain mind on an organic basis. After some years, Freud abandoned this dichotomy and proposed an a-theoretical, methodological solution to the dualist problem.

Freud's new schema errs, however, for various reasons:

1) He continues to propose that the necessary condition for consciousness is the encounter of quality with a minimal quantity of energy. It makes no difference if the encounter takes place in psi or in omega. In the first instance, quality enters psi; in the second, quantity enters omega.

2) In the new schema, quality does not pass through psi; it only excites it. Although the new model simplifies the mechanism involving consciousness or reality indications, it does not solve the central reductionist problem: consciousness still needs quantity.

3) It is not clear whether Freud now denies the presence of quality in psi. His statement regarding omega neurones, which do not transfer quantity and quality to psi but excite psi and mark the conduction paths along which energy will travel, hints at the passage of quantity or quality from omega to psi.

4) Freud does not explain how quality can move within phi and omega neurones in the absence of quantity. In the two models, original and revised, the essential problem of psycho-physiology and psychology remains unsolved. That is, no psychological or physical concept appears able to abolish the gap between consciousness and energy, quality and quantity, body and mind.

In addition to these issues, Freud proposes a yet-undiscussed advantage. According to his new proposal, perceptual processes involve consciousness '*eo ipso* [from their very nature]' and produce psychic results only after becoming conscious (sic, CL 160). This proposition is more appropriate to objectivism: perceptions are described as directly observed, without the involvement of internal processes. Freud thus appears to have no longer needed to distinguish the time of a quality's reception in the neuronal system from the appearance of the primary perceptual consciousness, nor does he require a complex process to explain it. It is only later, when attention (hypercathexis) participates in the perceptual process, that conscious perception acquires psychic, subjective meaning.

In the new model, the problem of quality's passage through psi (almost) disappears. Hence, omega discharges are now superfluous (CL 160). In the *Project* Freud writes that this discharge takes place in order to explain reality indications and to distinguish them from primary (initial) consciousness. Simplification of Freud's description of reality indications abolishes the need for omega discharge towards the body's motor mechanisms as well as renewal of sensorial excitation of psi. Omega is now situated before psi and can directly activate psi.

In the previous schema, Freud imposed a heavy energetic load on omega neurones while assuming that they work with only small quantities, or without quantity at all. The new schema simplifies omega system functioning by situating it between phi and psi. That is, in the old schema, to distinguish between primary consciousness and reality indication, Freud proposed that reality indications contain information announcing an omega discharge, with the latter received by psi. The problem is that when an omega discharge to motor mechanisms takes place, the neuronal movement ceases. In consequence, any perception, even the simplest one, awakens never-ending quality indication production, that is, 'information'. This information is always imprecise because if transmitted in the wake of a motor discharge, this information pertains to quality indications, not to initial perceptions. Furthermore, in Freud's previous model, it is impossible to judge perceptions with any degree of exactitude. In the new model, the problems related to primary consciousness no longer exist. The main problem solved is the elimination of psi's participation in perception. This process thus takes place only in the phi and omega systems, without quantity. Regarding secondary consciousness, its issues remain untouched.

From a mechanical perspective, the most important advantage of the new model is the elimination of a backward discharge to phi neurones to explain hallucinations although this feature retained with respect to omega (CL 160). Freud argued that he no longer required this process. We should recall that the source of the stimulus in hallucinations is in psi and not phi (the physical world). But why is it preferable for a backward movement to exist solely in relation to omega?

To answer this question, we should recall that the mechanical problem plaguing the explanation of hallucination is the most crucial and difficult of those raised in the *Project*. For Freud, hallucinations are not always pathological phenomena; rather, he considers them to be part of the normal process of cathexis of the object's memory:

> I do not doubt that in the first instance this wishful activation will produce the same thing as a perception - namely a hallucination. (319)

To reiterate, the first stage in the wish process is always hallucinatory, as it is in the case of cathexis of a hostile object memory. Freud also considered any affect (painful feeling) as analogous to the hallucinatory process. The memory of painful experiences is hallucinatory until the ego tames it (381). Hallucinatory cathexis of mnemic images regularly occurs in the ego's early developmental stages, such as when children need help in satisfying their needs.

As previously noted, Freud posited a backward discharge from psi to phi for the purpose of explaining secondary (perceptual and verbal) consciousness because he assumed that psi neither receives nor functions with qualities of physical objects. Hence, the psi system can awaken qualities in omega only if it (psi) motivates sensory stimuli in phi. Perceptual stimuli then pass from phi through psi, to awaken consciousness in omega, which is discharged in the direction of the body's motor mechanisms. Information on omega discharges thus constitutes the reality indication received in those psi neurones already endowed with hallucinatory cathexis.

For Freud, the difficulty in the initial schema rested on the supposition that discharge from psi to phi must be accomplished in a direction contrary to the current's natural reflex direction. Freud understood the concept of reflex precisely as his teachers did,[1] that is, he maintained that based on integration of the quantitative and neuronal hypotheses, the principle of inertia can be viewed as a current travelling from dendrites to axons (paragraph 2). Once Freud

---

1   Amacher, 1965: 14-20; 31-33; 43-48; 61-64.

proposed the backward discharge of the mnemic images activating reality indications, he was required to accept that the psi system discharges energy into phi. Such a scenario implies that the neuronal system works against itself.[2]

Freud goes on to argue in the *Project* that backward movement is possible upon the weakening of ego control, a condition that can explain, at most, free displacement of cathexes. It cannot explain passage contrary to the conduction pathways established during evolution, before the ego began developing. This is the problematic situation that Freud attempted to correct in the letter now examined.

I repeat my query: why is backward movement to omega preferable to the same movement toward phi? My response is that this solution is simpler than the one Freud had originally suggested. In the new schema, Freud assumes that phi and omega absorb only qualities, without quantities, and that only psi conducts the path of endogenous energy. One alternative might be that a natural direction of discharge is from psi to omega (the second being in the direction of motor mechanisms). This would not disrupt basic neuro-physiological assumptions although it is also problematic because it eliminates the prospect of backward movement from psi to omega. We therefore remain confounded as to why Freud continues to speak of backward movement to omega.

In the new schema, Freud offers three mechanical advantages to his account of defence and neuroses:

1) The law of defence is now applicable only to psi processes (mnemic images and thought) but not to perceptions. Freud preferred his new, revised premise, which reinforces his depiction of how pathological defence works. In assuming that defence does not act on perceptions, Freud paradoxically bolstered the psycho-physical conception of an objective picture of the world irrespective of his tendency to stress the importance of endogenous factors in this portrayal.

---

2   This means that movement flows in a direction contrary to that of the reflex discharge, according to Freud and his teachers, and constitutes a very early stage of phylogenetic development.

2) With secondary consciousness now appearing later, during psychic development, a simpler description of neurotic processes is possible. As stated, high-level secondary consciousness develops when thought processes connect to verbal associations. This account helps us to understand how a memory can anticipate ego activity and thus 'surprise' it (the concept *Nachträglichkeit*, 'deferred action', as described in the *Project*'s Part 2).

3) An explanation is given for the release of unpleasure during the conflict between purely quantitative endogenous cathexes and the processes that conscious sensations initiate in psi. It is difficult to understand, from a mechanical perspective, why this explanation is preferable to that found in the *Project*. The issue at hand refers to the source of unpleasure. In the *Project*, Freud posits that there are special neurones that release unpleasure. In the current letter he does not straightforwardly say whether he continues to accept this premise.

Freud's new proposals express further radicalization of three major dichotomies motivating his theorizing: conscious/unconscious, quantity/quality, external/internal world. Most of his constructs are guided by the distinction between two kinds of qualities: the perceptual and the verbal.[3] In this same letter, Freud betrays a substantial preference for quality and the consciousness/unconsciousness dichotomy in contradiction to quantitative considerations. He verily begins to conceive of defence as a qualitative problem.

A general mechanistic issue arising from the new model is especially worth noting. Freud apparently divided the neuronal system into two parts. The first, charged with dealing with the excitation arriving from the external world, is wholly conscious (its aim, it seems, is to become acquainted with the world). The second deals with unconscious endogenous stimuli (those that express and satisfy

---

3   I maintain that the main problem of defence is found in the distinction between qualities and not in the opposition between the principles of inertia and of constancy.

needs and wishes). These two parts ostensibly operate in isolation. This conceptualization differs from that of the psycho-neuronal system found in the *Project*, where any external *or* internal stimulus can activate the entire system.

The new division hints at Freud's feelings of failure regarding his inability to conceive of an integrated system that deals uniformly with diverse stimuli. The neuronal system's division can be thought of as a symbol of the collapse of his attempt to reconcile between the psycho-physical conception, in which knowledge of physical world is the neuronal system's primary aim, and the redefinition of the system's primary aim: elaboration and satisfaction of endogenous stimuli.

In the *Project,* Freud tried to integrate two exhibiting opposing mechanisms into one neuronal system. From the beginning, he understood that the challenge consisted in elaborating the mechanisms that make high-level psychological phenomena possible. He believed that he could solve the problem if he succeeded in anchoring mechanical in evolutionary processes. In his letter to Fliess, he gives no indication of any advantage to be found in renouncing evolutionary explanations, which were meant to allow Freud to treat primary systems as remnants of earlier developmental stages, when these 'systems' worked only according to the principle of inertia, with no need to store quantity. The mechanical obstacles noted, especially that of backward discharge, expressed the same evolutionary enigmas that Freud had been unable to solve until now.

The solutions Freud offers in this letter for the elimination of previous localizationist and mechanical impediments nonetheless raise many questions, not less than does the *Project*. The difficulties with the quantitative explanation of consciousness remain as they were, leaving how qualities are integrated with quantities unclear. The consciousness/unconsciousness dichotomy now acquires centre stage as a substitute for the inertia/constancy dichotomy, in which the *Project* was grounded. The letter also stresses the continued conundrums to be resolved with respect to explanations of consciousness as well as the relationship between body and psyche, which Freud was never able to solve by means of the common neuro-psychological notions used to integrate the two entities. Their continued insolvability became the main cause of Freud's abandonment of his biological and physiological project.

The fate of the evolutionary-mechanical model of pathology and transition to the new science

When compared with his frame of mind following the failure of the general evolutionary and mechanical explanations, Freud felt very optimistic regarding what he called the 'secret' and the 'clinical solution' for hysteria and obsession. He renounced his comprehensive reductionist dream and slowly became satisfied with his discussion of neurosis -- the theory of seduction and the concept of *Nachträglichkeit* (deferred action) -- found in the second part of the *Project*.

In the following two years he became absorbed in developing a new evolutionary-mechanical theory of neurosis. Freud had dwelt on the elaboration and functioning of the nervous system in the *Project*; he now drafted different versions of the stages marking the development of illness, sexuality and the psyche. These theories were not, however, less mechanical than the previous ones. Freud cannot, after all, be presented as more of a physiologist or biologist in the period studied here; his mechanistic stance, however, had been altered.

After some months of working on developmental premises, Freud attempted to ground these evolutionary theories in Fliess's chemical theory (letter of April 26, 1896), which suggested that chemical interactions could explain all life processes. After some failures in this direction, Freud expressed the desire that his friend provide him with the organic and physiological bases of those theories and describe how the chemical substances interacted (letters from June 30, 1896, July 7, 1897 and October 3, 1897). Although Freud gradually freed himself of his commitment to Fliess's theories, it is difficult to ascertain how much he truly believed that Fliess could ground psychology on physiology after he himself had failed. We therefore find Freud distancing himself from physiological explanations while immersing himself in the investigation of dreams and fantasies.

My purpose in turning to the evolutionary psycho-pathological theories that Freud expounded after he had deserted the *Project* is to show that he likewise abandoned his evolutionary and physiological explanations of neurosis. The evolutionary aspects of this project, embedded mainly in Fliess's evolutionary mechanics, failed for different reasons. However, it should be stressed that the evolutionary ideas that Freud took from Fliess, and those he himself developed, were not lost. They re-emerged as the premises guiding his later psychological theories.

We can list the three main causes for the failure of the evolutionary model of neuroses:

1) The weakness of the Fliess-Freud chemical model, according to which feminine and masculine chemical substances combine to influence normal and pathological psychic functioning throughout life (Fliess, 1923, 118-126; 247-298; 314-328). After several attempts, Freud abandoned this theory, which relied on the calculation of two gender-related periods (feminine=28 days; masculine=23 days) the course of significant life events.

2) Freud's rejection of the seduction theory consequent to his understanding of the importance of fantasy in psychic life. Premature seduction was an indispensable element of his developmental theory, which assumed that sexuality appears only with puberty. He therefore viewed a child's seduction by an elder as the cause of the early release of sexual substances, an event he thought explains, developmentally and physiologically, the later release of unpleasure but also the continuity of sexual pleasure.

3) Parallel to his formulation of the evolutionary model, Freud agonized over his delineation of psychology's essentials. Freud's soul was steeped with psychological ideas. They appeared in the Fliess letters as sporadic outbursts, as expressions of the idea driving Freud toward important revisions of his theory: the value and meaning of any psychic element depends on its changing relations with other psychological elements. This idea can be considered the main cause for the failure of the biologically based *Project*. Most crucially, this new conception led Freud to erase every organic premise from the fundamentals of his epistemic system even though organic and

biological notions would persist in his thinking, what I consider a reflection of Freud's enduring yet increasingly circumscribed allegiance to his mentors' ideas.

In the second part of the *Project,* Freud offers an evolutionary and mechanical description of pathological defence: hysterical patients are those who have undergone a traumatic sexual experience that was not understand until they reached puberty. At that point, together with the release of sexual substances, the memory intensifies and the patient comes to understand its meaning retroactively. This leads to an early activation of the memory, an event that takes the ego by surprise. The absence of a real-time response by the ego's attention mechanism results in the failure of the defence mechanism, manifested as pathological defence. Freud's new notion, pointing at differences in repression, the primary traumatic experience and the patient's psychic and sexual development, led him to distinguish between neuroses according to the specific defence activated. Freud shows himself at this point to be experimenting with developmental elements no less mechanical than the physiological ones.

Evidence of the mechanical character of his evolutionary explanation of pathological phenomena already appears in Freud's letter of October 8, 1895, to which he attached his manuscript of the *Project*. Some pivotal aspects of the letter, centring on Freud's difficulties with the 'elucidation of repression', remain unclear. The major issues requiring clarification are: a) those factors Freud considered unclear with respect to repression; and b) his use of the term 'mechanical' in two different meanings without indicating which meaning was employed in each case. It is very difficult to decipher Freud's intentions on the basis of his statement that although the mechanical aspect of repression 'does not hang together', his inability to include a mechanical factor in his explanation does not disturb him. His letter thus betrays his confusing, even contradictory use of 'mechanical', resulting from the severe difficulties he encountered when attempting to adequately integrate his rich clinical discoveries into his developmental model .

Further evidence that Freud's core worry involved application of an evolutionary framework also appears in this letter: After stating that he is troubled by the task of elucidating repression, but not its mechanism, he notes that he has made great advances in his clinical knowledge of pathology. When demonstrating his progress, he writes that he now thinks that the requisite condition for the appearance of hysteria must be an early sexual trauma, prior to puberty, that was accompanied by 'revulsion and fright', as opposed to obsessive neurosis, the outcome of a pleasant experience. He then states once more that he thinks he has failed in elucidating its mechanical elements (CL 141). I next attempt to unravel the confusion.

Freud had many doubts regarding his depiction of the different neuroses' elaboration and the manner in which to harmonise the various stages in which early sexual experiences may took place. He agonized most over the evolutionary aspects of his model. In his article 'The aetiology of hysteria' (1896c), Freud clearly announces that defence and repression are purely psychological issues, by which he means those childhood experiences retained in traumatic memories (1896c, III: 219-220).

My own review of the clinical discoveries Freud discussed has led me to identify the *'mechanical'* element troubling him as evolutionary mechanics. Freud focused on this approach only briefly, without further clarifying the clinical expressions of the various neuroses, of early sexual experiences and of repression.

Freud returns to the evolutionary solution in his letter of October 15, 1895, where he adds a number of details. He now argues that hysteria results from a pre-sexual (i.e., pre-pubescent, preceding release of sexual substances) sexual trauma, and obsession from pre-sexual sexual pleasure, later transformed into reproach.

On January 1, 1896, to reiterate, Freud sent Fliess a proposal aimed at revision of the mechanical project. The letter included *Draft K*, a broad outline for the evolutionary explanation of neuroses on the same grounds of the proposal introduced into the second part of the *Project*. He subsequently described the same proposal in the two papers he sent for publication on the same day (February 5, 1896a, b). In the following, I comment on these works, primarily *Draft K*.

Freud, as stated, grounds his new suggestions on the integrated evolutionary and mechanical premise expounded in the *Project*: defence is a normal tendency directed toward preventing unpleasure; it does not act against perceptions but only against memories and thoughts. Defence becomes negative when directed against ideas capable of releasing new unpleasure, a sensation absent during the initial experience, as in the case of sexual ideas. The condition for release of unpleasure is the onset of puberty, if occurring between the experience and its recall. Puberty strengthens the memory's intensity at a time when the psychic apparatus is unprepared to cope with that memory (CL 163).

Here Freud poses an intricate question: What is the source of the unpleasure that early sexual excitation releases? Freud sensed that it must be an independent, additional or different source of unpleasure, distinct from key neurones, the source of normal unpleasure (see the *Project*, p. 320), implying that he did not consider key neurones as the source of sexual unpleasure. He writes that without a good theory of the sexual process, it would be impossible to explain the origins of the unpleasure that activates defence. To explain this process, he applies the model behind anxiety neurosis, in which a psychic disturbance is produced by an energetic quantity, sexual in origin.

Interestingly, Freud does not present this problem as exclusively mechanical and physiological, but as existing 'deep in psychological riddles' (CL 163). The first solution he presents is essentially social in nature. There he argues that shame and morality act as repressive forces; without them there is no repression. This is the first time that Freud considers social phenomena as involved in producing psychic phenomena despite his preference for independent (and organic) sources to explain these sensations. He begins with the developmental view of neurosis he had already adopted, drafted into a general five-stage model:

1) An early traumatic sexual experience, to be repressed.

2) Repression of the sexual experience that arouses a memory of the traumatic experience, with the simultaneous formation of primary symptoms.

3) Successful repression; persistence of primary symptoms.

4) Repressed ideas return and struggle with the ego, leading to formation of new symptoms, i.e., the illness itself.

5) Adjustment, devastation, or recovery with malformations.

The different neuroses are thus distinguished by the manner in which repressed ideas return and symptoms are formed, by the course the illness took, but especially by the manner in which repression was achieved. During this stage of Freud's thinking, any new quandary acquires a developmental rather than a mechanical solution, with each chronologically positioned. This aspect of his thinking points to the change in the criteria that guided his work.

In obsessive neurosis, the primary experience is considered to be accompanied by pleasure, which is active in boys and passive in girls. An experience of this kind takes place in girls relatively late, at about 8 years of age. The reason for his differentiation is clear: the need to distinguish between two passive sexual experiences, the unpleasant, which leads to hysteria, and the pleasant, which produces obsession. Repression, of course, acts only in response to unpleasant cathexes. To explain the unpleasure released by memories of pleasant experiences, Freud posits that obsessive, like hysterical patients had experienced a passive experience prior to the pleasant experience. The passive experience must take place early so as not to block the pleasant experience. Hence, the temporal order of the two experiences and the onset of puberty is crucial for the syndrome's aetiology. After reaching sexual maturity, the patient reproaches himself for feeling pleasure in connection with the said activity. The relationship between the primary passive experience and the later pleasant experience prompts the attachment of unpleasure to the pleasant memory. Repression is activated and the first defensive symptom appears.

Freud distinguishes different stages in repression and in the formation of obsessive symptoms. When the primary experience causes the initial repression, the release of unpleasure appears as self-reproach. At first, the relation 'memory-self-reproach' is conscious. Later, these elements are repressed and antithetical symptoms – conscientiousness, shame and self-doubt – appear as the primary manifestations of defence. The third stage of the illness -- a state of pseudo-healthiness – then beings. Freud does not elaborate on this stage's constituents. He may well have intended to say that at this stage, a fragile yet temporary equilibrium arises between the antithetical forces.

Two criteria -- return of the repressed memory's content and self-reproach – determine the next of Freud's five stages of obsessive neurosis. Although defence begins to fail, it does not fully lose its force. Memories and self-reproach are altered, to return to consciousness as compromises between the repressed memories and the repressive ideas.

The fourth stage can manifest itself in two different forms, the first being typical obsessive ideas. The content of the child's experience is thus distorted in two ways: a contemporary event appears in place of a past one, or a sexual event is replaced by something similar but not sexual. An obsessive idea, the result of compromise, marks it as emotionally true but substantively false.

In the second form, repressed self-reproach manifests itself. Affect penetrates consciousness while being transformed into other feelings of unpleasure: shame, hypochondria, religious or social anxiety, persecutory delusions, and so forth.

In the fifth stage, the ego begins to battle the compromises. It attempts to stop the repressed memories as they try to return. This is the secondary defence that leads to the formation of new, secondary symptoms, expressed in obsessive brooding, hoarding, dipsomania, obsessive rituals. The criterion by which Freud distinguished three types of symptoms -- primary defensive, compromise, and secondary defensive -- is also developmental.

In the case of paranoia, Freud declared that he had not yet identified the clinical conditions and chronological relations of pleasure and unpleasure within the primary experience. Despite this admission, he was convinced that it is possible to explain paranoia by means of defence, with the primary paranoid experience being similar to that of obsessive neurosis, and repression occurring subsequent to memory's release of unpleasure. In paranoia, however, in place of self-reproach, projection appears. Others are consequently blamed for causing unpleasure. The primary symptom is, therefore, distrust. In paranoia, as in obsessions, different compromise symptoms are formed when the repressed memory returns. The content of the projected experience can return as an idea or as a visual or sensory hallucination although repressed feelings always return as hallucinated voices.

In paranoia, the symptoms of secondary defence will not appear because defences cannot act on self-reproaches when these are (a) not believed to be true and (b) projected onto others. When patients find themselves in this state, the ego tries to accept the imaginary ideas and resolve their contradictions. Rather than fight the symptoms, the ego explains them. Assimilatory delusions are consequently created as symptoms of ego defeat rather than those of secondary defence. The process ends in melancholia or defensive delusions (megalomania), with the ego completely transformed.

As to hysterical symptoms, these, too, emerge from sexual and traumatic childhood experiences, again before puberty and likewise provoking excitation in the sexual organs. A passive primary experience of unpleasure also appears. That is, the specific pre-condition of hysteria is sexual passivity in a pre-sexual stage. Another condition is that the primary experience occurs not very early in children, but when the release of unpleasure is still weak and pleasant experiences likely to subsequently occur. In this respect, Freud assumed that a pleasant sexual experience may occur in childhood, contiguous to an unpleasant one, because children do not understand the significance of such experiences. In this case, obsession will appear. This chain of events is meant to explain the transformation of many mixed cases of hysteria into obsession among men. In contrast, Freud believed that passivity led to the appearance of hysteria in women.

In *Draft K*, Freud provides his most complete description of hysteria. He states that hysteria begins with the ego being overwhelmed[4] because the primary experience of unpleasure is very intense. The ego, being unable to cope, must allow for unpleasure's discharge, most frequently in the form of exaggerated excitation. For Freud, this 'fright hysteria' is the opening phase of hysteria. Its main symptom, fear, is 'accompanied by a *gap* in the psyche' (CL 169, italics in the original), although Freud admitted that he could not state just when the primary overwhelming of the ego took place.

He was, however, convinced that repression and the formation of primary defence symptoms appear later, together with the memory

---

4 Here Freud wrote: 'which is what paranoia leads to' (CL 169). Freud seems to say that hysteria, a less-serious condition by today's standards, is initiated by paranoia. This pronouncement is very difficult to understand in terms of contemporary psychiatric classifications. Here I only mention it due to its place in Freud's theorizing but leave its interpretation to others.

of the primary experience. In hysteria, repression is not instigated by a strong antithetical idea but through a boundary idea pertaining to the ego and to the traumatic memory; it is, in essence, a product of compromise. Furthermore, contrary to the conditions of other illnesses, the substitution of the repressed idea does not proceed on the basis of logical categories but through the displacement of attention along a series of ideas linked by simultaneity. If the traumatic experience is discharged through motor activity, it will be transformed into a boundary idea and become the first symbol of the repressed content. There is no need to assume that the idea is repressed during repetitions of the hysterical attack, because it is the gap in the psyche that returns.

Freud's extension of the developmental theory of repression, based on the concept of the deferred action as described in the *Project*, raised new issues requiring resolution: Why is a woman's passive experience sometimes traumatic and sometimes pleasant? Why does the same passive experience cause hysteria in some women and obsession in others? How is the traumatic integrated with the pleasant experience in obsession? Why and how do primary traumatic experiences allow the appearance of later pleasant experiences and cause hysteria rather than obsessive neurosis?

These questions, together with the attempt to improve the classification of neuroses on developmental principles led Freud to a pure but often convoluted evolutionary solution, which he transmitted in some of the letters written to Fliess a few months after completing *Draft K*. In the course of his theorizing, Freud's adherence to organic, mechanical and evolutionary explanations had been repeatedly undermined. In these letters, the denotations as well as connotations of organic concepts are so deeply revised that they are almost unrecognizable.

In the letter dated May 30, 1896, Freud sketches the different phases of psychosexual development as follows:

Ia - Preconscious, up to 4 years of age.

Ib - Childhood, up to 8 years of age.

A - First transition period, up to 10 years of age, repression.

II - Prepubescence, up to 14 years of age.

B - Second transitional period, repression.

III - Maturity.

Freud characterizes the three neuroses discussed in *Draft K* according to the date of the primary experiences at their core. The outline's guiding principle was that the recall of early sexual experiences engenders a surplus of sexuality in the psyche that inhibits thought and colours their memory with obsessiveness. In the same letter, Freud employs the term 'translation' for the first time, in reference to the surplus of sexuality that impedes the 'translation' of phase Ia experiences into a psychic phenomenon. By this he means that repression is a failure of translation. Freud's formulation thus provides one of the first expressions of his emerging linguistic view of psychic phenomena, a framework that increasingly influenced Freud's theories and steadily but firmly distanced him from biological explanations. Although these linguistic aspects had previously received his clinical attention in *Studies on Hysteria*, it is only now that they affected his theorizing, his 'metapsychology' (CL 216).

As part of his blueprint for an aetiology of neurosis, Freud states that each neurosis has its own chronological requirements for primary sexual scenes to exert their influence (CL 188). In hysteria, where traumatic memories lead to conversion and not to psychic consequences, the primary experiences occur in the first stage of childhood (up to 4 years of age). The remnants of memories from this period are not translated into verbal images. More crucially, hysteria always concludes in conversion, unrelated to the period in which the primary scenes return, whether after the second stage of dentition (between 8 and 10 years of age [sic]) or after puberty.

In obsessive neurosis, the scenes pertain to period Ib and are translated into words; should they be aroused in period II or III, obsessive symptoms appear. With respect to paranoia, the scenes occur during period II, after the second dentition, and are aroused in III (puberty). In this case, defence is expressed in disbelief.

In this highly significant, telegraphic letter, Freud proposed new hypotheses regarding the repression's operation in the different neuroses, some of which were very surprising but all of which spoke of deep conceptual changes in Freud's thinking. I now turn to the major of these hypotheses.

Freud now focuses on the timing of the scene rather than repression, with the primary experience determining the 'choice of neurosis'. We also find a serious attempt to shift hysteria away from its central role in the theory of defence. Freud declares that paranoia is the defence neurosis par excellence, being independent of morality and the rejection of sexuality that motivate defence in hysteria and obsessive neurosis during the transitional periods A and B. Freud's conclusion now derives from his view that paranoia was almost free of roots in early childhood; it is a neurosis belonging to puberty, when repression appears. Freud also declares that defence is normal if sexual scenes are absent during periods Ia, Ib, and II. In this case, excessive sexuality in puberty produces anxiety, not neurosis. No longer does Freud have any reservations about formulating psycho-social hypotheses.

Towards the end of this letter, Freud points to a general temporal feature of his developmental approach and stresses the importance of intervals between sexual experiences. The continuation of scenes during periods of transition may thus avoid repression; in such a case, no surplus of sexuality is aroused between the scene and its memory because the scene recurs in consecutive stages of sexuality. This scenario hints at a simple explanation for perversions in childhood and puberty.

In the letter of December 6, 1896 we find Freud sketching, for the first time, an evolutionary mechanism to explain neuroses according to Fliess's conception of feminine and masculine periods. He also explains why pleasant experiences later cause unpleasure. Despite Freud's continued belief that evolutionary mechanics would solve psycho-pathological issues, we can already identify the erosion of this kind of thinking.

The new-old idea Freud develops is that from time to time, memory registrations enter into new arrangements according to changing circumstances. Freud labelled these rearrangements 'retranscriptions' (*Umschrift*). The novelty of his formulation is that memories are registered several times and in different kind of indications. In *On Aphasia*, Freud presented a similar arrangement with respect to the pathways leading from the body's periphery to the cortex (1891: 53). This early proposal did not then lead to a significant change in his psycho-physical view of memory and the inscription of perceptions. In the *Project*, a memory remains constant throughout all its vicissitudes. Freud's great innovation, as we see here, is his conceptualization of a general principle that directs the inscription of memories and perceptions. According to this principle, inscription in memory is not dictated by the objective characteristics of external objects but by the inscription's network of relations. It follows that the value and meaning of any psychic element is established in the context of all its relations, not just by its relations with external objects or events. This revision is important because it shows that Freud was gradually coming closer to a more precise presentation of empirical linguistic phenomena within the framework of his reductive thinking.

Two other implications of this principle guiding inscription are that endogenous, as well as external stimuli, acquire another significance, independent of the biological drive they serve. This idea gives the evolutionary model a decisive blow because it stresses the event's relations in memory, as well as negates the possibility of establishing the value and meaning of psychic elements according to their objective physical value, their physiological functioning, or their historical meaning. This notion is one of the main factors causing Freud to abandon biological and psychological conceptions of empirical phenomena.

The new principle sheds significant light on the character of Freud's conceptual and methodological development. The transition to his new science resulted not simply from explanatory failures but from a process of abstraction. The new principle states that the different elements of stories, fantasies and dreams are weighed and evaluated according to the diverse relations that they maintain with one another and not according to their biological, physical and psychological origins. The significance of this abstraction lies in Freud's gradual departure from concrete physical and organic explanations of psychic processes. Freud, a relentless materialist, had found himself with a very obstinate and enduring problem: the absence of a material substratum for his abstract theorizing. This problem and his inability, even in his mature thinking, to achieve an adequate formulation of his new empirical view motivated Freud to continue maintaining, to some degree, biological-evolutionary and physiological ideas throughout all his life even though they did not provide the material basis to his science. It is important to note that Freud makes no hints regarding any problem he might have with his new notions. He understood their implications: that the brain does not work according to evolutionary and mechanical biological laws exclusively but, rather, according to linguistic (i.e., social) laws and that memories change with any new association attached. This new comprehensive principle expresses his deepening understanding that the analysis of narrative and linguistic phenomena is impossible if we assume that meanings are established *a priori* by some biological, physiological or evolutionary process.

We can now return to the December 6 letter where Freud states that there are at least three main types of inscriptions (or registrations). He lists them by means of a developmental description of the psychic mechanism, rooted in the old distinction between perceptual and mnemic neurones. The three types of inscription are:

a) Wz, indications of perception, the first registration of perceptions, which cannot reach consciousness and are arranged according to association by simultaneity.

b) Ub, the second, unconscious registration; its arrangement in the unconscious occurs according to causal relations and may be appropriate for 'conceptual memories'. Consciousness does not penetrate this stratum. Although Freud did not provide a definition for conceptual memories, it appears that he was referring to memories of perceptions, to 're-presentations'.

c) Vb, the pre-conscious and third registration, associated with word presentations. It is our official ego. Freud declared that consciousness of preconscious inscriptions (secondary thought consciousness, CL 208) occurs subsequent to and is linked to the hallucinatory activation of word presentations.

Freud depicts the three stratified stages without providing any organic, biological validation for this arrangement. He makes no mention of how these stages are integrated, nor of their localization in the nervous system. Moreover, he does not treat the related psychological issues: What is the psychological import of inscriptions if they are unconscious? How do they influence psychological functioning if they do not appear in consciousness? How are they created? Freud leaves these and other questions unanswered and bereft of any discussion of the biological problematics raised by his new idea.

In truth, this letter is more complex than my presentation so far suggests. For example, when Freud argues that the different registrations are separate, he writes 'not necessarily topographically' between brackets. With this comment, Freud hints at his old conceptualization of inscriptions as found at different energy levels, as if he has yet to decide which premise to adopt.

Together with the premise that new perceptions are inscribed in new places, Freud offers another: any further re-transcription inhibits the previous inscription and empties it of its energy. That is, a new transcription completely neutralizes the earlier one. Due to the fact that the newer inscriptions are linguistic, we must presume that psychological and even physiological phenomena behave according to linguistic laws. By this, Freud comes close to the essential leap he will make in his later revolutionary works, when he positions linguistic phenomena at the centre of his empirics. His evolutionary model was thus collapsing through a process of slow internal disintegration.

Freud also began to use his new psycho-linguistic evolutionary model to explain neurotic traits and repression. He describes neuroses as arising when part of the psychic material is not translated into the new developmental stage. In the absence of such a translation, excitation is treated according to the psychological laws relevant to the earlier stage. To illustrate the process, Freud employs a political analogy: neurosis is similar to a province in which archaic laws are still enforced. This phrasing introduces the style he would use when speaking of psychic energy in his later works, irrespective of the field, the psychological or the biological, in which he was working.

With Freud now conceiving of repression as a failure of translation, he proposes that this failure occurs when the translation releases unpleasure. This unpleasure causes a disturbance of thought-blocking translation. Should defence be initiated within the same psychic stage and type of inscription, it is to be considered normal. Pathological defence still depends on the sexual nature of the early event. When this sexual event is recalled later, repression fails and memory releases new unpleasure.

Freud subsequently devises a new classification of neuroses on these grounds, one combining psychic and sexual development while indicating the stages in which each sexual event occurs:

1) Hysteria, from 1 and a half to 4 years of age.

2) Obsessive neurosis, from 4 to 8 years of age.

3) Paranoia, from 8 to 14 years of age.

Freud also explains sexual perversions here, for the first time. To do so, he describes the fate of sexual experiences that release pleasure. The reproduction of a great proportion of those experiences is accompanied by obsessive pleasure, which is impossible to inhibit. If a sexual experience is reproduced in a later stage, he continues, the release of pleasure is accompanied by compulsion, while unpleasure is accompanied by repression. In both cases, none of these experiences is translated (re-transcribed) into indications of a new stage. In perversions, no repression of pleasant sexual experiences occurs prior to formation of the psychic system. The sexual event is experienced at all stages as a current experience, accompanied by the release of compulsive pleasure.

Freud includes two problematic tables representing his new classification within the same letter (CL 210):

	$1\frac{1}{2}$	4	8	14–15
Psych.	Ia	Ib	II	III
Sex.		I	II	III

	Wz Up to 4	Wz + Ub Up to 8	Wz + Ub + Vb Up to 14–15	Ditto
Hysteria	current	Compulsion	Repressed in Wz	
Obsessional neurosis		Current	Repressed in Ub indications	
Paranoia		—	Current	Repressed in Vb indications
Perversion	current	Current	Compulsion (current)	Repression impossible or not attempted

In the notes accompanying the first table, Freud indicates that the psyche and sexuality do not develop in parallel because, as he had already mentioned, repression does not appear before the age of 4. Freud then appears to hint at the possibility that repression occurs after that age. This proposition differs from the second diagram, where he indicates the age of 8 as the time when repression begins. We may wonder whether he meant that psychic contents appearing up to 4 are neither repressed nor translated into words, as shown in the second diagram.

Two major problems appear in this vague second table: Freud argues here that in hysteria (occurring between ages 4 and 8), compulsion appears before the sexual event is repressed and behaves according to the laws applied at the stage of perceptual indications (Wz). This suggestion contradicts a previous one, according to which compulsion appears only in cases of sexual experiences accompanied by pleasure, not unpleasure, as in hysteria.

Another issue relates to the two contradictory premises reflected in the tables. Freud indicates that the sexual event causing obsession is repressed in Ub (unconscious) indications once the child reaches 14 years of age. But obsessive symptoms, differently from hysterical symptoms, are verbal. And yet, when classifying the different psychic stages, Freud only refers to Vb, not Ub, indications characterized by their connection with verbal associations. In addition, his chronology of psychic development inadequately reflects his empirical observations. In the first diagram, verbal associations are unimportant until age 4 and perhaps age 8. Freud, however, does not explain these inconsistencies.

After these two descriptions of psycho-neuronal and psycho-pathological stages of development, Freud writes to Fliess stating that these tables represent his model's psychological 'superstructure' (210) and that its organic basis in sexual processes must now be looked for. Freud no longer believes that neuronal explanations can provide the bases for understanding psychic processes and the solution of the mind-body problem. He nonetheless continues to maintain an organic-mechanical stance, which forces him to continue to attribute importance to neuronal components. However, at this period and for a short time, his thoughts are dominated by another organic-mechanical notion, revealed in his belief that Fliess's biological mechanics would provide the sought-for organic basis.

To solve this problem Freud applies Fliess's theory of periods, which maintains that all of life's problems result from the activity in fixed periods of two sexual substances. As evidence for the existence of these substances, Fliess had calculated these periods, which rest on different dates (birth, death, pregnancy, menstruation, illnesses, etc.).[5]

Taking up Fliess's model, Freud proposes that it is possible to mark the development of sexual stages (masculine and feminine) in terms of multiples of the duration of the feminine period ($\Pi = 28$ days). The first sexual stage, until primary repression at 8, is equal to 100 feminine periods (7 and 3/4 years). Primary repression continues during 20 Π (pi) (1 year and 6 1/2 months). Secondary repression, around the age of 15, is equal to 200 Π. Another 50 Π (3 years and 10 months) pass until puberty.

Freud found only two disadvantages in this schema: first, masculine periods of 23 days were left unused, and second, no explanation arose as to why the sexual and psychic stages appear simultaneously at age 4 and why perversion develops during some phases and neurosis at others.

Freud tries to explain *psychic* development on the grounds of a masculine substance and periods lasting 23 days. These calculations include the period of pregnancy, which equals 276 days=12 masculine Π (equal to 10 feminine Π=280 days). Freud provides various

---

5 Fliess assumed the existence of other, not only sexual, 'substances' [sic]: life and family (1923, VIII; 46-51; 60-65; 68-87; 334-341).

examples while arguing that these calculations indicate the presence of more stages, translations and innovations in the psychic system than previously assumed. But here he ceases to elaborate the translation process. It seems that he has wearied of this approach and its poor results. We may also venture that Freud developed the periodic theory mainly to preserve good relations with Fliess. On December 17, Freud writes that when an idea causes delight, it is not due to its proof but because it indicates a common ground. He also remarks that he was able to collect only psychological facts, while Fliess had compiled 'organological' facts, with the gap between them filled by a hypothesis (CL 215). From the tone of the text, I suggest that by this point, Freud may have desired to be freed from the shackles of his friend's theory and to disengage their respective fields.

In the said letter of December 17, 1896, Freud continues to explain a range of illnesses as resulting from the abnormal production of the two sexual substances. He argues that his 'metapsychology' ('my ideal and woebegone child', CL 216) lies hidden deep within this explanation. While elaborating his developmental model, Freud reaches the conclusion that he must ground *all* his psychological theories on the two biological substances even though his calculations did not provide good results. He further notes than in the wake of new yet still inadequate calculations, he had concluded that a core notion underlying his calculations is the differential deployment of the two substances. In his new formulation, the two substances are released daily; the differences between the sexes induces a surplus (in one or the other substance, according to the person's sex); and this surplus is felt at different times according to the various summations.

He further states that we must take into account abnormal release of the substances, abnormal deployment of these substances at any given moment, and the totals obtained, meaning the eruption of illness. Mania and melancholia thus result from the abnormal production of the substances, anxiety from the somatic deployment of the feminine substance when its discharge is inhibited, and neurasthenia from the somatic deployment of the masculine substance. Menstruation necessarily leads to the release of undischarged substances. Symptoms show neurasthenic features when discharge takes place in 23-day periods, and anxiety in 28-day periods. It thus appears that Freud assumed that masculine menstruation, similar to the feminine variety, occurred every 23 days for the purpose of discharging accumulated sexual substances. This is, in fact, the last letter in which Freud tried to present a comprehensive theory of psychic illness in terms of the two sexual substances.

In his following letter, dated January 3, 1897, Freud clearly states that the developmental model of neuroses had failed. Yet, he conversely points out that in his field of research, neuroses, he had discovered solid foundations for his model (I assume that Freud refers to a clinical perspective) despite the fact that neuroses 'resist the determination of time more than any other factor' (CL 219). What can be left of this developmental model if it is impossible to establish a clear chronology for the appearance of neuroses? He does comment that every development apparently focuses on early childhood, up to three years of age. This comment reflects the fact that his temporal explanations do not agree with his new clinical findings on the importance of early sexuality, findings contradicting Fliess's theories. It thus appears that sexuality is most essential in one's earliest years than in puberty.

We now come to the letter of January 11, 1897. Here Freud presents his new explanations of neuroses, psychoses, perversions and even epilepsy, based on the integration of the seduction theory with the significance of age. He also stresses the importance of seduction by a family member. In psychoses, this seduction occurs at a very early stage, between 1.25 and 1.5 years and prior to completion of the psychic apparatus. He also presents his budding theory of (oral and anal) erotogenic zones in addition to the importance of erotic sensations, especially those associated with the sense of smell.

Within this context, Freud makes a crucial yet obscure statement, which only Moussaief Masson pointed to its lack of clarity (CL 223, note 4). In the following I provide what I consider to be as precise an interpretation within the limits of Freudian exegesis. Freud wrote:

> The fact that the groups of sensations have much to do with psychological stratification presumably follows from the distribution in dreams and presumably has a direct connection with the mechanism of hysterical anaesthesias. (CL 223)

This statement should be interpreted according to his new notions regarding the inscription of perceptions and memories as mentioned in his letter dated December 6, 1896. Freud apparently intended to say that sensations go through a process similar to the translation and re-transcription of any perception. In addition, and different from the *Project*, he now appears to believe that in dreams, sensations go through a process of psychic redistribution. That is, they receive new meanings, differing from their original ones. According to this interpretative line, the connection of sensations with hysterical anaesthesia implies that a change in the value and meaning of sensations is essential if anaesthesia is to appear. Hysterical anaesthesia thus results from the symbolic -- not biological -- value and meaning of bodily organs. Freud thereby explains the infinite modifications in the values and meanings of sensations, perceptions, emotions and thoughts.

Freud's notion of the repeated reorganization of psychic elements is a central factor in his departure from the need for an organic substratum. By means of this premise, Freud paved the way for his increasing interest in the psychic fantasy world, which was then considered to be abstract and lacking any material basis in psychology, physiology, or philosophy.

As to the letter dated April 6, 1897, Freud writes here that until now, he had not identified another important source of hysterical phenomena -- hysterical fantasies -- originating in what little children hear and only later comprehend. The concept 'fantasy' is not straightforward. Freud understood the term differently from its current meaning as a more or less voluntary product of conscious imagination, as I demonstrate in what follows.

By the time he wrote the letter dated May 2, 1897, different concepts had begun to acquire new and unexpected meanings in Freud's thought. He tells Fliess that he has obtained clear proof of the structure of hysteria: everything is related to the reproduction of the original scene. This is the first occasion that Freud speaks of the 'structure of hysteria', outlined in *Draft L*, which he attached to this letter. He saw this structure as a conglomerate of fantasies that interpret and alter the content of earlier experiences. He argues that some scenes are directly reproduced while others return in the form of fantasies. The sources of fantasy lies in what is 'heard' [sic] and later interpreted; these are defensive structures, which aim is to embellish the facts and provide relief. Their everyday source is, perhaps, masturbation (or fantasies about this act). The definition of 'fantasy' becomes more complicated once Freud argues that these psychic structures are not memories but impulses derived from primary scenes. That is, Freud suggests that fantasies are not only defences but also repressed drives. His premise is that repressed fantasies continue to elaborate and change during unconscious transformations of its contemporary meaning, now referring to an unconscious process that evolves independently of our imagination.

We also find further precise expression of Freud's abandonment of the evolutionary, chronological model in this letter. He argues here that all neuroses contain the same components: memories, impulses (derived from memories) and protective fictions. The three neuroses also exhibit the same aetiology; the difference between them depends on the points where these components break through into consciousness and produce compromise symptoms. Freud clearly rejects the attempt to distinguish between neuroses on aetiological and developmental grounds, discerned in their variations, which lie in structure, in how they appear in consciousness. In hysteria, they penetrate through memories; in obsessive neurosis, in perverse impulses, and in paranoia, through protective fantasies. This process of characterizing neurosis according to penetration points leads Freud to his swift retreat from the evolutionary theory of neuroses.

Freud indicates a further turnabout in his theorizing in his letters of July 7 and September 21, 1897. He writes in the first letter that the entire psychology of neuroses originates in the falsification of memories and fantasies. These falsifications, which comprise the structure of hysteria, are more powerful than true memories. His premise that psychic elements are subject to retranslation and reinterpretation now has pathological import. The thin boundary between normality and pathology is replaced by the difference between the retranslation and falsification of memories. When a memory of a primary experience loses importance, the developmental-mechanical explanation of neuroses loses its core component, meaning that pathological repression results from the ego's surprise by memories of traumatic childhood experiences.

Continuing in this direction in the second letter, Freud explicitly rejects the entire developmental theory of neuroses that he had previously upheld. He points to four reasons for this reversal:

1) His disappointment from his inability to obtain the anticipated successes with patients with the aid of his analyses. He argues for the possibility of explaining his partial successes in other ways.

2) His surprise that in all the cases encountered, the father can be accused of being a pervert (even his own father). I believe that Freud rejected the seduction theory once he realized that the value and meaning of memories change constantly, and that the essential factor in the formation of illness is the falsification of memories by fantasies.[6]

3) None of the reality indications that allow one to distinguish between truth and cathected fantasy are present in the unconscious. That is, on the level of the unconscious, there is no difference between a true and objective perception and memories resulting from the activity of fantasies cathected with endogenous energy.

4) The fact that the secret of childhood experiences and unconscious memories is absent even in psychoses (which Freud conceived to be the direct penetration of the unconscious into the conscious), had led him to conclude that it is impossible to expect treatment to fully 'tame' unconscious memories.

After accepting the impossibility of explaining repression with the traumatic seduction theory and delayed understanding, Freud tried to explain repression on the basis of new evolutionary assumptions, as he relays in his letter of November 14, 1897. He writes that he is currently occupied with the 'essential thing' that stands behind repression. This organismic premise defines repression as a result of the abandonment of early sexual zones. Freud posits that when

---

6   These conclusions are almost identical to those of Blass and Simon, 1994.

human beings began to walk upright, earlier smell sensations became disgusting by means of a still-unknown process.

When explaining the development of disgust sensations biologically, Freud uses terms apparently taken from the organic lexicon but in a special and unusual way. With respect to the nose (and smell sensations), he offers the following equation: 'He turns up his nose = he regards himself as someone particularly noble'. What have the nose and smells to do together with nobility? What relationship is there between the organic rejection of bad smells and the psychic rejection nobles may feel towards simple people? This is one of the first examples of a phenomenon that will become a central mark of his theories: the use of terms simultaneously psychological and biological in their meanings. And yet, Freud's theory of sexual zones is essentially psychological, with organic sensations determined by linguistic associations.

Although Freud had rejected the seduction theory and stressed fantasies instead of memories in his letter of September 21, 1897, in the current letter (November 14, 1897) he returns to those theories and integrates them into an explanation of repression as the abandonment of sexual zones. He proposes that during childhood, the sexual release zone has yet to be located. That is, the sexual zones, in fact the entire body, cause secretion in a manner resembling what happens during later sexual release. Freud further states that this early sexual release is experienced as an internal libidinal event. The preferred zones for release are the anus, mouth and throat. He also revises his theory of deferred action, arguing that in the presence of a deferred neurotic understanding, originating in the excitation of sexual organs by the seducer, a similar normal deferred action occurs that instigates compulsive behaviour (CL 279-280). The deferred understanding, connected with the memory of excitation of abandoned sexual zones, produces unpleasure, an internal sensation similar to disgust.

The development of sexuality (or its repression) is described by Freud as resulting from developmental waves (*Entwicklungschuben*). After each wave, the child feels piety, shame, and the like. If the sexual zones are not repressed, the result is what Freud calls 'moral insanity'. Freud adds, without details, that developmental waves have different chronologies in boys and girls. Differences between the sexes appear in puberty. Whereas girls feel repugnance, boys are seized by libido. At this stage, another sexual zone -- the genital zone -- awakens in boys but remains dormant in girls.

Freud's description of the developmental waves again illustrates how he assigns dual psychological and biological meanings to his concepts. He writes that a memory 'stinks' much as an object might 'stink'. Similar to how we turn our noses away when an object stinks, the preconscious and conscious distance themselves from the memories that 'stink'. This process captures the crux of repression (CL 280). It follows that the distinction between normal and pathological repression passes along the fine line separating late sexual release (originating in the deferred action of memories of excitations of the abandoned sexual zones) from the sexual release originating in memories of the normal excitation of sexual organs.

The new distinction between the normal and the pathological implies a significant blurring of the traditional acute opposition between these two notions. Freud himself states that the main value of his new proposal resides in 'its linking the neurotic process and the normal one' (CL 281). This closeness was absent from his earlier theories because Freud was apparently only partially convinced at the time that it is possible to explain normality by means of sexuality.

Following his new theory of repression, Freud asked: 'What, now, does normal repression furnish us with?' (CL 280). His answer: normal repression provides us with something that, if freed, will produce anxiety, and if bound, rejection. Rejection, in turn, becomes the affective basis for many intellectual developments, including morality, shame, and so forth.

His revised view of the repression of memories associated with the sexual zones accordingly implies another defeat for organic approaches because Freud implicitly raises the possibility of the transformation of biological into psychological sexual energy. The organic aspect of the new idea was, however, itself problematic given the need to find a new explanation for neurasthenic anxiety for example, which had previously been attributed to purely somatic sexual factors. As Freud himself conceded, his achievement was the proposition that normal as well as pathological phenomena can be explained as resulting from sexual causes, that the causes of libido and anxiety were distinct, and that libido was a masculine whereas repression a feminine element.

The November 14 letter is therefore important for two reasons: first, it contains the denial of any essential difference between normal and pathological processes while attributing every phenomenon, not only the abnormal, to the repression of sexual contents; second, it is Freud's last attempt to propose a comprehensive evolutionary biological theory.

The three letters to Fliess written during 1898 essentially sound the formal death knell of Freud's adherence to evolutionary causation. With his letter of February 23, 1898, Freud informs Fliess that he has completed several chapters of his book on dreams. He writes that the book is leading him more deeply into psychology, that all his new formulations are aimed at the philosophical pole, and that he has nothing new to say about the organic-sexual aspect. On March 10, 1898 Freud writes that he has concluded that the theory of wish fulfilment engenders only psychological, but no biological solutions. He now asks Fliess if it would be possible to apply the term 'metapsychology' (previously referring to biological explanations) to his (Freud's) psychology, which leads behind consciousness. The question effectively completes Freud's shift to psychological theorizing.

Lastly, in his letter of September 22, 1898, Freud presents what may be considered his final word on his psychology's relationship with biology. Freud writes that he agrees with Fliess in not wanting to leave his psychology bereft of some organic basis although he does not know how to continue, that he is even unable to imagine a connection of the organic with the psychological. As a result, he has decided to confine himself to psychology exclusively. In short, Freud is announcing that biological theories have contributed nothing to solving the psycho-physical problem.

PART 3: The Scientific Revolution

Parallel with his unsuccessful attempts to arrive at an evolutionary solution for the mind/body problem, Freud began to direct his efforts toward investigating empirical phenomena -- specifically, dreams -- by means of the self-analysis of his own associations. His impressive results led to the publication in 1900 of his magnum opus, *The Interpretation of Dreams*. This book, a product of the turning point in his work, contains the essentials of his revolutionary approach to the human sciences. Freud revealed his research method in two other works as well, published subsequently: *The Psychopathology of Everyday Life* (1901) and *Jokes and Their Relation to the Unconscious* (1905). My concluding chapter covers the essentials of his revolutionary approach and his new methodology for the research of human phenomena.

5

The New Science

Freud grounded his study of dreams on the explanation of this phenomena he had formulated in 1895 but transmitted to Fliess after five years, in a letter dated June 12, 1900 (CL 417). This point is crucial for our understanding of how his thinking had changed between conclusion of the *Project* and his final attempts to discover a material, evolutionary solution to psychological phenomena, and publication of *The Interpretation of Dreams*. Beginning in 1895, Freud began viewing dreams as linguistic, objective and material events belonging to empirical reality, to be understood in terms free from the distortions introduced by the psycho-physiological lens. His approach clearly countered the position taken by his colleagues. I should first note that dreams are normal phenomena, a fact countering the common opinion that Freud's is mainly a psycho-pathological enterprise. In what I consider his pre-revolutionary period, Freud repeatedly pointed to similarities between normal and pathological phenomena, even alluding to the absence of any essential differences between them, a view he clearly expressed in his many studies of people's normal phenomena published as of 1900.[1]

---

1 Freud also rejected the idea of categorizing psychoanalysis as just another medical or psychiatric theory or approach, in fear that a medical framework could even be harmful to prospective analysts and discourage would-be analysts from the study of medicine (Jones, 1957, Vol. 3, Ch. 9). Jones stated with regret that Freud 'proclaimed as a principle that in his opinion it was a matter of indifference whether intending candidates for psycho-analytic training held a medical qualification or not' (id., 311).

Analysis of the way in which Freud investigated dreams illuminates his early work and its conundrums. His ambition throughout that period, in which he increasingly strove to study the human brain, was to examine brain functioning during thinking and speaking, as revealed by his essay *On Aphasia* and the *Project,* as well as to discover some way to scientifically research and explain linguistic phenomena.

The seven chapters comprising *The Interpretation of Dreams* can be divided into three 'parts'. The first includes only the first chapter, essential for understanding Freud's early but also late work. This chapter discloses Freud's approach to the relation between the body-brain and the psyche-mind. It contains a comprehensive, detailed critique of the early scientific literature on dreams and begins to disclose how Freud perceived his object of investigation, which he elaborates in later chapters. The subjects and problems that Freud criticizes embody those factors he viewed as hampering the development of his innovative approach.

The book's second 'part', Chapters Two-Six, constitutes the main body of the text. In these chapters, Freud proceeds to develop his interpretative-explanatory approach, according to which a dream represents the fulfilment of wishes. Following his teachers, Freud subjects the dream to precise, microscopic scientific observation. The empirical matter observed is the dream's text, a linguistic phenomenon. According to this view, a dream's manifest content (like that of actions and jokes), must be investigated in exhausting detail.

The third 'part' contains the last chapter, Chapter Seven. Here Freud presents his conception of the mind's composition and its functioning. Although written with a neuro-physiological lexicon, these theories are already free of any attempt to achieve physiological and evolutionary reductionism; a new kind of reductionism has taken their place. Instead of reduction of psychological into neurological phenomena, linguistic phenomena are now reduced to accepted psychological elements.

In this last chapter, Freud demonstrates renunciation of his outstanding achievements in the *Interpretation*'s previous chapters, where it clearly appears that ideas (representations) cannot be independent from one another. Moreover, psychological processes are themselves not to be considered ideational. To the contrary, in

Chapter Seven, Freud grounds his theory not on linguistic phenomena but on the basic assumptions of modern psychology, a discipline that identifies ideas as the psyche's elementary components and psychic activity as resulting from the associations constructed between them.[2] Freud appears unable to stop speaking in psycho-physiological terms and, as I will show, to reach a level of theorizing equivalent to his empirical and methodological achievements.

Dreams and solution of the material problem in psychology

The psycho-physical problem had already found a central place in Freud's first psychiatric studies. The *Project* (1895) and the attempt to develop some evolutionary premises after its abandonment can be thought of as a desperate effort in direction of its resolution. Its failure left Freud with a very serious problem from the perspective of the material paradigm because he was unable to establish his psychology on biological, physiological or evolutionary explanations. As previously discussed, Freud and natural scientists together considered psychology, in the absence of a material substratum, simply as metaphysics and thus of no scientific importance.

Most surprising is the evidence that despite the long history of Freudian studies, even scholars troubled by the material problem have paid no attention to the fact that an impressive solution to the mind-body dualism can be found in *The Interpretation of Dreams*. This neglect may possibly be explained by the fact that Freud's was a concrete and practical solution (the study of objective linguistic phenomena) that he was unable of elaborate in theoretical terms. The solution he does offer has dual significance: its turn from reductionism reveals mind-body dualism to be an ill-conceived problem; and it clearly diverges from the naturalistic materialism of psychology and neurology, a position maintained to this very day.

Freud's interpreters have almost completely neglected the book's first chapter, where Freud presents a comprehensive critique of the contemporary theories applied to explain dreams according to what

---

2   Marx stressed the proximity of Freud's linguistic psychology to 19th century psycho-neurological associationism (1967: 822).

was then considered strict scientific criteria. The main aim of his criticism was to prepare the groundwork for the conception of dreams as an autonomous phenomenon, independent of any physical, somatic and psychological stimuli. Such a phenomenon stands by itself, with every element receiving its psycho-linguistic value and meaning from its relations with other conscious and unconscious elements rather than from the stimuli that might have caused it.

Freud harshly criticized theories on two main issues: the idea that organic and psychic stimuli caused dreams; and that dreams were meaningless phenomena lacking psychic value, or the result of a decrease in psychic activity. Freud considered the latter attitudes as dominant among physicians, physiologists and philosophers. He was convinced that theories negating the psychic importance of dreams were based on the assumption that they are caused by somatic stimuli (4: 64).

In *The Interpretation*'s first chapter, Freud's aim was to reject all organic theories and to stress acceptance of the small number of theories that treated dreams as meaningful phenomena. According to his approach, a psychic or organic stimulus cannot explain a dream's content; furthermore, as stated, the value of any dream's (manifest or latent) elements are established by their relations to other dream contents.

In Chapters Two (The method of interpreting dreams), Three (A dream is a fulfilment of a wish) and Four (Distortion in dreams), Freud elaborated his explanation of dreams, which exhibits impressive simplicity: a dream is the fulfilment of wishes. Desires do not receive direct expression in a dream's manifest content; they are submitted instead to significant distortion and concealment so as to make them appropriate to appear in the manifest content. Dreams, therefore, take part in the chain of psychical activities (4: 96). This view completely opposed 'scientific' theories of dreams, which considered dreams to be somatic processes expressed through signs appearing in the psychic system. Freud, in contrast, had no doubts that dreams are exclusively psychic phenomena, with somatic elements elaborated according to a dream's contents and desires; hence, for him, they had no organic value. Although Freud's psychological elaboration does not come close to the precision of his empirical linguistic perception of dreams, it offers some insights into the path he took towards this achievement.

In Section C of *The Interpretation*'s first chapter, where Freud examines the sources together with the factors stimulating dreams as part of his program to prove the dream's independence of organic sources, he nonetheless argues that in-depth research will one day discover dreams' organic causes. We should recall that despite Freud's objective of demonstrating the dream's psychic character, he continued to pay lip service to biological reductionism.

Freud thus perceived the psychic value of dream elements as dependent on other, latent or manifest elements of the same dream. That is, one main feature of dream representations is that their value is not established by their relations with stimuli external to the dream, but by their relations to all associated elements at any given moment. Freud conceived a dream's manifest content to be a 'transvaluation of all psychical values' (5: 330, 339). Hence, to assess the value of any representation, the researcher must examine its different relations with all the dream's other elements while bearing in mind that the dream fulfils unconscious desires in a distorted manner. It thus becomes incumbent upon us to use the term 'linguistic elements' rather than the more-common 'representations'. By this I am not referring to the classic meaning of language, according to which words are conceived as expressions of representations registered in memory but in a different sense, as an element taking part in a linguistic chain. Freud's shift in his approach must therefore be seen as the conclusion of his renunciation of physical and physiological models.[3]

Where, then, was Freud to look for the material basis of his new research paradigm? What I find to be most impressive is that Freud, without elaborating his reasoning, relied on the researched phenomenon's simple empirical materialism, an approach gradually gaining strength. This kind of materialism, which began to develop when he turned to the study of his patients' life stories, expressed Freud's deep need to prevent his science from hanging in the air, from emerging as another metaphysical theory of human nature. Once he understood that neurological processes and explanations cannot

---

3 Quite notable is the fact that Freud's development preceded by only a short time the development of a similar conception in the field of linguistics. Ferdinand de Saussure, the Swiss father of modern linguistics, formulated a model in which the word receives its value and meaning solely within its linguistic framework rather than from its relations with extra-linguistic objects.

supply the required material substratum, he began to investigate 'psychic' phenomena (fantasies, dreams, jokes, parapraxes) while focusing on their empirical material characteristics. We can therefore conclude that during this period, Freud was transformed into an empirical materialist, like any ordinary natural scientist.

Freud's efforts are marvellously expressed in *The Interpretation of Dreams*. Empirically, the uniqueness of his study of dreams lies in the focus on each and every aspect of the dream's text. We can compare Freud's approach to the difference between a literary critic's analysis of a literary work and a linguist's analysis of linguistic phenomena. Despite the close relation between the two fields and the fact that the literary critic analyses many of the work's linguistic aspects, his aim, as a rule, is to characterize his object of study according to its themes, styles and rhetorical figures as they appear within the work's content and structure. The object of the linguist's study is, in contrast, the language used in the work down to its most minute components, from the phrase to its sounds, syllables, words (Ducrot and Todorov, 1972: 375). Freud integrated the two kinds of research, with the materialistic character of his work coming from his linguistic perspective.

Freud did not explicitly state his practical solution; and yet, the scientific study of linguistic phenomena as psychology's material infrastructure is a unique and incomparably better solution than classic 'brain materialism'. I argue that despite his abandonment of biological and neurological models, Freud's huge confidence in the scientific character of his work came from his intuitive certainty that he was studying concrete and material, not abstract and metaphysical, phenomena.

From the naturalist perspective, psychic events are abstract and immaterial phenomena. Neuronal explanations are intended to provide them with materiality. Within their framework, the researched phenomenon is immaterial while the neurones are used only to fulfil an explanatory need rather than being the subject of direct study. I refer to this kind of materialism as *theoretical materialism*, in contrast to Freudian *empirical materialism*, in which the researched phenomena are material and concrete and explanatory theories are abstract. I suggest calling Freud's passage from theoretical to empirical materialism as his *'material transformation'*. Empirical materialism is much more appropriate than theoretical materialism to normal hard science. The same applies to neurology but only if it constrains itself to the study of nervous systems. Freud, apparently, gradually reached the conclusion that the fact that we need a brain, and a body, to think, to act, to feel, and to relate to others, does not mean that neurology has much to teach us about human behaviour. On the contrary, neurology must incorporate the understanding that it cannot explain human activity, that the brain functions in response to the conditions imposed upon it by social interaction at all stages of its long evolution.

In the following I present some examples of the manner in which Freud's empirical materialism was expressed in different aspects of his revolutionary trilogy and in his investigation of different phenomena. Consider his famous analysis of his inability to recall the name of the artist who painted the Orvieto frescos -- Signorelli – which he explained by means of his associations with the syllable 'bo' (1901, 6: 5). Another example is found in the dream I call 'Marcinowski', which has only one phrase. In this dream, the syllable 'se' and the sole sound 'c' play a central role (1900, 4: 302-303). A further example is the joke where the main elements are the sounds 'är' and 'amili', sounds that have neither value or meaning outside the word 'familionär', invented by the joke's author (1905, 8: 18-19). These three examples exemplify Freud's rigorous examination of even the smallest purely material linguistic elements.

Another material aspect of his new methodology is expressed in Freud's dealing with memory and oblivion in dreams (1900, 4: 11-21; 5: 468-484). Freud wanted to make clear that the distortions found in dreams are anything but casual. The appearance of disguised memories results from censure. Freud was not interested in the events that occurred in 'psychic' reality, nor if the dream pictures presented them faithfully, but in what was remembered and how it was remembered. To him, the dream as dreamt was not important, only the dreamer's telling of the dream (Litowitz and Litowitz, 1977: 431). That is, the dream as a verbal, material phenomenon was essential, not what happened in the brain or the psyche when dreaming.

Hence, the distinction between the dream as it is dreamt and the dream as it is told is fundamental. If the research object is the dream as dreamt, we have no direct access to the phenomenon. In this case, the dream as told provides only external testimony that transmits some information about the event. We therefore find that Freud, different from other dream researchers, related to what is actually said as the phenomenon to be investigated, and not simply as a source of information.

The study of the dream's text, as a linguistic phenomenon, represents Freud's greatest achievement and a fundamental advance of the research in the human sciences in general. Freud had proposed an empirical conception where materiality is inherent to the phenomena. The materiality of the spoken and written text needs no scientific or philosophical proof, nor any other basis, to substantiate itself beyond its presentation. I re-emphasize that this step is important because: a) it solves the material or dualism problem, making it irrelevant for the study of mankind; b) establishment of the written text as a research object fulfils the demands of exact science because texts are material and totally objective phenomena that anyone can research; and c) Freud showed how human phenomena can be precisely investigated, free of their distortion to comply with the demands of quantitative and experimental methods. Freud, in fact, established a new guiding principle for the precise and accurate investigation of mankind in general: to obtain true knowledge about people, the research must take the character of the specific phenomenon, that is, the human phenomenon, into consideration. Furthermore, scientists must apply methods appropriate for this kind of investigation. The method must thus adapt itself to the object under study, rather than vice versa. This approach is not easy to apply and brings with it many methodological difficulties, but warns against introducing distortions into the human sciences by turning to inadequate and inappropriate quantitative and experimental methods, as is overwhelmingly practiced today.[4]

By proposing this innovative solution to the material phenomena, Freud ended a very important period in his intellectual life, the pre-revolutionary period. Freud no longer had any need of a

---

4 Without elaborating here, I stress that implicit to my assertion is the argument that these methods may be useful when the investigation is directed by economic, academic, and political interests that do not provide true and reliable knowledge about human beings, given that the research is not aimed at this objective.

neurological infrastructure thanks to his anchoring his investigations on objective material phenomena. From now on, a new dichotomy would worry him.

Linguistic phenomena and psychological theories (metapsychology)

By positing linguistic (material) phenomena as a practical solution to dualism, Freud took his anthropology to the same level of the natural sciences. By relocating the material basis of psychology, the psyche-body/immaterial-material dichotomy was shown to be scientifically irrelevant, without any fear of a decline into subjectivity, metaphysics, biological materialism or idealistic spiritualism. Another highly important facet of Freud's move comes from its implications for the relationship between language and thought. In this context, the question arises as to what precisely defines and demarcates research objects in the human sciences.

To answer this question it is worthwhile reviewing what I previously wrote on language and thought, specifically that despite his innovations, Freud continued to adhere to accepted conceptions of the language-thought relationship, revealed in *On Aphasia*. That is, different from most of Freud's interpreters, I argue that it is possible to distinguish two different views of this relationship throughout his work: first, the traditional philosophical and psychological parallelism between the two, in which language reflects thought and representations; and second, a new conception in which linguistic phenomena, considered as independent from thought, take the lead, with the concepts 'thought' and 'representation' losing their scientific legitimacy as indicators of empirical phenomena.

The first conception appears in *On Aphasia*, where Freud argues that from a psychological point of view, words are the functional unity of speech, comprised of auditory, visual and kinaesthetic elements (1891: 73). Furthermore, they acquire their meaning from their connection to representations, the images of physical objects (1891: 77-78). I label this conception *'psycho-physical linguistic parallelism'*. By adopting this view (despite his critique), Freud retained the psycho-linguistic approach of his physicalist mentors. The philosophical and psychological tenets of his psycho-physical education comes to light most clearly in Freud's parallelist view of the relations between language and thought, which strongly influenced his meta-psychology and later psycho-pathological classifications.

However, in this same work, Freud, without rejecting the psychological approach to words, proposes a theory in which the psycho-physical parallelism is eliminated on the physiological level, together with his partial rejection of localizationist theory. Although Freud does not complete this new physiological theory with a new theory of language-thought relations, he introduces two propositions, implicitly addressing a new psychological perspective. In the first proposition, he describes the cortical speech area as a large area in which no functional differentiation appears, and in which it is impossible to distinguish between perceptions, memories, ideas (in general) and their associations. The second proposition denies the existence of differences in physiological processes parallel to those of perception and association as distinct from a psychological perspective. Hence, I consider those propositions as early expressions of an intuitive understanding of language's independence and its priority over thought, especially regarding the infinite combinatorial possibilities of its elements. This also applies to the forced and unnatural distinction of psychic elements (perceptions, memories, ideas) inside the linguistic stream.

The following stage in his conception of language-thought relations appears in the *Project*, in Freud's exposition of the basic structure of judgement used to analyse all primary and secondary processes (Part 1, paragraph 21; Part 2, paragraph 4). Freud divides judgement into two segments, the 'thing' and the 'predicate'. His use of the term 'thing' to refer to the object of judgement is suggestive; it indicates the complete identification of verbal grammatical elements with the external object. This traditional parallelism again appears in Freud's argument that the two components of judgement correspond to the constant and the variable components of perceptions and representations, respectively (I: 328).

This parallelism is eroded by Freud's new theories and doubts. The tension between the two, the old and the new, became the source of many reductionist problems. As I have shown, Freud attempted to explain representational phenomena by means of a neuronal system capable of working with two kinds of stimuli, external physical and internal biological. According to his evolutionary approach, endogenous stimuli became the dominant evolutionary factor at a very early stage in nervous system development. That is, in neuronal systems that come to cope with somatic stimuli, the reception of external perceptions are influenced by internal stimuli. The dominance of endogenous factors is expressed in Freud's analysis of perception and thought as based on experiences of satisfaction and unpleasure. Freud's evolutionary and physiological theories thus result in his conclusion that all representations are influenced by endogenous factors and do not present an exact reproduction of reality. Hence, representations and thought processes are influenced by impulses and desires.

Freud's fluctuations between his two contradictory approaches reached its peak when he dealt with one of the most difficult reductionist issues in the *Project*: the permanence versus change of memory registrations. This conundrum led Freud to revise his views, with his new model entailing interaction between allegedly objective perceptions and wishful representations, which achieved fuller expression in Freud's later theoretical work on desire and its influence on reality perception as well as the relationship between fantasy and reality. Still, the new theory of representation, which denies that perceptions and representations receive their meaning from the objects they supposedly reflect, does not upset the assumption of a fixed relationship between representations and words. However, a search of Freud's writings nonetheless reveals clear moves toward dissociation of the relation between language and thinking as assumed by modern philosophy.

These developments complete the erosion of the parallelist linguistic psycho-physical approach and supports a clearer understanding of Freud's heterogeneous theories. To the physiological theory on a continuous language area as found in *On Aphasia*, we can now add Freud's new notion regarding the incessant reorganization of representations, what he labelled 'translations' (see letters to Fliess dated May 30 and December 6, 1896). By means of the new model, in which representations may be registered anew with each energy passage, Freud was intent on painting a better picture of the changes undergone by each memory and thus of its multiplicity of values and meanings. With this revision, Freud was able to reject the fixed relationship between representations and words: with any new translation, the word-representation receives new meanings and possibly enters into new sound associations. What becomes important now are the relations between the associations.

Freud gradually transformed linguistic phenomena, rather than representations, into the focus of his practical investigations because he felt that his notion 'translation' of representations still did not provide an exact account of those phenomena. I therefore argue that an important factor influencing the redirection of his research originated in his doubts concerning his ability to precisely explain narrative and linguistic phenomena by means of his representation-based psychological theories. My conclusion rests on the simple fact that Freud turned to the study of recounted and transcribed dreams in the wake of his dissatisfaction with his theoretical constructs regarding the explanation of normal high-level thought processes. The posing of the written text of dreams as his new empirical object of research constituted a new method that totally diverged from those of the theoreticians who had attempted to explain dreams as psychological or physiological phenomena, the dream as dreamt and during dreaming. Freud had become a student of language, conceived as a product of human activity and social interaction. This transition represents the third and final, the effectively most important in relation to language and thought, being a practical methodological proposal.

In light of the developments traced in this book, I maintain that a new approach for interpreting Freud's work must be formulated, one based on the structure of his new science. To properly understand Freud, we must first understand the essential transformation that his psychological theories underwent once assembled into a scientific structure in which linguistic phenomena became the focus of practical research. The important questions raised consequent to his brilliant empirical shift, aimed at solving psychology's material problem, do not refer to whether those theories became more psychological and less biological, nor if they continued to preserve some aura of biologism. Rather, they pertain to the relationship between the perception of linguistic phenomena as empirical phenomena and the suitability of the psychological theories that Freud devised to explain them.

To respond to these questions, we must take in account the various linguistic phenomena that are incapable of explanation within Freud's theory of representations. Freud related to the most finite of linguistic phenomena, such as sounds and syllables. When we relate to these sounds outside their specific contexts, they exhibit no semantic, logical, or psychological meaning. We therefore find many of these are beyond comprehension as representations in the common meaning of a verbal-conceptual unit.

A comparison between Freud's empirical perspective and research methodology on the one hand, and psychological theories on the other, indicates that the latter, all of which are grounded in the notion of representation, do not provide a comprehensive description and explanation of the respective empirical phenomena. A gap exists between the linguistic phenomenon and its associated theoretical conceptualization. This fact raises a fundamental question regarding the character of the theories discussed in Chapter Seven. Despite his impressive turn toward empirical linguistic phenomena as his objects of investigation, Freud's theories continued to rest on representation. Although he revised the traditional psycho-physical assumption of representations as reflections of external objects, that he began to view the perception of reality as dependent on our wishes and words as functioning independently of representations, he stopped short of constructing full-fledged theories based on his innovative view of the language-thought relationship. Freud therefore continued to build his theories, especially those belonging to the economic (energetic) model, on the assumed parallelism of the object, word and representation.

These facts have led me to a further conclusion: Freud's later psychological theories are reductive. What differentiates this reduction from the earlier, pre-revolutionary explanations is that Freud now reduces linguistic phenomena to purely psychological events.

All previous interpreters have erred in their evaluation of Freud's theories because they did not attach any importance to Freud's perspective on the empirical phenomena he researched or to his theoretical inadequacies. Freud's practical methodological yet implicit answer to the previous questions is that any conceptualization of linguistic phenomena in terms of the concepts 'psyche' and 'representation' is unsubstantiated and distortive.

Freud's later theories must also be examined according to the tension between his polar tendencies: the conservative and the revolutionary. Freud's science was not created as a complete whole; it still awaits the introduction of adequate anthropological rather than psychological theories.

I also argue that the Freudian principles for the scientific research of human beings may initiate a scientific revolution, not inferior in its value and implications to those of the revolution in the 17th century's in the natural sciences and that of quantum physics. To complete his achievement, we should apply the basic principle of Freudian research, according to which maximal compatibility between the empirical phenomenon, its description and the method used for its investigation is maintained. This principle is more important than any hastily built theory. Today's research in the human sciences applies this principle loosely, if at all. These sciences, developed randomly and designed so as to satisfy numerous religious, academic, political, cultural, economic interests, prevent any logical or rational discussion on their core principles, or what is and what is not empirically appropriate for the study of mankind specifically.

Freud's incomplete enterprise also left open the question of what methods are appropriate for the study of distinct human phenomena in a manner that would free them of any subjugation to the demands imposed by established agencies or interests, most especially those of positivistic and hermeneutic-humanistic philosophy of science. After Freud and thanks to him, the question of how empirical phenomena are to be perceived in order to allow for their exacting scientific study must be placed at the centre of any scientific inquiry into human phenomena.

An outstanding example of the want of this kind of debate involves the concept 'psyche'. Despite the serious philosophical criticism of this concept,[5] it remains central to the academic division of the human sciences, with psychology still conceived as a scientific discipline (so long, of course, as research is practised by means of the purportedly

---

5 For comprehensive criticism of the concept 'psyche' as well as references to the argument I develop here on the nonexistence of a real problem body-mind, see Rorty, 1980.

empirical methods of quantification and experiment). It is therefore crucial to mention that my argument about the incompatibility of the concept psyche to the study of human phenomena is very different from the ontological argument of materialist philosophers and positivistic (psycho-neurologists, psycho-biologists) psychologists. Different from these, who deny the existence of an independent psyche (mind) and argue that psychological processes are essentially neurological, I reject entry into any ontological debate over the concept; instead, I prefer to discuss its epistemic inadequacy exclusively. Hence, I propose using other concepts (primarily 'human phenomena') in its place.

Now, and only by way of epilogue, I examine Freud's later studies and their implications for a scientific methodology targeted at the human sciences and their inadequate and illogical academic organization.

Expanding the empirical field of the new science: The new core dichotomy of Freudian research

As stated, Freud's research objects and methodology, more than his theories, are the keys to understanding Freud's nascent science. Although unstated, it appears that the social character of the linguistic phenomena Freud studied opened up a new world for him, a fascinating world of new objects, to which he enthusiastically turned. It is also clear that while linguistic phenomena constituted an essential part of Freudian research, they did not exhaust the empirical world given to study with his methods. One of the outstanding features of his late research is that it goes beyond 'psychological', individual phenomena, observed in the fact that most of his research was directed to the study of social phenomena. However, because Freud chose to refer to his enterprise as 'psychoanalysis', we must conclude that he apparently had great difficulty in freeing himself from the academic divisions still in force. These contradictions in Freud's oeuvre created much confusion among disciples and other researchers.

We can locate the different approaches they adopted on a continuum, with those situated at one pole completely ignoring the sociological aspects of his works, through those acknowledging them while ignoring their methodological significance, to those viewing Freud's theories as social psychology, an integrative effort between the two disciplines, at the other pole. Contemporary psychoanalysts, philosophers and thinkers from other fields, when relating to any analysis of social -- rather than clinical -- phenomena conducted according to Freudian theories, regularly apply the label 'applied psychoanalysis' to this work. One latent assumption underlying this term is that a field exists, naturally appropriate for Freud's research method, with another field existing in which that method can be applied only by extension, meaning that his method is inappropriate there in principle. Another assumption is that Freud researched social objects only from a psychological point of view, as if offering psychological explanations for social phenomena. This view, however does not fully acknowledge the character of Freud's research methods and the range of fields to which they may be applied.

We have ample evidence indicating that it is impossible to relate to Freud's late work only as fitting for the study of individuals (that is, as psychology). First, we have the studies in which he related to aesthetics as social phenomena. His three most elaborate and representative works in this direction are: *Jokes and Their Relation to the Unconscious* (1905); *The Moses of Michelangelo* (1914); and *The Uncanny* (1919). In these, Freud conducted no analysis whatsoever of the feelings, fantasies or personality of the artist studied. Jokes, for instance, were conceived by him as essentially social phenomena (8, Chapter 5). Even in his biographical studies, such as those on Leonardo, Goethe and Dostoyevski, which appear suitable to the application of psychologistic arguments, we can easily find sociological interpretations. I need only mention that he always studied the relations of the artist with his parents and significant figures in his childhood.

Second, his studies of early and late familial relations led Freud to formulate a fundamental theoretical approach according to which a person's love/hate relations to his parents determine his behaviour and life course. Known as the Oedipus complex, this approach embodies a sociological theory on the important role of the family for human development; it has since became a cornerstone of Freudian 'psychology'. For instance, the Freudian psyche is formed according to the vicissitudes of the Oedipal process, that is, through parental influence on the child.[6]

---

6   See Lacan, 1938.

Third, Freud proposed, in 1923, a new model of the psyche's structure. In this model he demarcated three areas with overlapping boundaries: the id, the ego and the superego. The ego emerges from the struggle between the id, representing nature and composed of drives, and the superego, representing parental, that is social, influences. Here we have a socio-biological theory explaining the structure of the psyche.

Fourth, Freud explains his treatment method as conducted according to the theory of transference,[7] which involves the patient transferring his thoughts and feelings, created in his early relations with his parents, to the analyst. The aim of treatment is to explore this transference, a pattern of behaviour frequently observed in social relations. The difference between Freud's concept of this relationship and other social relationships is that transference itself is transformed into the object of investigation.

Fifth, Freud published his major investigations into the structure of society in *Totem and Taboo* (1913) and *Group Psychology and the Analysis of the Ego* (1921). Freud's engagement with the psychology-sociology dichotomy is clearly expressed in *Totem and Taboo* by his classification of explanations of totemism into two groups: sociological and psychological (13: 113-119). The exposition of the individual (psychological) element on the one hand, and the sociological on the other, is quite balanced. Most striking is the fact that Freud engaged in so full a description of the Oedipus complex, one of the core theories directing management of analytical treatment in precisely this book rather than in his clinical elaborations. According to the prevalent terminology, this is a sociological theory par excellence, with the psychological playing a secondary role.

The essay *Group Psychology and the Analysis of the Ego* is a direct continuation of *Totem and Taboo*. In this work, relations between the individual and society stand at the centre. Freud's aim here is dual: to deny the theory explaining social phenomena as consequences of the social instinct appearing in the psyche once a person enters in contact with other people, and to explain those phenomena as rooted in familial relations. Freud argues in this essay

---

7 See entry Transference, Laplanche and Pontalis, 1973.

that the church and the military, two of the social institutions on which Freud focuses his analytical sights, exist precisely because their members are connected by libidinal relations to the leader in the first instance and to the masses (their comrades) in the second instance.

Most meaningful in this work is the swing between the psychological and the sociological, also found in all of Freud's late thought. In section X of *Group Psychology,* Freud explains mass behaviour as a revival of the archaic horde, and concludes that social psychology (sociology) is the oldest form of human psychology. He, then offers a sociological explanation for psychology: individual psychology, he writes, is extricated from social psychology only at a later stage, gradually and partially (13: 123). That is, Freud's view opposed psychologism. Freud wanted to show that the psyche, and perhaps the very belief in its existence, has its source in social processes.

After this 'sociological' explanation, Freud nonetheless proposes psychological explanations. He argues that individual psychology must be as old as social psychology because from the beginning, two psychologies were in place: one, that of the individuals belonging to the group, and two, that of the father, chief, or leader. He explains that the possibility of transforming collective into individual psychology is, by necessity, implicit in the assumption that the ancestral father denies his sons the satisfaction of their sexual needs, actions compelling them to develop emotional relations among themselves but also with him. That is, the ancestral father forces a collective psychology upon his sons. The father's sexual envy and intolerance -- his individual psychology -- are thus the source of social psychology.

It is difficult to understand why Freud thought that only the father's behaviour toward his sons could be considered as an expression of individual psychology and that of his sons as social psychology or sociology. The two explanations may certainly be considered sociological as well as psychological. We may venture that his model expresses two tendencies in his thinking about the relationship between the individual and society. On the one hand, it reflects his deep understanding that there is no psychic phenomena that is not social and vice versa; on the other, it points to his discomfort with the attempts of sociologists, politicians and social reformers to deny the importance of the individual and even erase psychology from the human sciences. Freud's internal contradictions may therefore reflect the sterile debate undertaken by the two disciplines during this period.[8] Practically speaking, neither Freud nor sociologists were able to ignore the alternative view: there is no sociology that does not include, at least implicitly, a conception of the individual person. Alternatively, even Freud's most individual explanations, such as the Oedipus complex, are sociological.

As stated, the relationship between the individual and society was one of the major subjects of Freud's later work. Although Freud exposed the social character of human relations, we should note that in Freud's *New Introductory Lectures On Psycho-Analysis* (1933), an additional motive surfaces when he deals with the sociology-psychology dichotomy: to reduce sociological phenomena to psychological explanations. As he writes:

> 'For sociology, too, dealing as it does with the behaviour of people in society, cannot be anything but applied psychology. Strictly speaking there are only two sciences: psychology, pure and applied, and natural sciences.' (22: 179).

And yet, the fact that one's psychic life is *always* related to other persons led Freud to conclude that individual psychology is also social psychology (sociology)[9] and that no valid reason exists to warrant their separation. He criticizes the principles on which sociology was grounded, isolated from psychology and denying the study of the individual's relations with his or her parents and siblings (18: 69-71).

Recalling that Freud himself considered interpersonal relations to be social phenomena, a clearly reductionist stance to psychology that raises many problems for the human sciences, should not stop us from examining the various fragments written in which Freud attempts to balance those statements. In his writings we thus find two different attempts to solve the tensions associated with the opposition between psychology and sociology. The first, a theoretical endeavour

---

8   See Levy Bruhl, 1973 (1900): 206-209.

9   'In the individual's mental life someone else is invariably involved, as a model, as an object, as a helper, as an opponent; and so from the very first individual psychology, in this extended but entirely justifiable sense of the word, is at the same time social psychology as well.' (18: 69)

that has been studied by many researchers, is lodged in his effort to bridge between the two disciplines, as indicated above.[10] The second is an empirical attempt never explicitly formulated. It is reflected in Freud's tendency to identify new objects for investigation. This search hints at a new direction in his perception of empirical phenomena and in the character of research in human sciences, resting on abrogation of the differentiation between psychological and sociological objects.

Towards a new empirical object in the study of human phenomena

Freud's attempts to integrate a psychological with a sociological perspective and to offer a psycho-social explanation of the phenomena he studied point to his dissatisfaction with the division of human phenomena in academic disciplines. This issue led him to attempt another solution, one that, in my opinion, is the only successful approach to the difficulty of assigning human phenomenon to only one of two distinct categories.

As I have shown, Freud's science is free from the material problem confounding psychology and philosophy. It has no need of a biological basis because it relies on the materiality of the researched phenomenon. It also offers a new, although undeveloped, direction for resolving the questions arising from the traditional division of human phenomena into sociological and psychological events.

The clearest evidence of this inherently different approach appears quite early in Freud's work. In 1907, Freud published the paper 'Obsessive Actions and Religious Practices', his first on a phenomenon commonly considered sociological in nature. Importantly, it was written a short time after publication of his book on jokes. The paper should be considered as his initial attempt to broaden the fields in which his method could be applied and to study what had originally been defined as sociological together with psychological phenomena.

I would stress that Freud makes no attempt in this paper to outline a collective or social psychology; nor does he expend any effort in showing that there is no essential difference between obsessive

---

10 See Wallerstein and Smelser, 1969; Mittscherlich et al., 1970; Endelman, 1981, Part 1; Craib, 1990.

and religious phenomena. Freud's aim is clear: to show that both phenomena express unconscious meanings. If a difference exists between the two, it may be that religious phenomena, do have meaning whereas obsessive behaviour, appears senseless (9: 119-120). Although Freud does not reject the accepted distinction between the social and individual character of the two phenomena, respectively, he viewed that distinction as negligible and undeserving of deep consideration.

Freud's avoidance of this central differentiation in human sciences is deeply rooted in all his thinking. It found expression in diverse ideas, such as the similarities between the structure of social organizations and the psyche, and in the parallels he found between totemism and fetishism. Stated differently, Freud's theorizing eventually aspired to negate the importance of the individual/society dichotomy, in a process similar to what he had undergone with respect to the mind/body dualism. On a theoretical level, he constantly proposed integrative explanations, considering them as psychological explanations of social phenomena, which may have been motivated by his inability to find unifying psychological and sociological concepts. In parallel, he did not allow the sociology-psychology dichotomy to distort his empirical perception of human phenomena. Freud understood that human phenomena are simultaneously psychological and sociological, implying that it is impossible to use this distinction as a classificatory principle, or to establish bounded scientific fields, each exploring one class of phenomena in isolation, as is currently practiced in academia.

His methodology and empirical approach consequently invite a deep change in the classification of the human sciences and the organization of academic departments. It may be that all the human sciences could be reduced to only one, an expanded anthropology. This new anthropology would embrace all the disciplines that investigate mankind but only with the aim of obtaining knowledge for the sake of humanity's progress. That is, the new anthropology would not serve any economical, religious or political interests and not aspire to control people. Research not abiding by this principle would be excluded from the scientific field. Another important feature of this new science would be its assimilation of Freud's linguistic perspective and its implications for our understanding of the brain, now considered a social tool, the means by which a bodily organ complies with the demands originating in the universal collective character of mankind as it evolved during the species' infinite attempts to communicate and cooperate. Neurological research of the human brain would then become conceived along the principles of the new science.

Bibliography

Freud, S. (1886a) 'Report on my studies in Paris and Berlin'. SE 1. 3-15. London: Hogarth.
- (1886b) 'Preface'. *Translation of Charcot's Lectures on the Diseases of the Nervous System*, SE 1. 19-22. London: Hogarth.
- (1886c) 'Observation of a severe case of hemi-anaesthesia in a hysterical male'. SE 1. 23-31. London: Hogarth.
- (1888a) 'Hysteria'. SE 1. 39-57. London: Hogarth.
- (1888b) 'Preface', in 'Translation of Bernheim's "Suggestion"'. SE 1, 73. London: Hogarth.
- (1889) 'Review of August Forel's *"Der Hypnotismus"'*. SE 1, 90. London: Hogarth.
- (1891) [1953]. *On Aphasia. A Critical Study.* Trans. by E. Stengel. London: Imago.
- (1891) *Zur Auffassung der Aphasien: Eine Kritische Studie.* Leipzig und Wien: Franz Deuticke.
- (1892). 'Sketches for the "Preliminary Communication" of 1893'. SE 1: 145-154. London: Hogarth.
- (1892-93) 'A case of successful treatment by hypnotism: With some remarks on the origin of hysterical symptoms through "Counterwill"'. SE 1. 116.
- (1892-94) 'Preface and footnotes to the translation of Charcot's Tuesday Lectures'. SE 1. 131. London: Hogarth.
- (1893a) 'On the psychical mechanism of hysterical phenomena (A lecture)'. SE 3: 25. London: Hogarth.
- (with Breuer, J.) (1893b) 'On the psychical mechanism of hysterical phenomena: Preliminary communication'. SE 2: 1-17. London: Hogarth.
- (1893c) 'Some points for a comparative study of organic and hysterical motor paralyses'. SE 1:157. London: Hogarth.
- (1893d) 'Charcot'. SE 3: 7. London: Hogarth.

- (1894a) 'The neuro-psychoses of defence (An attempt at a psychological theory of acquired hysteria, of many phobias and obsessions and of certain hallucinatory psychoses)'. SE 3. 43. London: Hogarth.
- (1894b) 'On the grounds for detaching a particular syndrome from neurasthenia under the description "anxiety neurosis"'. SE 3: 87. London: Hogarth.
- (1894c) 'Obsessions and phobias: Their psychical mechanism and their etiology'. SE 3: 71. London: Hogarth.
- (1895a) 'Studies on hysteria' (with Breuer's additions). SE 2: 1. London: Hogarth.
- (1895b). *Project for a Scientific Psychology.* SE 1. 281-391. London: Hogarth.
- (1896a) 'Heredity and the etiology of neuroses'. SE 3. 142. London: Hogarth.
- (1896b) 'Further remarks on the neuro-psychoses of defence'. SE 3, 159.
- (1900) *The Interpretation of Dreams.* SE, 4-5. London: Hogarth.
- (1905) *Jokes and Their Relation to the Unconscious.* SE 8. London: Hogarth.
- (1913) *Totem and Taboo.* SE 13, vii-162. London: Hogarth.
- (1914) *The Moses of Michelangelo.* SE 13. 209. London: Hogarth.
- (1915) *The Unconscious.* SE 14. 159. London: Hogarth.
- (1916/7) 'Introductory lectures on psycho-analysis'. SE 16. London: Hogarth.
- (1919) 'The uncanny'. SE 17. 217. London: Hogarth.
- (1921) *Group Psychology and the Analysis of the Ego.* SE 18. 65. London: Hogarth.
- (1925) *An Autobiographical Study.* SE 20. 1-74. London: Hogarth.
- (1933) *New Introductory Lectures on Psycho-Analysis.* 22: 1-182. London: Hogarth.
- (1950) *Aus den Anfangen der Psychoanalyse: Briefe an Wilhelm Fliess, Abhandlungen und Notizen aus den Jahren 1887-1902 (Anf).* Einleitung von Kris, E. Herausgebern: Bonaparte, M., Freud, A. und Kris, E. London: Imago.
- (1953-1974) *The Standard Edition of the Complete Psychological Works of S. Freud* (SE), 24 vols. Translated and edited by James Strachey, in collaboration with Anna Freud, assisted by Alix Strachey and Alan Tyson. London: Hogarth and the Institute of Psycho-Analysis.
- (1954). *The Origins of Psychoanalysis: Letters to Wilhelm Fliess, Drafts and Notes, 1887-1902.* Ed. by Bonaparte, M., Freud, A., and Kris, E.; trans. by Mosbacher, E. and Strachey, J. New York: Basic Books.
- (1985) *The Complete Letters to Wilhelm Fliess 1887-1904* (CL). Translated and edited by J. Moussaieff Masson. Cambridge, MA: Belknap.
- (1986) *Briefe an Wilhelm Fließ 1887-1904. (Briefe). Ungekürzte Ausgabe.* Hg. von J. Moussaieff Masson. Bearbeitung der deutschen Fassung von M. Schröter. Frankfurt am Main: S. Fischer.
- (1991) *Gesammelte Werke* (GW). 18 vols. Edited by Anna Freud, with the collaboration of Marie Bonaparte, E. Bibring, W. Hoffer, E. Kris, and O. Isakower. London: Imago.

Ackerknecht, E. H. (1959) *Short History of Psychiatry.* Second Ed. Trans. by S. Wolff. New York: Hafner.

Amacher, P. (1964) 'Thomas Laycock, I.M. Sechenov, and the reflex arc concept'. *Bull. Hist. Med.* 38:168-183.

- (1965) 'Freud's neurological education and its influence on psychoanalytic theory'. *Psych.* Issues 4, No. 4, Monograph 16. New York: International University Press.
Andersson, O. (1962). *Studies in the Prehistory of Psychoanalysis: the Etiology of Psychoneuroses and Some Related Themes in Sigmund Freud's Scientific Writings and Letters, 1886-1896.* Stockholm: Svenska Bokforlaget.
Apprey, M. (1994) 'Translator's note and preface', in G. Politzer (Ed.). *Critique of the Foundations of Psychology,* pp. x-xxii. Pittsburgh, PA: Duquesne University Press.
Beard, G. M. (1890) *Die Sexuelle Neurasthenie.* 2. Auflage. Leipzig und Wien: Franz Deuticke.
Bernfeld, S. (1944) 'Freud's earliest theories and the school of Helmholtz'. *Psy. Quart., 13*:341-62.
- (1949) Freud's scientific beginnings. *The American Imago,* 6:163-96.
- (1951) 'Sigmund Freud, M.D., 1882-85'. *International Journal of Psycho-Analysis,* 32:204-216.
Blass, R. and Simon, B. (1994) 'The value of the historical perspective to contemporary psychoanalysis: Freud's ʽseduction hypothesis'. *Int. Journal of Psychoan.* 75:677-694.
Brazier, M. (1959). The historical development of neurophysiology, in *Handbook of Physiology. Section 1: Neurophysiology.* Edited by Field, J., Magoun, H. V. and Hall, V. E. Washington, DC: American Physiological Society.
Boring, E. G. (1950) *A History of Experimental Psychology.* 2nd. Ed. New York: Appleton-Century-Crofts.
Brett, G. S. (1953) *History of Psychology (1912-1921).* Ed. and abridged by Peters, R. S. London: Allen & Unwin.
Bruecke, E. (1874) *Vorlesungen ueber Physiologie.* Wien: W. Braumuller.
Brunner, J. (1994) '"Every path must end in darkness," or: Why psychoanalysis needs metapsychology'. *Science in Context* 7:83-101.
Cassirer Bernfeld, S. (1955) 'Sigmund Freud: The origins of psychoanalysis' book review, Psy. Q. 24:284-91.
Charcot, J.-M. (1991) *Clinical Lectures on Diseases of the Nervous System (1889).* Edition and Introduction by Ruth Harris, London: Tavistock/Routledge.
Centonze, D., Siracusano, A., Calabresi, P., and Bernardi , G. (2004) 'The *Project for a Scientific Psychology* (1895): A Freudian anticipation of LTP-memory connection theory'. *Brain Research Reviews* 46:310– 314.
Chertok, L. (1970). 'Freud in Paris'. *Int. J. Psy.,* 51: 511.
Chertok, L. and de Saussure, R. (1989) 'The birth of psychoanalysis', in *S. Freud: Critical Assesments,* V. I., L. Spurling, ed. New York-London: Routledge.
Cioffi, F. (1998) *Freud and the Question of Pseudoscience.* Ill: Open Court.
Craib, Ian. (1990) *Psychoanalysis and Social Theory.* Amherst: Univ. of Massachusets Press.
Cranefield, P. F. (1957) 'The organic physics of 1847 and the biophysics of today'. *J. Hist. Med. and Allied Sci.* 12(10):407-23.
Crews, F. (1986) *Skeptical Engagements.* New York: Oxford University Press.
Danziger, K. (1998 [1990]) *Constructing the Subject. Historical Origins of Psychological Research.* Cambridge: Cambridge University Press.

Darwin, Ch. (1877) 'A Biographical Sketch of an Infant'. *Mind* 7:285-294.
- [1988 (1859)] *On the Origin of Species*. In *The Works of Charles Darwin*, V. 15. P. H. Barrett & R. D., Freeman, eds.. London: Pickering.

Davar, B. V., & Bhat, P. R. (1995) *Psychoanalysis as a Human Science-Beyond Foundationalism*. New Delhi: Sage.

Davison, C. (1955) 'Review of Freud's "On Aphasia"'. *Psych. Quart.* 24:115-119.

Dilthey, W. (1989). *Selected Works; V. 1: Introduction to the Human Sciences*. Princeton, NJ: Princeton University Press.

Dorer, M. (1932) *Historische Grundlagen der psychoanalyse*. Leipzig: F. Meiner.

Draenos, S. (1982) *Freud's Odyssey. Psychoanalysis and the End of Metaphysics*. New Haven: Yale University Press.

Ducrot, O. et Todorov, T. (1972). *Dictionnaire encyclopedique des sciences du langage*. Paris: Editions du Seuil.

Endelman, R. (1981) *Psyche and Society*. New York: Columbia University Press.

Erneling, C. E., & Johnson, D. M., eds. (2005) *The Mind as a Scientific Object*. Oxford and New York: Oxford University Press.

Exner, S. (1894) *Entwurf zu einer physiologischen Erklarung der psyschichen Erscheinungen*. Leipzig: Deuticke.

Fancher, R. E. (1973) *Psychoanalytic Psychology: The Development of Freud's Thought*. New York: Norton.

Flanagan, O. (1984) *The Science of Mind*. Cambridge, Mass. and London: MIT Press.

Fliess, W. (1923). *Der Ablauf des Lebens: Grundlegung zur Exakten Biology. (The End of Life: Foundation for the Accurate Biology)* (2nd edn.). Leipzig and Vienna: Franz Deuticke. 2e. Auf.

Freud, S. (1886a) 'Report on my studies in Paris and Berlin'. SE 1. 3-15. London: Hogarth.
- (1886b) 'Preface'. *Translation of Charcot's Lectures on the Diseases of the Nervous System*, SE 1. 19-22. London: Hogarth.
- (1886c) 'Observation of a severe case of hemi-anaesthesia in a hysterical male'. SE 1. 23-31. London: Hogarth.
- (1888a) 'Hysteria'. SE 1. 39-57. London: Hogarth.
- (1888b) 'Preface', in 'Translation of Bernheim's "Suggestion"'. SE 1, 73. London: Hogarth.
- (1889) 'Review of August Forel's "*Der Hypnotismus*"'. SE 1, 90. London: Hogarth.
- (1891) [1953]. *On Aphasia. A Critical Study*. Trans. by E. Stengel. London: Imago.
- (1891) *Zur Auffassung der Aphasien: Eine Kritische Studie*. Leipzig und Wien: Franz Deuticke.
- (1892). 'Sketches for the "Preliminary Communication" of 1893'. SE 1: 145-154. London: Hogarth.
- (1892-93) 'A case of successful treatment by hypnotism: With some remarks on the origin of hysterical symptoms through "Counterwill"'. SE 1. 116.
- (1892-94) 'Preface and footnotes to the translation of Charcot's Tuesday Lectures'. SE 1. 131. London: Hogarth.

- (1893a) 'On the psychical mechanism of hysterical phenomena (A lecture)'. SE 3: 25. London: Hogarth.
- (with Breuer, J.) (1893b) 'On the psychical mechanism of hysterical phenomena: Preliminary communication'. SE 2: 1-17. London: Hogarth.
- (1893c) 'Some points for a comparative study of organic and hysterical motor paralyses'. SE 1:157. London: Hogarth.
- (1893d) 'Charcot'. SE 3: 7. London: Hogarth.
- (1894a) 'The neuro-psychoses of defence (An attempt at a psychological theory of acquired hysteria, of many phobias and obsessions and of certain hallucinatory psychoses)'. SE 3. 43. London: Hogarth.
- (1894b) 'On the grounds for detaching a particular syndrome from neurasthenia under the description "anxiety neurosis"'. SE 3: 87. London: Hogarth.
- (1894c) 'Obsessions and phobias: Their psychical mechanism and their etiology'. SE 3: 71. London: Hogarth.
- (1895a) 'Studies on hysteria' (with Breuer's additions). SE 2: 1. London: Hogarth.
- (1895b). *Project for a Scientific Psychology.* SE 1. 281-391. London: Hogarth.
- (1896a) 'Heredity and the etiology of neuroses'. SE 3. 142. London: Hogarth.
- (1896b) 'Further remarks on the neuro-psychoses of defence'. SE 3, 159.
- (1900) *The Interpretation of Dreams.* SE, 4-5. London: Hogarth.
- (1905) *Jokes and Their Relation to the Unconscious.* SE 8. London: Hogarth.
- (1913) *Totem and Taboo.* SE 13, vii-162. London: Hogarth.
- (1914) *The Moses of Michelangelo.* SE 13. 209. London: Hogarth.
- (1915) *The Unconscious.* SE 14. 159. London: Hogarth.
- (1916/7) 'Introductory lectures on psycho-analysis'. SE 16. London: Hogarth.
- (1919) 'The uncanny'. SE 17. 217. London: Hogarth.
- (1921) *Group Psychology and the Analysis of the Ego.* SE 18. 65. London: Hogarth.
- (1925) *An Autobiographical Study.* SE 20. 1-74. London: Hogarth.
- (1933) *New Introductory Lectures on Psycho-Analysis.* 22: 1-182. London: Hogarth.
- (1950) *Aus den Anfängen der Psychoanalyse: Briefe an Wilhelm Fliess, Abhandlungen und Notizen aus den Jahren 1887-1902 (Anf).* Einleitung von Kris, E. Herausgebern: Bonaparte, M., Freud, A. und Kris, E. London: Imago.
- (1953-1974) *The Standard Edition of the Complete Psychological Works of S. Freud* (SE), 24 vols. Translated and edited by James Strachey, in collaboration with Anna Freud, assisted by Alix Strachey and Alan Tyson. London: Hogarth and the Institute of Psycho-Analysis.
- (1954). *The Origins of Psychoanalysis: Letters to Wilhelm Fliess, Drafts and Notes, 1887-1902.* Ed. by Bonaparte, M., Freud, A., and Kris, E.; trans. by Mosbacher, E. and Strachey, J. New York: Basic Books.
- (1985) *The Complete Letters to Wilhelm Fliess 1887-1904* (CL). Translated and edited by J. Moussaieff Masson. Cambridge, MA: Belknap.
- (1986) *Briefe an Wilhelm Fließ 1887-1904. (Briefe). Ungekürzte Ausgabe.* Hg. von J. Moussaieff Masson. *Bearbeitung der deutschen Fassung von M. Schröter.* Frankfurt am Main: S. Fischer.

- (1991) *Gesammelte Werke* (GW). 18 vols. Edited by Anna Freud, with the collaboration of Marie Bonaparte, E. Bibring, W. Hoffer, E. Kris, and O. Isakower. London: Imago.

Friedman, J. and Alexander, J. (1983) 'Psychoanalysis and natural science: Freud's 1895 "Project" revisited'. *Int. Rev. of Psy.* 10:303-318.

Fullinwider, S. (1983) 'Sigmund Freud, John Hughlings Jackson, and speech'. *J. Hist. Ideas* 44:151-58.

Galaty, D.H. (1974) 'The Philosophical Basis of Mid-nineteenth Century German Reductionism'. *J. H. Medicine and Allied Sciences*, 29. 295-316.

Gamwell, L. and Solms, M. (2006) *From Neurology to Psychoanalysis. Sigmund Freud's Neurological Drawings and Diagrams of the Mind*. Binghamton, NY: University Art Museum, State University of New York.

Gay, P. (1988) *A Life for Our Time*. London and Melbourne: Dent & Sons.

Gelfand, T. (1988) 'Mon cher docteur Freud: Charcot's unpublished correspondence to Freud, 1888-1893'. *Bull. Hist. Med.*, 62:563-588.

Ghiselin, M. T. (1973). 'Darwin and evolutionary psychology. *Science* 179:964-968.

Giorgi, A. (1994) 'Foreword: The psychology of Georges Politzer', in: Politzer, G. *Critique of the Foundations of Psychology* (Trans. M. Apprey) (pp. xxiii-xxxviii). Pittsburgh: Duquesne University Press.

Glick, B.S. (1966) 'Freud, the problem of quality and the "secretory neurone"'. *Psychoanal. Quart.* 35:84-97.

Gould, S. J. (1977) *Onthogeny and Philogeny*. Cambridge, MA: Belknap.

Greenberg, V. D. (1997) *Freud and his Aphasia Book. Language and the Sources of Psychoanalysis*. Ithaca and London: Cornell University Press.

Gregory, F. (1977) *Scientific Materialism in Nineteenth Century Germany*. Dordrecht: D. Reidel.

Haeckel, E. (1906 [1874]) *The Evolution of Man*. London: Watts. Trans. and abridged by J. McCabe from the 5th ed. of *Anthropogenie oder Entwicklungsgeschichte des Menschen*.

Haimovich, S. (2010) *Freud and Psychiatry. On "Studies on Hysteria"*. Tel Aviv: Resling. (Hebrew)

Harris, R. (1991) 'Introduction'. *Prof. Charcot's Clinical Lectures*. London: Tavistock/Routledge.

Havens, L.L. (1966) 'Charcot and Hysteria'. *J. Nerv. and Ment. Dis.* 141(5):505-516.

Holt, R. R. (1962) 'A Critical Examination of Freud's Concept of Bound vs. Free Cathexis', *J. Am. Psy. Ass.* 10:475-525.

- (1965). 'A Review of Some of Freud's Biological Assumptions and Their Influence on His Theories', in *Psychoanalysis and Current Biological Thought*, N.S.Greenfield and W.C.Lewis, eds. Madison, WI: University of Wisconsin Press.

Jackson, J. H. (1958) *Selected Writings*, James Taylor, ed.. London: Staples Press.

Jerusalem, W. (1895) *Die Urteilsfunktion*. Wien und Leipzig: W. Braumuller.

Jones, E. (1957) *The Life and Work of Sigmund Freud, Vol. 3: The Last Phase 1919-1939*. London: Hogarth.

- (1972 [1953]) *The Life and Work of Sigmund Freud, Vol. 1: The Young Freud 1856-1900*. London: Hogarth.

Kanzer, M. (1973) 'Two Prevalent Misconceptions about Freud's "Project"'. *The Annual of Psychoan.* I:88-103.

Kitcher, P. (1992) *Freud's Dream: A Complete Interdisciplinary Science of Mind.* Cambridge, MA: MIT Press.

Kleinpaul, R. (1972 [1888]) *Sprache ohne Worte. Idee einer allgemeinen Wissenschaft der Sprache (Language Without Words. The Idea of a General Science of Language).* The Hague: Mouton.

Knight, I. F. (1984) 'Freud's Project: A Theory for 'Studies on Hysteria'. *J. Hist. Behav. Sc.* 20:340-358.

Køppe, S. (1983) 'The psychology of the neuron: Freud, Cajal and Golgi'. *Scandinavian Journal of Psychology* 24(1):1-12.

Krafft-Ebing, R. v. (1890) *Lehrbuch der Psychiatrie.* 4. Auflage. Stuttgart: Enke.

Kris, E. (1950) 'The significance of Freud's earliest discoveries'. *Int. J. Psy.* 31:108-116.

- (1954). Introduction to *The Origins of Psychoanalysis: Letters to Wilhelm Fliess, Drafts and Notes, 1887-1902*, Bonaparte, M., Freud, A. and Kris, E., eds., Mosbacher, E. and Strachey, J., trans. New York: Basic Books.

Lacan, J. (1981). *The Four Fundamental Concepts of Psychoanalysis: The Seminar of Jacques Lacan, Book XI*, Alan Sheridan, trans. New York and London: W.W. Norton.

- (1992) 'The Ethics of Psychoanalysis, 1959-1960', in Miller, J. A. ed., *The Seminar of Jacques Lacan, Book 7*, D. Porter, trans. London and New York: Tavistock & Routledge.

- (2001 [1938]) '*Les complexes familiaux dans la formation de l'individu Essai d'analyse d'une fonction en psychologie*', in *Autres écrits*, Paris: Éditions Du Seuil.

Lacan, J. (2006 [1966]) *Écrits*, B.Fink, trans., in collaboration with H. Fink and R. Grigg. New York: Norton.

Lange, F. A. (1880 [1877]) *History of Materialism and Criticism of Its Present Importance.* 3 Vols. E. C. Thomas, trans. Boston: Houghton, Osgood & Co.

Laplanche, J. and Pontalis, J.-B. (1973) *The Language of Psychoanalysis*, D. Nicholson-Smith, trans. *The International Psycho-Analytical Library*, 94:1-497. London: Hogarth and Institute of Psycho-Analysis.

Levin, K. (1978) *Freud's Early Psychology of the Neuroses: A Historical Perspective.* Pittsburgh, PA: Pittsburgh University Press.

Levitt, C. and Turgeon, A. (2009) 'Sigmund Freud's intensive reading of Ludwig Feuerbach'. *Canadian Journal of Psychoanalysis* 17:14-35.

Levy Bruhl, L. (1973) *The Philosophy of A. Comte* [1900], K. de Beaumont-Klein, trans. [1903]. Clifton, NJ: A. M. Kelley.

Litowitz, B. and Litowitz, N. (1977) 'The influence of linguistic theory on psychoanalysis'. *Int. Review of Psy* 4: 419-448.

Major, R. (1974) 'The revolution of hysteria', *Int. J. Psy.*, 55:385-395.

Mancia, M. (1983) Archeology of Freudian thought and the history of neurophysiology. *Int. Rev. of Psychoan.* 10:185-92.

Marshall, J. (1974). 'Freud's psychology of language', in *Freud: A Collection of Critical Essays*, R. Wollheim, ed. New York: Anchor.

Marx, O. M. (1966) 'Aphasia studies and language theory in the 19th Century. *Bull. Hist. Med.* 4:328-49.

Marx, O. M. (1967) 'Freud and aphasia: An historical analysis'. *Amer. J. Psychiatry* 124:815-825.

– (1970). 'Nineteenth century medical psychology: Theoretical problems in the work of Griesinger, Meynert, and Wernicke. *Isis* 61:355-70.

Medawar, P. B. (1975) 'Review of I. S. Cooper, *The Victim is Always the Same*'. *New York Review of Books*, January 23.

Meynert, T. (1968 [1885]) *Psychiatry. A Clinical Treatise of the Diseases of the Forebrain*, B. Sachs, trans. New York and London: Hafner.

– (1892) *Sammlung von Popular Wissenschaftlichen Vorträgen über den bau und die Leistungen des Gehirns*. Wien und Leipzig: W. Braumüller.

Mills, J. (2004) 'Clarifications on *Trieb*: Freud's theory of motivation reinstated'. *Psychoanalytic Psychology*, 21(4):673-677.

Mitscherlich, A. et al. (1970) 'On psychoanalysis and sociology. *Int. J. Psy.* 51:33-48.

Möbius, P. J. (1895) *Uber die gegenwartige Auffassung der Hysterie. Monatschrift Geburtsh. Gynak.*, Band 1, pp. 12-21.

Oppenheim, H. (1890) *Thatsachliches und Hypothetisches uber das Wesen der Hysterie. Berliner Klinische Wochenschrift*, 23 Juni:553-556.

Politzer, G. (1965-1966 [1928-1929] *Escritos Psicológicos (Psychological Writings)*, E. Ramos, trans. Buenos Aires: Jorge Alvarez.

– (1994 [1928]) *Critique of the Foundations of Psychology*, M. Apprey, trans. Pittsburgh, PA: Duquesne University Press.

Popper, K. R. (1972) *Conjectures and Refutations. The Growth of Scientific Knowledge* (4th ed., rev.). London: Routledge & Kegan Paul.

Preyer, W. (1973 [1882, 1890). *The Mind of the Child*, Part I, H. W. Brown, trans. New York: Arno.

– ([1973 [1882, 1889]). *The Mind of the Child*. Part II. H. W. Brown, trans. New York: Arno.

Pribram, K. H. (1962) 'The neuropsychology of Sigmund Freud', in *Experimental Foundations of Clinical Psychology*, A. J. Bachrach, ed. New York: Basic Books, pp. 442-468.

– (1965) 'Freud's *Project*: An open, biologically based model for psychoanalysis', in *Psychoanalysis and Current Biological Thought*, N. S. Greenfield and C. Lewis, eds. Madison, WI: Univ. Wisconsin Press, pp. 81-92.

Pribram, K. H. and Gill, M. M. (1976). *Freud's 'Project' Re-assessed: Preface to Contemporary Cognitive Theory and Neuropsychology*. New York: Basic Books.

Ricoeur, P. (1970 [1965]) *Freud and Philosophy: An Essay on Interpretation*. New Haven: Yale University Press.

Riese, W. (1958a). 'Freudian concepts of brain function and brain disease'. *J. Nervous Mental Disease* 127:287-307.

– (1958b). 'The pre-Freudian origins of psychoanalysis', in *Science and Psychoanalysis, V. 1*, J. Masserman, ed. New York: Grune & Stratton, pp. 29-72.

– (1959). *A History of Neurology*. New York: MD Publications.

– (1965). 'The sources of Hughlings Jackson's view on aphasia. *Brain* 88:811-822.

Riese, W. and Hoff, E.C. (1950-1) 'A History of the Doctrine of Cerebral Localization'. *J. History Med.* 5:50-71 and 6:439-470.

Ritvo, L. (1965) 'Darwin as the source of Freud's Neo-Lamarckianism'. *J. Amer. Psychoanal. Assn.*, 13:499-517.
- (1972) 'Carl Claus as Freud's professor of the new Darwinian biology'. *Int. J. Psycho-Anal.*, 53:277-283.
- (1974) 'The impact of Darwin on Freud'. *Psych. Quarterly*, 43:177-192.
- (1990). *Darwin's Influence on Freud: A Tale of Two Sciences.* New Haven & London: Yale University Press.

Rizzutto, A. M. (1989) 'A hypothesis about Freud's motive for writing the monograph *On Aphasia*'. *Int. Rev. of Psychoan.* 16:111-117.
- (1990) 'The origins of Freud's concept of object representation (`Objektvorstellung`') in his monograph *On Aphasia*: Its theoretical and technical importance'. *Int. J. of Psychoan.* 71:241-248.

Romanes, G. (1883) *Mental Evolution in Animals. With a Posthumous Essay on Instinct by Charles Darwin.* London: Kegan Paul, Trench & Co.
- (1888) *Mental Evolution in Man: Origin of Human Faculty.* London: Kegan Paul, Trench & Co.

Rorty, R. (1980) *Philosophy and the Mirror of Nature.* Oxford: Blackwell.

Rothschuh, K. E. (1973) *History of Physiology.* G. B. Risse, ed. and trans. New York: Krieger.

Scherrer, F. (2003) 'Freud is not the author of the *Aphasia* article (1888): Some comments and observations on Freud's contribution to Villaret's medical dictionary of 1888-91'. *Neuro-Psychoanalysis* 5(2): 183-194.

Sirkin, M. and Fleming, M. (1982) 'Freud's *Project* and its relationship to psychoanalytic theory. *J. Hist. Behavioral Sc.* 18:230-241.

Solms, M. (2002) 'An introduction to the neuroscientific works of Sigmund Freud', in *The Pre-Psychoanalytic Writings of Sigmund Freud*, G. van de Vijver & F. Geerardyn, eds. London and New York: Karnac.

Solms, M. and Saling, M. (1986). 'On psychoanalysis and neuroscience: Freud's attitude to the localizationist tradition. *Int. J. of Psychoanal.*, 67:397- 416.

Solms, M. & Saling, M. (1990). *A Moment of Transition. Two Neuroscientific Articles by Sigmund Freud.* London: Karnac.

Solomon, R. (1974) 'Freud's neurological theory of mind' in *Freud: A Collection of Critical Essays*, R. Wollheim, ed. New York: Anchor, pp. 25-52.

Spehlmann, R. (1953) *Sigmund Freuds Neurologische Schriften.* Berlin: Springer.

Stengel, E. (1953) *Introduction to On Aphasia: A Critical Study.* London: Imago.

Stengel, E. (1954) 'A re-evaluation of Freud's book *On Aphasia*: Its significance for psychoanalysis. *Int. J. Psy.* 35:85-89.

Stewart, W. A. (1969) *Psychoanalysis: The First Ten Years, 1888-1898.* New York and London: Macmillan.

Strachey, J. (1956). 'Editor's Note to "Report on My Studies in Paris and Berlin"', in SE 1 (1886-1899), pp. 3-15.
- (1962a) 'The emergence of Freud's fundamental hypotheses. Appendix to *The Neuro-Psychoses of Defence*', in SE 3 (1893-1899), pp. 62-69.
- (1962b). 'Freud's views on phobias. Appendix to *Obsessions and Phobias*, in SE 3 (1893-1899), pp. 83-84.

- (1966). 'Editor's introduction and notes to *Project for a Scientific Psychology* (1950 [1895]).

Sulloway, F. (1979) *Freud, Biologist of the Mind. Beyond the Psychoanalytic Legend.* London: Burnet Books.

Tauber, A. I. (2010) *Freud, the Reluctant Philosopher.* Princeton, NJ: Oxford and Princeton University Press.

Temkin, O. (1946) 'Materialism in French and German physiology of the early nineteenth century. *Bull. Hist. Med.* 20:322-327.

Thornton, E. M. (1986 [1983]) *The Freudian Fallacy: Freud and Cocaine.* London: Paladin/Collins.

Trosman, H. (1976) 'Freud's cultural background', in *Freud: The Fusion of Science and Humanism. The Intellectual History of Psychoanalysis,* J. E. Gedo and G. H. Pollock, eds. New York: International University Press, pp. 46-70.

Wallerstein, R.S. and Smelser, N.J. (1969) 'Psychoanalysis and Sociology'. *Int. J. Psy.* 50:693.

Webster, R. (1995) *Why Freud was Wrong. Sin, Science and Psychanalysis.* Basic Books.

Wundt, W. (1969) *Principles of Physiological Psychology,* Vol. 1. E. B. Titchener, trans. (from the 5th German ed. (1902)). New York: Kraus. [Reprinted London: Sonnenschein, 1910].

Young, R. M. (1990) *Mind, Brain and Adaptation in the Nineteenth Century. Cerebral Localization and its Biological Context from Gall to Ferrier.* New York: Oxford University Press.

Glossary

Haimovich Freud Glossary*

This glossary provides mainly the evolutionary meanings of terms as used by Freud

Affect: a) as emotion, affect results from the endogenous cathexis of memories of pain experiences; it represents the third and most developed stage for coping with pain (unpleasure).

b) as a physiological concept: energy and quantity of energy (*Affekt-Affektbetrag*).

Association: a) physiologically, any connection between neurones.

b) psychologically, any connection between representations (sensations, perceptions, memories).

Associative passage: the free flow of energy through neurons.

Cognitive thought: the analysis of perceptions and memories, providing knowledge at any stage of thought development; Freud often uses the term judgement in its place.

Contact barrier: neuronal device opposing the free, associative passage of energy, making possible the storage of energy needed to fulfil biological needs and the parallel appearance and functioning of memory. Contact barriers appear relatively late in the evolution of nervous systems but prior to consciousness.

Experience of pain: the psychical state, to be distinguished from physical pain, in which traces remaining from physical pain are recathected, releasing unpleasure; emerges after the appearance of consciousness.

Facilitation: alteration of contact barriers after any passage of energy, making future passages easier (more associative).

Hallucination: intense cathexis of memory traces, awaking reality indications; a state similar to objective perception; leads to unpleasure.

Inscription (registration): memory trace embedded in neurones after any passage of energy.

Internal perceptions: recall and perception of memories.

Materialist psychology: a philosophical approach meant to endow psychology with scientificity by grounding it in neurology.

Motor mechanisms: mechanisms for the discharge of energy and the satisfaction of biological needs, comprising muscular and neural motor innervation (stimulation).

Pain: physical state resulting from eruption of large quantities of external energy into the nervous system.

Primary function of nervous system: the tendency of neuronal systems to rapidly discharge energy (see principle of inertia and facilitation)

Primary neuronal system: undeveloped systems that discharge energy immediately upon its reception.

Principles of inertia and constancy: principles directing the evolution and functioning of nervous systems.
- a) Neuronal constancy: the secondary function of neuronal systems, resulting from a compromise between the tendency for complete discharge of energy and the need for its accumulation in order to fulfil biological needs.
- b) Neuronal inertia: the primary function of neuronal systems, directing their initial evolution and functioning; tendency to completely discharge received energy.

Psycho-physical linguistic parallelism: the assumed existence of a mirrored and fixed relationship between external objects, their mental representations and the words naming them.

Reality or quality (consciousness) indications: signs received by the neuronal system indicating the presence of an object.

   a) perceptual indications: provide information about the presence of external objects and their attributes;

   b) verbal indications: provide information about the presence of memories (internal objects), thereby enabling them to become conscious and the object of observation and judgement; necessary for development of secondary thought

Reflex arc: the primary mechanism serving the principle of inertia; describes the fixed direction of energy discharge from dendrites to axons.

Representations: general name for any psychological element (sensations, perceptions, memories).

Reproductive thought: broadly speaking, any thought process involving memories, or mnemic images; more restrictedly, an advanced thought process, conducted only with memories (mnemic neurones), absent perceptions of external objects (perceptual neurones).

Secondary function of the nervous system: refers to the accumulation of energy by neurons for the purpose of fulfilling biological needs (see principle of constancy) and to the inhibition and control of the free passage of energy.

Secondary neuronal system:

   a) physiologically, neuronal systems in which the secondary function enables energy accumulation and inhibition of primary associative passages of energy.

   b) psychologically, nervous systems able to think and inhibit the free association of representations.

Side cathexis: cathexis of adjoining neurones, allowing inhibition of the free, associative passage of energy.

Verbal indications: quality indications enabling memories to become objects of knowledge and thought.

Transcription-Translation-Retranscription: terms designating new inscriptions of an original trace-inscription of a perception, at higher levels of ego development and ego functioning. Notions intended to strengthen the idea that the original perceptual traces are not changed by their posterior cathexis.

Wishful cathexis (wishful neurones): endogenous cathexis of mnemic neurons, residues of experiences of biological need-satisfaction.

Word presentation: the memory or recall of a word.

Index

A
abreaction, 57, 58, 62, 66
aetiologies, sexual, 71–2, 74, 78, 82, 84
affect, 62, 64–5, 129, 130
alienation, 82
Amacher, P., 124
anthropology, new, 247
anxiety melancholia, 84
anxiety neuroses, 68, 69, 70, 72–3, 205
  origins/features, 76–82, 84, 89, 218
  phobias, 92
aphasia, 50–3
  and mind-body problem, 43–6
Aphasia, 18, 19, 33–43, 49–51, 121, 211–12, 235, 237
artists, Freud's biographies, 242
association by simultaneity, 127
associations, psychological, 38–9, 40, 42, 53–4
attention, 135–6, 169, 170–8, 181, 196
auto-suggestion, 32–3, 55

B
Bernfeld, Siegfried, 33
Bernheim, Hippolyte, 32
Bhat, Parameshwar, 9–10
bodily experiences in knowledge acquisition, 156, 158
body-mind problem, 43–54, 81, 100, 121
Brentano, Franz, 17, 23
Breuer, Josef
  Freud's correspondence with, 19
  on hysteria, 56–7, 58, 61–2, 64, 66, 67, 68
Broca area, 39–40
Brücke, Ernest, 17, 24, 25, 124
Brunner, José, 9

C
catharsis, 62, 67
cathexes, 127, 131, 133–4, 147
  bodily, 157–8
  endogenous, 170, 173–4
  hyper-cathexis, 151, 152–3, 173–5
  psychical, 157–8
  wishful/purposive, 183
Charcot, Jean-Martin, 18, 24, 57, 64
  on hysteria, 28, 29, 30, 50, 56, 58–9
chemical theory, 201, 202
children/childhood
  dependence, 126
  ego development, 141–3, 149, 197
  memory development, 149, 151
  neuronal systems, 124
  sexuality, 202, 209–10, 223–4
  traumatic memories, 69, 203–11, 215

Claus, Carl, 17, 24, 25, 26
cocaine use, 24
cognition, 148, 152, 158, 175, 183
  of the human other, 153–4
coitus interruptus, 72, 76, 87
compulsion, in hysteria, 164, 216
concomitance theory, 43, 46–8
consciousness, 93, 113, 118–21, 196
  in dreams, 162–3
  quantitative model, failure of, 121, 133, 138
  and quantity, 195
  relation to unconscious, 181–2, 187
  secondary, 142, 179, 197, 199
contact barriers, 107, 108, 113–14, 115, 116, 119, 133

D

Damasio, Antonio, 33
Darwinism, 24, 25–6, 105, 108, 112, 116, 172
  and neurology, 28
Davar, Bhargavi, 9–10
defence psychoses, 93–6
defences, 59, 66–7, 73, 90–3, 139, 198
  alienation, 81–2
  anxiety, 80
  hysteria, 203
  normal vs. pathological, 99
  primary and secondary, 131, 132, 135, 177
  psycho-neuroses, 90–6
  . see also repression
deferred action, 223
Descartes, René, 5
disgust sensations, 223–4
Draft A, 77
Draft B, 68, 70, 74, 76, 77
Draft E, 76–7, 78, 80
Draft G, 82–9
Draft H, 93, 94, 95, 141
Draft K, 204, 208, 210
dreams, 20, 103, 160–3, 201, 226, 229–30, 233–4
  and consciousness, 162–3
  and displacement, 164
  dream: 'Marcinowski,' 233
  forgetting, 162
  and hallucinations, 96, 161, 169
  linguistic phenomena, 228
  memory and oblivion, 233
  psychic redistribution, 220
  as wish fulfilment, 161, 163, 228, 230
Du Bois-Reymond, Emil, 25

E

education, Freud's, 17, 18, 23–4
ego, 103, 105, 106, 125, 243
  evolution of, 148–9
  in hysteria, 208
  independent action of, 180
  mechanical explanation, failure of, 113
  primary, 130–4, 197
  and repression, 167–8, 207
  secondary thinking, 134–8, 176–7
  and speech indications, 183
  three stages of development, 141–3
  and wishful cathexes, 183, 185
Elizabeth (case), 67
Emmy (case), 67, 93
emotions, 63–5
empirical materialism, 232–3
errors and contradictions, 188–9, 190
evolutionary model, 20, 124, 143, 147, 169, 171–2, 176–7, 200
  failure of, 181
  Freud's abandonment of, 221, 225
  . see also Darwinism

F

fantasies, 201, 202, 220–2
fathers, 244
Fliess, Wilhelm, 201–2
  Freud sends *Project* to, 20, 193, 203–4
  Freud's letters to, 99–100, 138, 140, 156, 193–4, 200, 209–10, 213–15, 225
  periodic theory, 217–19
Forel, August, 33
Foundationalism, 9–10
free association, 67
frigidity, 86–7

G

Gay, Peter, 23
gender differences
  neurasthenia, 75
  sexual development/experiences, 206, 223–4
Gill, Martin, 99, 132, 144–5, 146–7
Greenberg, Valerie, 34
Group Psychology, 243–4

H

Haeckel, Ernest
  biogenetic law 108, 109, 110, 112, 116
hallucinations, 93, 95–6, 137, 161, 175, 190, 196–7
  avoidance of, 177, 178
  and perceptions, 127, 140–1
hallucinatory confusion, 68, 73, 94, 207
Helmholtz school, 25, 26
hermeneutic approach, 6–8, 9
human sciences, contemporary, 240–1
humanities, 8, 9, 10, 14
hypnoid states, 66, 68
hypnosis, 18, 29, 32–3, 55, 67, 68
hysteria, 18, 28, 164–8, 203, 204
  and anxiety, 77–8, 79
  and aphasia, 50–3
  and compulsion, 164, 216
  conversion, 210
  as defence, 68, 69, 73, 91, 211, 215, 221
  definition, 28–33
  early works, 25
  and sexual passivity, 206, 208
  and trauma, 55–67
hysterical anaesthesia, 87, 220

I

id, 243
impulses, 125, 237
inertia, 107, 108–9, 111, 112, 132, 197
infantile cerebral palsy, 25
instincts, 125–6
Interpretation of Dreams, The, 4, 13, 19, 20, 226, 227, 229–32, 239
Introductory Lectures (1916–17), 65

J

Jackson, John Hughlings
  concomitance theory, 46–8
  Darwinism, 28, 43–4
  influence on Freud, 42, 52, 54, 123
  on localization, 40
  on primary thought, 156–7
Jerusalem, Wilhelm, 140, 150, 156
jokes, 233
Jokes and their Relation to the Unconscious, 4, 13, 226, 242
judgment, 139, 144–6, 147–8, 154, 236
  and memory, 155–6

K

Kanzer, Mark, 44
Kitcher, Patricia, 9

L

Lacan, Jacques, 15
Lange, Friedrich, 35, 40
language. *see* aphasia; linguistic phenomena
Laplanche, J., 125
Levin, Kenneth, 31, 49, 55, 59, 67–8, 140
libido, 80, 83, 224–5
Lichtheim, Ludwig, 36
linguistic phenomena, 18, 19, 20, 100, 181, 213, 214
  aphasia research, 33–4
  dreams, 228, 232, 233–4
  Freud's research focus, 235–41
  and thought, 235
  . *see also* aphasia
linguistics, modern, 54
localization theory, 35–43, 45–6, 48, 52–3
Lucy (case), 67
Ludwig, Karl, 25

M

mania, 208, 218
Marx, Otto, 46, 47, 48–9, 54
masturbation, 72, 75, 83, 87, 93
melancholia, 68, 70, 82–90, 218
memories, 117, 128–9, 142, 146, 148
  and change, 184–7, 213, 237–8

child development, 149, 151
  falsification of, 221–2
  and judgment, 146, 156
  and pain, 188–91
  registration of, 211–12
  sexual, and defence, 164–8, 203–11
metapsychology, 225, 236
Meynert, Theodor, 17, 24, 27, 28, 31, 123, 124
  localization theory, 36, 39
mind, concept of, 14–15
mind-body problem, 43–54, 81, 100, 229
morality, origins, 126
Moses of Michelangelo, The, 242
motor discharge/mechanisms, 151, 156–7
mourning, 83, 84, 89–90

N

narratives, 103–4, 213
nervous system, 105–6, 116
  . see also neuronal systems
neurasthenia, 68, 69, 70, 75–82
  and periodic theory, 218
  and sexuality, 74–7, 79, 89
  and traumatic memories, 72
neurology as theoretical materialism, 25, 33–4, 44, 49, 233
neuronal systems, 106–8
  energy storage, 113–14, 117
  functions, 121–4, 132
  hysteria, 59, 62–3
  primary, 109–10, 112
  secondary, 111–14, 117
neurone theory
  . see Project
'Neuro-psychoses of Defence,' 92
neuroses, 26–8, 202
  developmental model, 205, 215–17, 219, 222
  evolutionary-mechanical theory, 201, 221
  general theory of, 61–96
  psycho-linguistic evolutionary model, 214
  somatic, 68, 69, 71–3, 81
New Introductory Lectures (1933), 245

O

objectivity-subjectivity, 174, 182, 183–4
obsessions, 68, 94, 204, 210, 211, 246–7
  as defence, 73, 92, 93, 215
  and hysteria, 208
  and pleasure/self-reproach, 206–7
  verbal symptoms, 216
Obsessions and Phobias, 92
Oedipus complex, 242-3, 245
omega neurones, 118–19, 120, 128, 135, 136–8, 180, 196–8
  and psi, 194–5
On Aphasia
  . see Aphasia
ontogeny, 109–10
Oppenheim, Hermann, 64

P

pain, 127–8, 150
  memories of, 188–91
  and reflex defence, 131, 159
paralysis, hysterical, 55, 58, 63
paranoia, 68, 73, 94–5, 207–8, 210, 215
  and puberty, 211
  and fantasies, 221
perceptions, 42, 114, 146, 156
  facilitated by attention, 170–8
  and hallucinations, 127, 140–1
  hyper-cathexis, 151, 152–3, 173–5
  registrations of, 212, 213–14, 220
  and speech, 38–9, 53–4
perceptual identity, 142, 146, 151–2, 154
periods, feminine and masculine, 211
perversions, sexual, 215
phi neurones, 114–15, 116–17, 118–19, 122–3, 128
philosophy, 10, 12, 13, 15, 19, 23
phobias, 70, 92–3
phylogeny, 109–10, 112
pleasure principle, 119, 149, 177, 206
  unpleasure, 188–91, 199, 204–5
Politzer, Georges, 15
Pontalis, Jean-Bertrand, 125
Popper, Karl, 5–6, 10

positivism, 6–8, 9, 14
practical thought, 184–8
Preliminary Communication (1893), 18, 51, 56, 57, 64, 67
Pribram, Karl, 99, 132, 144–5, 146–7
primary theoretical thinking, 152
Project, 4, 19–20, 34, 42–5, 61, 81, 103–91
   on consciousness, 93, 118–21
   failure/completion, 68, 70, 98–9, 169
   fate of, 193–225
   four stages and structure, 103–6
   Jackson's influence on, 52
   language-thought relations, 236
   and mind-body problem, 100
   neuronal systems, 106–12, 200
   on psychic pain, 90
   secondary thought processes, 168–88
   thought processes, 138–68
projection, 95
psi neurones, 114–15, 116–17, 118–19, 122–3, 125, 128, 129–30
   for endogenous energy, 198
   and omega, 194–5, 196–7
   and phi, 198
   in repression/attraction, 133
   . *see also* omega neurones
psyche, 32, 44, 240–1, 243
psychiatry, 17
   Freud's early steps, 26–8
   on hysteria, 28–9, 50
   neuro-anatomic, 28
   on paranoia and obsessions, 94
   pre-scientific, 12, 13
   and psychology, 49
psychology, 31, 44, 49, 225, 229
psycho-neuroses, 90–6
Psychopathology of Everyday Life, The, 4, 13, 226
psychoses, 5, 73, 93–6

Q

qualities, 118–19, 122–3, 136, 138, 175, 179–80, 181, 182–3, 196
in new model, 198, 200
perceptual/verbal, 199

quantities, 112, 118, 119, 122–3, 138
   definition, 106–7
   endogenous, 126
   in new model, 200

R

reality, and wishes, 239
reality indications, 134–8, 139–40, 147, 151, 154, 196, 222
   ego development, 141–2, 178, 179
reductionism, 25, 98, 103–4, 106, 120–1, 169, 239
reflex mechanism, 122–3, 124, 197
relationships, human, and cognition, 153–4
religion, 12, 246–7
repression, 68, 72, 91, 133, 136, 203–11
   normal vs. pathological, 99, 224–5
   in paranoia, 94–5
   secondary thinking, 169
   and translation, 215
reproductive thinking, 144–6, 148, 149, 150–1, 154, 158
   and judgment, 155–6
retentive hysteria, 91
Riese, Walther, 34, 47, 49

S

Saling, Michael, 43–4
satisfaction, 126–7, 176, 237
Schematic Diagram of Sexuality, 84–5
secondary ego, 134–8
seduction theory, 202, 222
sentences, and meaning, 54
sexual anaesthesia, 78, 82, 84–90
sexuality
   development of, 202, 209–10, 223–4
   and melancholia, 82–90
   and neurasthenia, 75–82, 89
   and neuroses, 67–74, 158, 164–8, 202, 205–11, 215
   physiology of, 79–80, 84–5
smell sensations, 223
social phenomena, 205, 241–8
social psychology (sociology), 244–6
Solms, Mark, 43–4

somatic actual neuroses, 74–82
speech associations, 40, 175–6, 179, 199
speech centres (cortical), 39–40
speech indications, 180, 181, 183, 187
speech pathology, 50–3
  . see also aphasia, *Aphasia*
speech phenomena, normal, 53–4
Stengel, Erwin, 43
Stewart, Walter, 78
Strachey, James, 97, 115, 125, 166
Studies on Hysteria, 69, 93, 162, 210
substitution, 92
Sulloway, Frank, 98, 99
superego, 243
symptoms, hysterical, 55, 56–8, 62–3, 64
symptoms, types, 207

T
Tauber, Alfred, 6
theoretical thinking, 151–2
thought, 138–60
  bodily experiences and, 158–60
  as dialectical, 157
  and language, 235
  as mostly unconscious, 181–2, 187
  nonverbal, 151, 154, 155
  primary processes, 144–68
  regulated by ego's cathexes, 159–60
  secondary processes (verbal), 142, 146, 154, 168–91
  unpleasure, 188–91
  . see also linguistic phenomena
Totem and Taboo, 243
totemism, 243, 247
transference, 243
transposition, 92, 95
traumatic memories, 56–8, 62–6, 69, 166–8, 203–11, 215

U
Uncanny, The, 242
unconscious
  endogenous stimuli, 199–200
  reality indications, lack of, 222
  relation to conscious, 181–2, 187

V
verbal identity, 142, 146, 154
Vienna, 24–7
Villaret, Albert, 27

W
Wernicke, Carl, 37, 49
Wernicke's area, 39–40
wish fulfilment, 139, 161, 163, 183, 225
  dreams as, 228, 230
wishful cathexes, 183, 184–5
women
  anxiety, 78, 82
  hysteria, 28, 52, 208
  melancholia, 88–9
  neurasthenia, 75
  repression, 225